THE FLETCHER JONES FOUNDATION
HUMANITIES IMPRINT

The Fletcher Jones Foundation has endowed this imprint to foster
innovative and enduring scholarship in the humanities.

The publisher gratefully acknowledges the generous support of the Fletcher Jones Foundation Humanities Endowment Fund of the University of California Press Foundation.

Walt Whitman and the Civil War

Walt Whitman and the Civil War

America's Poet during the Lost Years of 1860–1862

Ted Genoways

UNIVERSITY OF CALIFORNIA PRESS

Berkeley   Los Angeles   London

University of California Press, one of the most distinguished
university presses in the United States, enriches lives around
the world by advancing scholarship in the humanities, social
sciences, and natural sciences. Its activities are supported by
the UC Press Foundation and by philanthropic contributions from individuals and institutions. For more information, visit www.ucpress.edu.

University of California Press
Berkeley and Los Angeles, California

University of California Press, Ltd.
London, England

Library of Congress Cataloging-in-Publication Data

Genoways, Ted.
    Walt Whitman and the Civil War : America's poet during
the lost years of 1860–1862 / Ted Genoways.
        p.   cm.
    Includes bibliographical references and index.
    ISBN 978-0-520-25906-5 (cloth : alk. paper)
    1. Whitman, Walt, 1819–1892—Political and social views.
2. Whitman, Walt, 1819–1892—Knowledge—United States.
3. Poets, American—19th century—Biography.   I. Title.

PS3232.G46   2009
811'.3—dc22
[B]   2009003369

Manufactured in the United States of America

18 17 16 15 14 13 12 11 10 09
10 9 8 7 6 5 4 3 2 1

This book is printed on Natures Book, which contains 30%
post-consumer waste and meets the minimum requirements
of ANSI/NISO z39.48-1992 (R 1997) (*Permanence of Paper*).

CONTENTS

ACKNOWLEDGMENTS

This book would not have been possible without the steady support and constant encouragement of Ed Folsom. He has guided my work with patience, insight, and enthusiasm. No one could ask for a better mentor or friend. I also owe a debt of gratitude to Sherry Ceniza, my first professor of Whitman studies, for her own scholarship on the 1860 edition of *Leaves of Grass* and for directing me toward continuing my study with Ed. Thanks, too, to Jerome Loving and Kenneth M. Price for comments and suggestions during the editing stage of this manuscript; to Kathleen Diffley for her instruction and scholarship in Civil War periodicals; and to David Hamilton, Christopher Merrill, and John Erickson for their enthusiasm and support.

I am grateful to the libraries and archives that house the manuscripts from which I have quoted and to the Walt Whitman Archive (whitman-archive.unl.edu) for making many of those manuscripts available to me in electronic form. Special thanks to the Office of the President of the University of Virginia for supporting this research by granting me the hours to complete this work.

Last, but certainly not least, I want to express my thanks to my family: my parents; my wife, Mary Anne Andrei; and my son, Jack, who grew up with this project.

Quicksand Years

Quicksand years that whirl me I know not whither,
Schemes, politics fail—all is shaken—all gives way.
Notebook draft, January 1863

"The real war will never get in the books," Walt Whitman wrote in 1876.[1] It is a statement that frequently has been misread as a critique of the printed page and its inability to encompass anything so large as the Civil War. But more than a decade after the guns had fallen silent at Appomattox, Whitman knew full well that the war was already the subject of countless books—just not what Whitman considered the *real* war. He rankled against the emerging national narrative that focused on "the few great battles" rather than the countless days spent by common soldiers in camp, on the march, in hospital wards, or in prison pens.[2] He felt that his own war-era prose writings had languished unpublished because he favored a narrative that highlighted "not the official surface-courteousness of the Generals," but the "two or three millions of American young and middle-aged men, North and South, embodied in those armies."[3]

Whitman worried that, in the nation's eagerness to make sense of the war, an unambiguous version of events had been written into history to the exclusion of what he called "that many-threaded drama." That true version of the war would not focus merely on "the bloody battles" but would interweave political concerns, such as "the dread of foreign interference," and "the immense money expenditure, like a heavy-pouring constant rain," as well as the "unending, universal mourning-wail of women, parents, orphans." Collectively, he believed they formed an "untold and unwritten history," one that defied epic sweep by its very fractiousness, but a history "infinitely greater (like life's) than the few scraps and distortions that are ever told or written."[4]

In Whitman's estimation all historians—not merely the historians of the Civil War—tended to overlook the common man. Near the end of his life he told one of his literary executors, Thomas Harned, that he had something of a "distaste for history": "So much of it is cruel, so much of it is lie. I am waiting for the historians who will tell the truth about the people—about the nobility of the people: the essential soundness of the common man. . . . Think of the things in everyday life—we see them everywhere—that never are exploited in print. Nobody hunts them up—nobody puts them into a story."[5] Despite this grim view, Whitman himself had been a participant in a powerful collective counternarrative of the war that had already been written, an impromptu and impressionistic narrative, "jotted down . . . at the time and on the spot" by the nation's newspaper writers.

Many years after the war, Whitman still vividly remembered gathering with a crowd after midnight on April 13, 1861, to hear the telegraphic dispatch from the *New York Times* announcing the outbreak of war. In the days and weeks following the first Battle of Bull Run he faithfully read the editorials of Horace Greeley because they "restored the Union energies with determination five times magnified."[6] On December 16, 1862, he recognized the misspelled name of his brother in the *New York Herald* among the lists of wounded at Fredericksburg. He saw a giant broadside tacked outside a Washington newspaper office proclaiming "Glorious Victory for the Union Army!" on the night of July 4, 1863—that Independence Day that both Vicksburg and Gettysburg were won.[7] When news of Lincoln's assassination reached New York on April 15,

1865, Whitman spent the morning with his mother passing the newspapers back and forth in silence, and in the afternoon ventured into the rain to join the crowds around the bulletin boards where the evening editions were posted.[8]

For Whitman, the real history of the war lay in these moods and moments, which were dramatized—and often created—by the daily stream of information and misinformation that drove the anxiety of the period.

It would take a century for these works to receive serious attention from historians and another generation for literary scholars to begin studying them. In *Patriotic Gore*, published for the war's centennial in 1961, Edmund Wilson lamented, "The period of the American Civil War was not one in which belles lettres flourished."[9] But Wilson believed that there was an unmatched flowering of effective and moving writing in genres usually classified outside literature:

> The elaborate orations of Charles Sumner, modeled on Demosthenes and Cicero; Lincoln's unique addresses, at once directives and elegies; John Brown's letters from prison and final speech to the court; Grant's hard and pellucid memoirs and John Mosby's almost picaresque ones, together with the chronicles and apologetics of innumerable other officers of both the armies; the brilliant journal of Mary Chestnut, so much more imaginative and revealing than most of the fiction inspired by the war; the autobiographies of the Adams brothers . . . such documents dramatize the war as the poet or the fiction writer has never been able to do.[10]

Yet Wilson was unwilling to claim a literary status for these works—even those he went on to discuss in *Patriotic Gore*—for the very reason that they amounted to a fractured and often contradictory narrative. He compared the experience of piecing together these texts to reading Browning's *The Ring and the Book*, "in which the same story is told from the points of view of nine different persons."[11]

Wilson's argument found still firmer footing in Daniel Aaron's *Unwritten War*, published in 1973, at the end of the Vietnam era. Aaron argued that the Civil War had profoundly affected a number of important writers but had inspired a "paucity of 'epics' and 'masterpieces.' "[12] Referring to Whitman's claim that the "real war will never get in the books," Aaron argued that "many aspects of the 'real' War can only be discovered in some of the published and unpublished memorabilia. A glance at this material shows how much of the War escaped even Whitman's searching and sympathetic eye." Like Wilson before him, Aaron did not view these items of "memorabilia" as superior to the "literature" of the war, despite his claim that "as yet no novel or poem has disclosed the common soldier so vividly as the historian Bell Wiley does in his collective portraits of Johnny Reb and Billy Yank."[13]

Aaron wrote at perhaps the last moment in the American study of (war) literature in which New Critical and Romantic standards of beauty and truth were used to judge the greatness of a work. After Vietnam the unknowability of truth and the confusion and moral relativism of war become the primary subjects of American war narratives. Tim O'Brien's seminal piece, "How to Tell a True War Story," published in 1990, uses this confusion as its central conceit. The more the narrator insists on the truth of the story, the more invented it seems to become, until finally the narrator concedes that it is only through lying that any truth about war can be constructed: "In any war story, but especially a true one, it's difficult to separate what happened from what seemed to happen. What seems to happen becomes its own happening and has to be told that way. . . . And then afterward, when you go to tell about it, there is always that surreal seemingness, which makes the story seem untrue, but which in fact represents the hard and exact truth as it *seemed*."[14]

Such postmodern, post-Vietnam realizations of relative truths in the fog of war were part of a new critical paradigm. No longer did critics lament, as Aaron did, "the impossibility of reproducing authentic sensations of war" or disparage a work of literature for telling "only part of the story."[15] In this new era, the fragmented narrative became the dominant mode. Any work that seemed to present too coherent or too crafted a vision aroused suspicion. Operating within this new framework, a new wave of scholars has returned to previously ignored works and gleaned a wealth of material in the occasional and ephemeral pieces published during the Civil War.

The two finest examples of this scholarship are Kathleen Diffley's *Where My Heart Is Turning Ever* and Alice Fahs's *The Imagined Civil War.* Diffley debunks the myth of the "unwritten war" by studying more than three hundred stories published in popular magazines between 1861 and 1876. She not only demonstrates the extent of this body of work but also maps its significant trends. Her considerable broadening of the Civil War canon not only provides valuable context but also suggests other, untapped opportunities for study of the popular press, especially where poetry is concerned.

Subsequent studies have sought to apply Diffley's sensibility to other aspects of periodical culture, but so far only Fahs has approached Diffley's level of meticulousness.[16] But whereas Diffley's analysis delves deeply into a circumscribed body of texts, Fahs offers a sweeping panorama of the war's "popular literature," a category that includes not only the histories, novels, and poetry of the war but also humorous tales, songs, children's stories, and various kinds of print ephemera. Most of this work was published "by obscure authors about whom little is known, or it was published anonymously, pseudonymously, or with initials that provide tantalizing—but often insoluble—clues to authorship."[17] Fahs uses this dearth of biographical information as an opportunity to study works and publications rather than focus on authors. As a result, *The Imagined Civil War* is more coherent and insightful than Wilson's *Patriotic Gore*, and, paradoxically, its comprehensiveness highlights the best writers of the war more effectively than does Wilson's exultation of the few.

These books, taken collectively, also suggest a new methodology for writing traditional author biography. Where past scholars have relied almost exclusively on an author's own view of himself or herself, this course of research opens the broader possibility of examining an author's place within the cultural context of a particular moment. In the case of a writer like Whitman, it also presents the opportunity to investigate periods previously considered too sketchy to analyze, if not lost altogether.

Given Whitman's proclivity for self-invention, perhaps it should come as no surprise that he distrusted biographers and historians. "What lying things, travesties, most all so-called histories, biographies, autobiographies, are!" Whitman told Horace Traubel in his late-life home in Camden. "They make you sick—give you the bellyache! I suppose it can be said that the world still waits for its honest historian, biographer, autobiographer. Will he ever come?" Traubel harbored the ambition of being Whitman's Boswell and jovially offered, "I'll be the first!" But Whitman responded with disgust. "It would be a worthy ambition," he huffed. "It would be revolutionary."[18]

Whitman's disdain for biography seems to have originated shortly after the Civil War, when official histories of every general and politician were rushed into print. In late 1866 he first published the poem "When I read the book, the biography famous," which he would later expand to read, in full:

> When I read the book, the biography famous,
> And is this, then, (said I,) what the author calls a man's life?
> And so will some one, when I am dead and gone, write my life?
> (As if any man really knew aught of my life;
> Why, even I myself, I often think, know little or nothing of
> my real life;
> Only a few hints—a few diffused, faint clews and indirections,
> I seek, for my own use, to trace out here.)

The poem contains Whitman's fundamental argument: no man—not even Whitman himself—could know the story of his life. How could anyone write a book that could capture anything so elusive as a man?

Yet Whitman spent his later years with his first biographer, Richard Maurice Bucke, and then Horace Traubel, recalling and explicating the minutiae of his life, lending significance to the false starts and missteps, shaping his random days into a coherent and meaningful narrative. Because of his many failures of memory, Whitman has often been accused of lying or stretching the truth in the construction of this story; more often, however, he was simply selective, choosing his details as carefully as any writer would. Contemporary critics saw his poems as indiscriminate auction catalogues, but Whitman was, in fact, a master of elision in all phases of his life. He emphasized touchstone moments that mattered most to him, returning to them almost obsessively, while remaining frustratingly mum about vast passages of time.

For years he teased Traubel with the promise of revealing a major secret, but when Traubel chided him, "You haven't yet told me your great secret," Whitman replied, "No, I haven't, but I will: you must know it: some day the right day will come." But it never did, and Whitman died without revealing the secret. The result of such withholdings is a series of famed silences. Gaps in the record. Lost years.

The most famous of these gaps is the span of years from 1850 to 1855, the period in which Whitman transformed himself from a dilettante story writer to the prototypical working-class poet—transformed himself, in other words, from Walter to Walt.

Walter had been born into a humble family of Quakers on Long Island, and his social standing had allowed him to rise no further than fleeting stints as editor of various small-time newspapers. For the better part of the 1840s, he had fashioned himself a dandy, complete with cane and boutonniere, in a vain attempt to boost his status. But for the frontispiece of the first (1855) edition of *Leaves of Grass*, Walt changed all that. His broad hat tipped back, his beard thick and mottled, he stood defiantly, one hand crooked at his hip, the other thrust in his pocket. Most importantly, he was dressed in the clothes of the common man. No waistcoat or tie, he posed with his collar open, revealing a working-man's undershirt.

The dramatic appearance in 1855 and the quickly ensuing issuance of the 1856 edition of *Leaves of Grass*, however, slipped into a second silence in 1857 that lasted until the final months of 1859. Whitman was editing the *Brooklyn Daily Times* for part of that time but, as Ezra Greenspan has noted, put so little of himself into the paper that it seemed almost as if it were edited by some other Walt Whitman.[19] The tone of the editorials bears almost no resemblance to Whitman's distinctive style; indeed, many scholars harbor doubts about his authorship—despite Whitman's own claim to have edited the paper from 1857–1859.[20]

That silence was ended by the publication of the greatly expanded 1860 edition of *Leaves of Grass*, but after its release tradition holds that Whitman disappeared a third time for more than two years. Jerome Loving, in his recent biography *Walt Whitman: The Song of Himself*, goes so far as to assign specific dates to this vanishing: "Whitman fairly disappears from all biographies between May 24, 1860, when he took the Shore Line Railroad back from Boston after seeing the third edition of *Leaves of Grass* through the press, to December 16, 1862, when the Whitman household at 122 Portland Street, near Myrtle Avenue in Brooklyn, got its first indication that brother George had been wounded at the Battle of Fredericksburg."[21]

Loving is hardly alone in his judgment. Ed Folsom and Kenneth M. Price describe the years leading up to the Civil War as "one of the haziest periods of Whitman's life."[22] Roy Morris Jr. described Whitman during these years as "strangely abstracted," until the war "showed up abruptly on the Whitmans' own doorstep."[23] M. Jimmie Killingsworth has gone one step further, writing that Whitman "seems to have worked at avoiding the reality of war."[24]

Whitman left a dauntingly complete record of his war years in Washington, D.C. By providing more than enough material for a book in his 1863 and early 1864 prose writings as well as his 1865 publications of *Drum-Taps* and *Sequel to Drum-Taps*, Whitman has freed scholars from the necessity of investigating the interstices.

For example, Roy Morris Jr.'s *Better Angel*, which claims to be the first book-length study of Whitman's Civil War period, instead focuses almost exclusively on Whitman in Washington during 1863 and parts of 1864 and 1865. Morris nods toward periodical history by mentioning

Whitman's numerous associations—friendships with Henry Clapp of the *New York Leader* in 1861 or William Swinton of the *New York Times* in 1863, for example—but he never considers how such friendships may have granted Whitman entrance to certain publications, much less how those editorial tastes or those readerships may have shaped his work. He also falls prey to a common desire to pinpoint a stable aesthetic and artistic vision, rather than recognize that Whitman's penchant for reinvention was only accelerated by the dynamism of war. In an effort to present a simple narrative, Morris's book, like so many studies before, grants only a few pages to Whitman's activities in 1861 and 1862. Likewise, Mark Daniel Epstein, in *Lincoln and Whitman: Parallel Lives in Civil War Washington*, claims only to document Whitman's years while he lived in Washington, but he freely includes New York passages—such as the printing of *Drum-Taps*—when the historical record is readily available.

A far better model for an account of Whitman during the war is Stanton Garner's *The Civil War World of Herman Melville*, a kaleidoscopic study encompassing Melville's life from the buildup to war to the beginnings of reconstruction. The encyclopedic range of the book is all the more remarkable when one considers that Melville left almost no direct record of his life during this time—no diary, fewer than two dozen letters, and almost no incoming correspondence. In order to sustain this work of more than 500 pages, Garner relies on a wealth of less conventional sources to recreate the world that shaped Melville's war experience—asserting in his introduction, "Thus if it is impossible to know much about the life of Herman Melville, it is possible to know a great deal about the world in which he lived."[25] This combination of archival sources, contemporary accounts from the popular press, military records, and Melville's own poetry weaves together into a rich and surprisingly coherent portrait. The method is especially appropriate and effective, because Garner does such an effective job of linking his source material to Melville's own works. Though Melville watched blockade ships being readied for duty in the Brooklyn Navy Yard and even rode out on a cavalry scouting expedition in 1864, it was primarily through newspapers, magazines, and the *Rebellion Record* that he learned of the progress of the war and created his own version of its events. Thus Garner's book is able to map Melville's intellectual engagement with the war in ways that conventional biography could not.

Proceeding along this same course, I have sought to fill in the gap of Whitman's years from 1860 to 1862. As with Melville, little of Whitman's outgoing correspondence of that period survives. For example, all of his letters to Thayer & Eldridge relating to the 1860 edition of *Leaves of Grass* and the abortive *The Banner At Day-Break* were likely destroyed when the firm sank into bankruptcy and saw its assets seized and auctioned. His letters to his brother George, who enlisted in April 1861 and then reenlisted in September 1861, were not preserved. George probably discarded them at the time. Indeed, only ten letters known to have been written by Whitman survive from 1860 through 1862—and four of those were discovered in the course of researching this book.

During that same period, however, Whitman was hardly hidden from public view. He published poems in the *Saturday Press*, the *New York Times*, *Harper's Weekly*, and the *New York Leader*; submitted other poems that were rejected; and began drafts of many more. He published more than thirty articles in the *Leader*, *Brooklyn Standard*, *Brooklyn City News*, and *Brooklyn Eagle* and was the subject of numerous others. He kept notebooks of poem jottings, ideas, and addresses and maintained a collection of incoming correspondence numbering nearly fifty letters.

In addition to these already known sources I have added a sizable body of new information, ranging from undocumented publications and new letters to numerous additions to the corpus of popular discussion that surrounded Whitman and his work. If Whitman's interior world is sometimes difficult to fathom, his public self is highly visible. Almost never did an issue of Henry Clapp's *Saturday Press* appear in 1860 without extended mention of Whitman. The publication of his poems in mainstream periodicals in 1861 drew responses from all over the country, many of which reflect regional attitudes toward the poetry and the democratic ideals they espouse.

Whitman was not merely contributing to the media of the time, however; his work was indelibly inscribed and shaped by the limits that the war imposed on the print culture. He sought particular audiences for his poems and articles; he published some works for artistic expression and others for financial gain; he wrote according to the schedules of newspapers as they published more or less frequently due to the war; and sometimes his work went unpublished when a periodical ceased publication or an editor was forced from his post. To date, scholars of Whitman's Civil War writings have not reckoned with these realities. This book is a step in that direction—an effort to fill a crucial gap in the biographical record and, in so doing, to debunk the myth that Whitman was uninvolved in and unaffected by the country's march to war. This long-standing characterization not only misjudges him during this period, it also ignores the quicksand events that whirled Whitman, as politics failed and the country threatened to tear itself in two.

CHAPTER ONE

The Red-Hot Fellows
of Those Times

I was a decided and outspoken anti-slavery believer myself,
then and always; but shied from the extremists, the red-hot
fellows of those times.

> Whitman's preface to William
> Douglas O'Connor's *Three Tales*

Just past two o'clock on the bitter-cold morning of December 5, 1859,
the body of John Brown was secreted from the steamboat landing in New
York City, where it had been unloaded several hours earlier, to McGraw
& Taylor undertakers in the Bowery district. The hope was to avoid a re-
peat of the scene in Philadelphia, where, days earlier, a throng of well-
wishers, many of them former slaves, had followed the funeral wagon
from the depot at Broad Street all the way to the Walnut Street wharf—
the massive spectacle drawing workers away from their stations at the
factories, the crowd increasing as it went. In New York, where the race
debate was now fevered, many feared that a public conveyance of Brown's
body would end in violence. Only the night before, on December 4, Reverend Antoinette Brown Blackwell had preached in support of Brown at
Goldbeck's Musical Hall on Broadway, and the Winter Garden Theater

was set to premiere the antislavery tragedy *The Octoroon*, which the *New York Herald* predicted would touch off riots.[1]

Worst of all, a public gathering to debate the morality of inciting slave insurrections had been called for the Peoples' Meeting, a public hall that, by coincidence, stood less than a block from McGraw & Taylor. Somehow word spread at the meeting that down the street Brown's corpse was being dressed for burial. By late afternoon the ranks of the curious shook the gate at the rear entrance to the funeral home, demanding admission. To satisfy the mob, police eventually allowed an orderly line to enter for a private viewing, including two of Brown's old associates, Richard J. Hinton and John Swinton.[2]

Hinton, an English émigré not yet thirty years old, had first become involved in militant antislavery activities in 1854 while working as a journalist covering the Anthony Burns fugitive slave case in Boston. So swayed was he by abolitionist rhetoric that he joined Thomas Wentworth Higginson and Martin Stowall in the failed attack on the Boston Court House. Within two years Hinton was in Kansas again, ostensibly to report for the *Boston Traveler* and the *Chicago Tribune* on Free Soil radicals, but in fact he was fighting with a new band led by Higginson and Stowall.[3]

At the Whitney House hotel in Lawrence, Kansas, Hinton formed lasting friendships with other activist-journalists, including Swinton, then managing editor of the *Lawrence Republican*, and James Redpath, a reporter for the St. Louis–based *Daily Missouri Democrat*. After the sack of Lawrence, Redpath joined John Brown himself and spent nearly two years gathering narratives from slaves across the South in hopes of gauging their readiness to join in armed revolt. In 1859 these narratives were gathered into a book, *The Roving Editor; or, Talks with Slaves in the Southern States*, which Redpath dedicated to Brown, writing, "You, Old Hero! believe that the slave should be aided and urged to insurrection, and hence do I lay this tribute at your feet."[4] After the failure at Harpers Ferry, Redpath, unlike many of Brown's followers, continued to support him publicly, authoring a series of high-profile defenses of Brown for the Boston *Atlas and Daily Bee*.

Redpath's editorials caught the eye of the Boston publisher Thayer & Eldridge. William Wilde Thayer and Charles W. Eldridge, former clerks at the publishing house Dayton and Wentworth, were just twenty-eight and twenty-one years old and had not yet published a book when they wrote to Redpath to suggest a biography of John Brown, but the two ambitious young men had bought out their former boss, Horace Wentworth, on credit secured from such influential backers as Senator Charles Sumner, the *Liberator* editor William Lloyd Garrison, and the orator Wendell Phillips, on the assurance that they would publish abolitionist texts on timely subjects. Seeing a great opportunity to launch their business they convinced Redpath to take on the task of writing Brown's life by promising that a portion of the profits would be given to Brown's bereaved family. Redpath later explained, "They believed in John Brown; they wished to do him justice; and they desired to assist his destitute family. . . . I could not resist it."[5]

Redpath quickly sought out Hinton to assist with research, but Hinton had cause for concern. A carpetbag of letters discovered at Brown's hideout at Harpers Ferry mentioned Hinton, so he agreed to work with Redpath only on the condition of anonymity. For most of November, while Brown awaited execution in Virginia, Hinton interviewed Brown's family in Kansas and Ohio and just happened to be in New York on his way back to Boston when he learned that the hanged man's body had arrived in the city.

As Hinton and Swinton stood before Brown's coffin in the failing light of the afternoon, the lid was removed and the head and shoulders of the abolitionist martyr were exposed. The undertakers had done their work well, removing the noose Brown's executioners had purposely left around his neck and covering the purple bruises that had blossomed on his brow as the arteries in his head ruptured and bled under the skin. There was no hint of his sudden, violent death; Hinton wrote that he "wore a calm expression as of one asleep."[6]

But Swinton, who had not seen Brown since he had grown his long grizzled beard, was struck by how the old man, under the flickering gaslights and long shadows of that late winter afternoon, bore a shocking resemblance to his friend Walt Whitman. Hinton, too, knew Whitman; they had met when Whitman personally delivered a review copy of the first edition of *Leaves of Grass* to the *Knickerbocker* magazine, where Hinton worked. The two reporters left the funeral home talking about their mutual acquaintance, Swinton saying that a new edition of *Leaves of Grass* was ready for press but could find no publisher, and Hinton replying that he was going to Thayer & Eldridge the next day and would put in a good word.[7]

But by then Thayer & Eldridge were focusing their efforts on the Brown biography. All their future books would depend on the success of this first title. The timing was problematic: across the South a movement was afoot to outlaw the distribution or sale of any printed material advocating an end to slavery. As early as 1857 a bookseller in Mobile had been expelled from Alabama for ordering a copy of Frederick Douglass's *Narrative* for a customer.[8] In the wake of Harpers Ferry, Hinton R. Helper's *The Impending Crisis of the South* was banned in several southern states because it called on poor nonslaveholders to oppose slavery rather than risk getting caught up in a war that did not directly affect them. To counter these book bans a Republican committee printed an abridged edition of *The Impending Crisis* that they distributed surreptitiously throughout the South. Sixty-eight Republican members of Congress signed an endorsement of the book.

Among the signatories was John Sherman of Ohio, who was nominated for speaker of the House when the new session of Congress convened on December 5, the very day Brown's body was dressed for burial in New York. The revelation that Sherman had endorsed *The Impending Crisis* touched off a scandal that resulted in more than two months and forty-four votes of hopeless deadlock over his nomination. This chaos on Capitol Hill also opened the door for Senator James M. Mason of Virginia, author of the Fugitive Slave Law, to call for the appointment of a committee to investigate the Harpers Ferry raid to determine whether "such invasion was made under color of any organization intended to subvert the Government of any State of the Union."[9]

The reaction to Brown's execution and the possibility of slave revolt helped spur interest in Redpath's biography. On the sole basis of a few advance advertisements in *The Liberator* and the *National Era*, orders flooded into the Thayer & Eldridge offices. By Christmas Eve, barely a month after the book was announced, ten thousand subscribers from New England alone had requested the book, and as the projected publication date of New Year's Day approached, the volume of orders increased to nearly a thousand per day.[10] Soon other publishers began advertising competing volumes, hastily assembled from newspaper accounts, but Redpath's book relied on his personal knowledge of Brown, his own and Hinton's hours of interviews, countless private letters retrieved by Redpath's wife from Brown's family in North Elba, and Brown's unpublished autobiography, which Redpath included as an appendix. Were this not enough, Thayer & Eldridge secured endorsements from Brown's widow and children, including a statement from one of the sons, Salmon Brown, that Redpath "above all others" was the man to write his father's biography.[11]

By the time the book finally was issued from the press on January 10, 1860, more than thirty thousand copies had been ordered in advance. In Boston's Suffolk County Thayer & Eldridge had to hire a half-dozen book agents to deliver copies and take additional orders.[12] Just two weeks after the book's publication, they sent over a thousand dollars to Brown's widow—her share of their remarkable windfall. It seemed that everything was going better than the two young publishers could ever have hoped.

But the intimate knowledge of Brown's clan that made the book such a sensation also aroused the interest of Senator Mason's investigatory committee. They issued a summons for Redpath to appear, along with the Concord radical Franklin B. Sanborn and John Brown Jr., no later than February 6. Redpath responded that pressing business detained him, but he was not excused from testifying. When the date passed and the men had not appeared before Congress, warrants were issued and federal marshals were dispatched to arrest them as material witnesses. But the warrants were too late in coming. On February 10, 1860, *The*

Liberator reported that Redpath had decided to "disappoint the expectations of the Committee" by fleeing for parts unknown, prompting *Vanity Fair* to muse, "The quickest path out of the country: Redpath."[13] Thayer & Eldridge's best-selling author—its only author—was a wanted fugitive.

Broadway, wrote Walt Whitman, was a "mighty ever-flowing land-river, pouring down through the center of Manhattan Island."[14] Along either side rose New York's signature landmarks: City Hall, City Hospital, Barnum's Museum, the Astor House, the Tabernacle, and the new grand theaters. Sandwiched between stood every conceivable caste of storefront and business: the offices of doctors and undertakers; the shops of haberdashers, hatters, and tailors; hotels and drug stores; booksellers and publishers; and always upstairs the skylit photograph and ambrotype establishments, the studios of portrait painters; downstairs, billiard halls and ten-pin alleys, brothels and opium dens, cheap rathskellers and oyster saloons. One such underground watering hole, on the west side of Broadway just above Bleecker, was Pfaff's Restaurant and Lager Bier Saloon—though to its patrons it was simply Pfaff's or, sometimes, "the Cave."

As its nickname would suggest, the amenities at Pfaff's were few. The main room held a handful of round tables clustered near the bar. The second room, which tunneled under the sidewalk, held a single long table, informally dubbed "the Bohemian table."[15] Early advertisements promised "the best viands, the best lager bier, the best coffee and tea, the best wines and liquors, the best Havana cigars, the best company; in fine, the best of everything."[16] But the reality was much humbler. The saloon's founder, a Swiss German immigrant named Charles Ignatius Pfaff, used the same pewter mugs to serve both Rhine wine and beer, and he dished up fried beefsteaks and German *pfannekuchen*.[17] One of the regulars later mused that Pfaff had begun his business with little more than a few kegs of beer and a special talent for making coffee, which was fortunate because Pfaff's most important customer, Henry Clapp Jr., "subsisted chiefly on coffee and tobacco."[18]

In addition to being the acknowledged ringleader at Pfaff's, Clapp was the editor of the *Saturday Press*, declared by the *New York Traveller* to be "the sprightliest, raciest, frankest, sauciest, sharpest, wittiest, most piquant, original, outspoken, and sententious American literary weekly."[19] William Winter, one of Clapp's associate editors, remembered the man himself in much the same way: "brilliant and buoyant in mind; impatient of the commonplace; intolerant of the smug, ponderous, empty, obstructive respectability; prone to sarcasm; and he had for so long a time lived in a continuous bitter conflict with conventionality that he had become reckless of public opinion."[20]

Each night after dinner Clapp assumed the head of the Bohemian table and became the sharp-tongued center of attention, whose special talent lay in whittling lofty figures down to size with his pithy quips. Asked his opinion of Horace Greeley, the editor of the *New York Tribune*, Clapp declared, "Horace Greeley is emphatically a self-made man," then quickly added, *"and he worships his Creator!"*[21] Of the high-and-mighty Reverend Samuel Osgood, Clapp said, "He is waiting for a vacancy in the Trinity."[22] It's no wonder that one detractor remembered, "When he talked it was like snapping glass under your heel," or that another wrote, "He is a born Yankee; speaks French like a native; plays poker like a Western man; drinks like a fish, smokes like a Dutchman; is as full of dainty conceits as a Spanish or Italian poet, is as rough in his manners as a Russian or a Russian bear."[23]

By the late months of 1859 Walt Whitman was always at Clapp's right hand. In sharp contrast to the wiry, effervescent Clapp, Whitman was broad-shouldered, his hair and beard mottled with gray, his face always ruddy and eyebrows always arched. He wore plain blue or gray coats with his shirt collars undone, revealing his thick neck and the hair on his chest. He rarely spoke, and when he did he was never an accomplished punster like Clapp; still, his comments could cut the young poets who revered him to the quick. Of William Winter he once said, "Willy is a young Longfellow," which Winter bitterly recalled decades later as "the perfection of contemptuous indifference."[24] When Thomas Bailey Aldrich asked Whitman's opinion of his poems, Whitman replied, "I like your *tinkles:* I like them very well." To which the wounded Aldrich replied in the pages of *Vanity Fair,* "You will kill me with laughter, some day, you dear owl!"[25]

Whitman may have dismissed the poor efforts of younger poets, but since self-issuing the second edition of *Leaves of Grass* more than three years earlier he had not published any poetry of his own. In the intervening time he had prepared an 1857 edition of *Leaves* but failed to find financial backing; he had been hired and fired as editor of the *Brooklyn Daily Times;* and he had slid into what he would later describe as his "slough."

All that changed when Henry Clapp offered to publish a new poem by Whitman, titled "A Child's Reminiscence" (later "Out of the Cradle Endlessly Rocking"), in the *Saturday Press* on Christmas Eve 1859. Appearing in the *Saturday Press* was an important reemergence for Whitman, largely because it carried with it the implied imprimatur of its influential editor. The *New York Dispatch* had praised Clapp's integrity, claiming he could not "be induced by money or patronage to puff anybody or anything not deserving free favorable mention."[26] But Whitman himself was not above such puffery.

To emphasize Clapp's endorsement Whitman took out ads in a half-dozen newspapers in Manhattan and Brooklyn, describing the poem as the "Saturday Press's Christmas present."[27] For the Brooklyn papers he had planned a six-line excerpt from the poem but apparently couldn't afford to buy the space. Instead, he wrote an anonymous article for the *Brooklyn City News* explaining the poem. He described it as "a curious ballad . . . after the same rude and mystical type of versification" as *Leaves of Grass* and played up the fact that the setting was "this island of ours, under its old aboriginal name of Paumanok." He warned readers, however, that "the whole poem needs to be read in its entirety—and several times at that."[28] Whitman also convinced Clapp to run an anonymous editorial to accompany the poem. Combining the language of the advertisements and the *City News* article, Whitman wrote:

Our readers may, if they choose, consider as our Christmas or New Year's present to them, the curious warble, by Walt Whitman, of "*A Child's Reminiscence*," on our First Page. Like the "*Leaves of Grass*," the purport of this wild and plaintive song, well-enveloped, and eluding definition, is positive and unquestionable, like the effect of music.

The piece will bear reading many times—perhaps indeed only comes forth, as from recesses, by many repetitions.[29]

As Whitman had hoped, the poem aroused a response, but the *Cincinnati Daily Commercial* scoffed at the editorial, writing, "Curious, it may be; but warble it is not, in any sense of that mellifluous word," and deriding the description of the poem as "well-enveloped, and eluding definition": "Indeed! We should think so. For our part, we hope it will remain 'well enveloped' till doomsday; and as for 'definition,' all we can do in that direction is to declare that either that 'poem' is nonsense, or we are a lunatic."[30]

Yet for all the vitriol directed at Whitman, the Cincinnati reviewer was particularly disappointed to see the poem represented in the *Saturday Press*. Clapp had built the paper's reputation on quick-witted and allusive verse, "sparkling *bons mots*." There was no trace of "juicy" puns or "charming piquancies" in Whitman's work:

How in the name of all the Muses this so-called "poem" ever got into the columns of the *Saturday Press*, passes our poor comprehension. We had come to look upon that journal as the prince of literary weeklies, the *arbiter elegantiarum* of dramatic and poetic taste, into whose well filled columns nothing stupid or inferior could intrude . . . [but] that unclean cub of the wilderness, Walt Whitman, has been suffered to intrude, trampling with his vulgar and profane hoofs among the delicate flowers which bloom there, and soiling the spotless white of its fair columns with lines of stupid and meaningless twaddle.[31]

Never able to resist coming to his own defense, Whitman published an anonymous review of his "lyric utterances," titled "All About a Mocking-

Bird," in the January 7 issue of the *Saturday Press*. He did not stop, however, at explaining the methods of his poem in response to the "tip-top
cutting-and-slashing criticism from the *Cincinnati Daily Commercial*." He
also claimed:

> We are able to declare that there will also soon crop out the true
> Leaves of Grass, the fuller-grown work of which the former two is-
> sues were the inchoates—this forthcoming one, far, very far ahead of
> them in quality, quantity, and in supple lyric exuberance.
>
> Those former issues, published by the author himself in little
> pittance-editions, on trial, have just dropped the book enough to rip-
> ple the inner first-circles of literary agitation, in immediate contact
> with it. The outer, vast, extending, and ever-wider-extending circles,
> of the general supply, perusal, and discussion of such a work, have
> still to come. The market needs to-day to be supplied—the great
> West especially—with copious thousands of copies.[32]

By this point Whitman may have been aware that Richard J. Hinton was
lobbying his publishers on Whitman's behalf. Certainly the article seems
less a defense of his one poem than an advertisement for the edition he
envisioned.

In service of this goal Henry Clapp was only too happy to continue the
controversy over "A Child's Reminiscence" into the next issue of the *Saturday Press*. First, "Umos," the paper's correspondent from Washington, delivered a humorous account of attempting to read Whitman's poem aloud
to his wife. He likened the experience to his first time on ice skates and won-
dered if Whitman wasn't upon his "*muse*-ical skates for the first time." He
asked his wife what Clapp could have seen in such "wretched trumpery," to
which she replied that "she didn't think it trumpery . . . she thought there
was something in it." The author did not press further, he said, in order to
maintain the peace of his household, but it was his "private opinion," he
wrote Clapp, that "Whitman found a lot of dictionary *pi* going off at auction, bought it for a song, employed a Chinese type-setter from the Bible
House to set it up in lines of unequal length, and then sold it to you as an
original Poem."[33]

In a neighboring column, Whitman's fellow Pfaffian, the actress and novelist Ada Clare, took issue with the denunciation of Whitman's style voiced by Umos. She declared that "a practiced versifier might go on rhyming until the seas were dry" without achieving any emotional effect; as an example, she pointed to the prim meters and rhymes of William Winter. Whitman's poem, however, "could only have been written by a poet, and versifying would not help it." She admitted, "I love the poem."[34]

Henry Clapp did not weigh in on the controversy directly, but he certainly recognized the value of a literary dustup. On the front page, in the same position he had published "A Child's Reminiscence" three weeks before, he published another Whitman poem, "You and Me and To-Day," and soon followed it with two more poems, each titled "Poemet," and another titled simply "Leaves."[35] At the same time Clapp began featuring regular parodies of Whitman's poems written by an anonymous Philadelphian, who identified himself only as "Saerasmid." The secret author, Charles Desmarais (an anagram of Saerasmid) Gardette, was a former reporter for the *New York Evening Post* who now wrote for the *Philadelphia Evening Journal* and also contributed frequently to the *Saturday Press*; whenever he was in New York he joined Clapp, Whitman, and the others at the Bohemian table.[36] An accomplished parodist, Gardette achieved his greatest fame when challenged by his friends to create a perfect imitation of Poe. His homage, published in the November 19, 1859, issue of the *Saturday Press*, was so convincing that it continued to surface in volumes of Poe's collected works into the twentieth century, even after Gardette published detailed accounts of its composition.

Gardette's "Yourn, Mine, and Any-Day" lampooned Whitman's "You and Me and To-Day" line by line. His send-up of "Poemet" was not so much a parody as a series of asides built within Whitman's own text—what the author called "parentheses, analytical, antithetical, philosophical, and explanatory." Thus Whitman's line "And if the memorials of the dead were put indifferently everywhere, even in the room where I eat or sleep, I should be satisfied" became Gardette's "And if the memorials of the dead (i.e. posthumous biographies, etc.) were put up indifferently, (i.e. not well bound) everywhere, even in the room where I eat or sleep, I should be satisfied, (i.e. to accept 'em as additions to my library)."

The constant attention, the fiery back and forth may finally have convinced Thayer & Eldridge that Whitman's work had captured the public's imagination and might match the sales he so brazenly promised. They may also have learned that Emerson had convinced James Russell Lowell to publish Whitman's "Bardic Symbols" (later "As I Ebb'd with the Ocean of Life") in Boston's highly influential *Atlantic Monthly*. Or they may simply have concluded that, if they intended to make their business an ongoing concern, they were now in need of authors. They had already written to the young fiction writer William D. O'Connor, offering to pay him a salary if he would write a novel, but Whitman bragged of having a book at the ready.[37]

On February 10, the day James Redpath was discovered to have fled Malden, Massachusetts, Thayer & Eldridge wrote, "We want to be the publishers of Walt. Whitman's Poems—Leaves of Grass," promising Whitman, "[We can] put your books into good form, and style attractive to the eye; we can sell a large number of copies." Their enthusiasm, however, exceeded their knowledge of Whitman's intentions; they were forced to conclude by asking of his poems, "Are they ready for the press? Will you let us read them? Will you write us? Please give us your residence."[38]

. . .

Late on the day that Thayer and Eldridge wrote to Whitman, they convened a meeting in the back room of their bookshop on Washington Street. The counting room doubled as the regular meeting space of a militant group of abolitionists in Boston, known as the Black Strings—for the thin black ribbons members wore under their collars to identify each other. This loose-knit network, hastily assembled after Harpers Ferry, formed a kind of Underground Railroad for Brown's confederates, providing them with safe houses and spiriting them from one place to another under cover of darkness. For several weeks Thayer had been concealing Charles Plummer Tidd, one of the Harpers Ferry Raiders, at his home on Myrtle Street, waiting for the opportunity to send him north to Canada but also relying on him for information about the area surrounding Harpers Ferry as plans were made for rescuing other members of Brown's party. The Unitarian minister, writer, and radical abolitionist Thomas Wentworth Higginson came to Boston from Worcester on February 10 to meet with Tidd at Thayer & Eldridge to discuss his plan to break two of Brown's accomplices, Albert Hazlett and Aaron Stevens, out of the jail in Harpers Ferry.

Despite Tidd's discouraging assessment of the terrain and the hostility of the populace around Charlestown, Higginson was determined to forge ahead. He had already sent Hinton to Kansas to gather a band of Brown's faithful followers, and Hinton had wired that the party, including the jailbreaker Silas S. Soule and Brown's close confidant James Montgomery, was on its way to the rendezvous point in Harrisburg, Pennsylvania, some fifty miles from the jail. Thayer offered Higginson eight hundred dollars for what was expected to be a long period in hiding. He gave nearly four hundred up front and promised to deliver the rest personally to Harrisburg the next day. Higginson took the money and left immediately.

The rash plan had all the earmarks of a second Harpers Ferry, with even longer odds and a more certain outcome. Higginson himself summarized the "difficulties" he perceived:

> The enterprise would involve traversing fifty miles of mountain country by night, carrying arms, ammunition, blankets, and a week's rations, with the frequent necessity of camping without fire in February, and with the certainty of detection in case of snow. It would include crossing the Potomac, possibly at a point where there was neither a bridge nor a ford. It would culminate in an attack on a building with a wall fourteen feet high, with two sentinels outside and twenty-five inside; with a certainty of raising the town in the process, and then, if successful, with the need of retreating, perhaps with wounded men and probably by daylight.[39]

Were this not ambitious enough, the plan was not to take Stevens and Hazlett north, but rather to go over the mountains to the south and all the way to the coast in hopes of buying passage—with the money supplied by Thayer—on a ship to Cuba or Haiti.[40]

Despite grave doubts, Thayer left the next day for Harrisburg with the remainder of the promised money "in small bills sewed in a bag that was fastened between my legs at the crotch" and a bag of tools, including "field glasses, saws and files for jail window bars." After a restless night at the Astor House in New York, fearful of being robbed, Thayer arrived at the United States Hotel in Harrisburg, where he met up with Higginson's Massachusetts men and Hinton's Kansas party. All agreed to spend the next days in reconnaissance.[41]

On February 18 Soule sneaked into Charlestown, feigned drunkenness, and was thrown into the same jail as Hazlett and Stevens. He told them of the plot to help them escape, but they asked Soule to call off the rescue, fearful that the jailer, who had shown such kindness to John Brown, would be killed in the attempt. Soule was released from jail the next morning and made his way back to Harrisburg with the discouraging news. At the same time, Montgomery returned with word that a blizzard was headed their way from the west. A meeting was called in the tavern of the hotel and a vote taken; all were in unanimous agreement that the mission should go forward despite the obvious risks. After the vote Montgomery, though he considered it folly, acceded. "I will lead you," he said.

But Higginson had changed his mind. Many years later Thayer remembered that Higginson pushed his chair back from the table and demanded, "Why then shall 15 men lose their lives and at that fail to save the prisoners? If the latter could be done, it might have some justification for the attempt. No, you must not go." He concluded his speech by saying simply, "I was the man who asked you to come here. I command you to disperse."[42] The Massachusetts men left for home, but the Kansas party decided to remain close, in case a better opportunity for the rescue should present itself. It never did.

On the morning of March 16 Aaron D. Stevens and Albert Hazlett were led to the gallows and, precisely at noon, were dropped by the neck. Hazlett died instantly, but the younger, stronger Stevens struggled and convulsed for several minutes before finally falling limp.

Back in Boston Whitman had arrived to see to the publication of his new edition of *Leaves of Grass* but found Thayer and Eldridge gone to a public memorial for the executed prisoners at Meionson meeting hall. Many of Brown's close confidants, including Soule and Montgomery, were in attendance, and several, such as Dr. John Doy and Higginson, addressed the crowd. But the evening belonged to Hinton. He spoke movingly of his friendship with Aaron Stevens and the urgent rage against slavery that the young man displayed, but Hinton reminded the more temperate members of the audience that political resolve was needed as well. He urged the crowd to support William Seward for the Republican nomination for president and to pressure Seward to stay true to his antislavery beliefs. "The contest is deepening," Hinton told the crowd. "And the time has come when we should fling out a new banner, writing thereon: 'The Abolition of Slavery—under the Constitution or over the Constitution; through the Union or out of the Union. It's abolition by all means and through every agency.' Marshalled under this banner, we can exert a moral force through the ballot-box never felt before."[43]

In faraway Ohio another rally had been organized at the Jefferson Courthouse in Ashtabula County, where John Brown Jr. and Owen Brown were in hiding from federal marshals. William C. Howells, the editor of the *Ashtabula Sentinel* and a supporter of John Brown, had assured his readers, "We can maintain secrecy; we can frown on, and refuse intercourse with spies; we have houses, and homes, and hearts, to lend refuge."[44] Howells had reason to be confident. James Redpath had not fled to Canada, as widely reported, but to Ashtabula, where he and Howells had started an Ohio branch of the Black Strings. A writer for the *National Democrat* who attended the rally reported, "There is a band here pledged to resisting, even unto death, whose distinguishing mark is a black ribbon worn around the neck."[45] The intention of the members in

Boston was that Ashtabula would serve as a stronghold to which Brown's conspirators could be smuggled.

But Redpath had larger—and more revolutionary—plans. Like Hinton, he had been a close friend of Aaron Stevens, and the news of his execution enraged him. "Stevens is dead," Redpath told the crowd packed into the courthouse. "His brave life was choked out of him for presuming, without asking Senator Mason's permission, to believe in the Declaration of Independence." Redpath called on his Ashtabula brethren to follow Stevens's example:

> *To those of you who are ready to imitate Stevens, this only need be said: "Be prepared; bide your time; ere long you will be called."* For I tell you, men of Ashtabula, that the strangling of John Brown was not the death of his cause; and that, ere many more moons revolve, the slave will be offered succor again. Six months before the blow at Harper's Ferry I stated that it would be made, and even indicated by whom: and again, *I give the slave driver a solemn warning to set his house in order, for his doom is pronounced—"he shall die and not live."*[46]

Redpath called on the crowd to give generously to support the cause. He was also planning a follow-up book for Thayer & Eldridge, a collection of sermons, essays, and poems in tribute to Brown that he hoped would sell as well as the Brown biography. The eventual volume would include William Dean Howells's poem "Old Brown," originally published in his father's *Ashtabula Sentinel* on January 25. The younger Howells, in addition to being an aspiring poet with a slim volume of poems coauthored with John J. Piatt and published by Follett & Foster, was also a writer for the *Daily Ohio State Journal* in Columbus. And he was a devoted reader of the *Saturday Press*.

Howells had mentioned Whitman several times in his *State Journal* columns during the early months of 1860, but it was Redpath who apparently gave Howells the new issue of the *Atlantic Monthly* with "Bardic Symbols," published that weekend without an author's byline (as was all work in the *Atlantic* at that time).[47] But Whitman's authorial hand was unmistakable. The *New York Times* declared that this "fantastical seadrift" of a poem needed "no ghost of a publisher's lead-pencil to inform [readers that it] came out from ocean-deeps of that remarkable 'Kosmos,' Mr. WALT. WHITMAN."[48] The *Saturday Press* recognized the poet's "unmistakable impress of genius" and took the opportunity "to congratulate the Magazine on the acquisition of Walt Whitman as one of its contributors."[49] Howells not only recognized the author but showed intimate knowledge of him. In a review in the *State Journal* he mentioned that Whitman had briefly driven a Broadway omnibus in late 1859 before "he suddenly flashed upon us in the New York *Saturday Press*, and created eager dissension among the 'crickets.' "[50]

Howells also denounced the critics who had too quickly dismissed Whitman, asserting that the poet had "higher claims upon our consideration than mere magazine contributorship" because *Leaves of Grass*, "whatever else you may think, is wonderful." But even Howells felt forced to admit that "Bardic Symbols" appeared "more lawless, measureless, rhymeless and inscrutable than ever." He may have recalled Whitman's warning months earlier that "A Child's Reminiscence" would "only [come] forth, as from recesses, by many repetitions," but Howells found repeated readings of no help: "No one, even after the fourth or fifth reading, can pretend to say what the 'Bardic Symbols' symbolize. The poet walks by the sea, and addressing the drift, the foam, the billows and the wind, attempts to force from them, by his frantic outcry, the true solution of the mystery of Existence, always most heavily and darkly felt in the august ocean presence. All is confusion, waste and sound. It is in vain that you attempt to gather the poet's full meaning from what he says or what he hints."[51] Despite Howells's professed ambivalence, he soon after wrote a Whitmanesque, free verse poem entitled "The Pilot's Story" and sent it to the *Atlantic*.

On the morning after the execution of Stevens and Hazlett, Ralph Waldo Emerson appeared unannounced in the counting room of Thayer & Eldridge. Emerson was to deliver his lecture "Moral Sentiment" for the Parker Fraternity at the Music Hall on that Sunday night and, arriving a day early from Concord, learned that Whitman was in Boston. A mutual friend had given him the address of Whitman's boarding house, where he learned that Whitman was at the printer. Charles Eldridge put everything aside to escort Emerson directly to the top floor of the Boston Stereotype Foundry, where Whitman was reading proofs.[52]

Emerson was no ordinary visitor. He was one of the select few who had championed the first edition of *Leaves of Grass* in 1855, sending Whitman what today stands as one of the most famous letters in American literature. A large measure of its fame is due to the fact that Whitman used the letter repeatedly to promote the first edition, publishing it first in the *New York Tribune*, then printing small broadsides that he pasted onto the marbled endpapers of the book, and finally printing it as part of a group of reviews that he included in later bindings of the book. Emerson had not given permission for the use of his letter and he considered Whitman's broadcasting of it "a strange rude thing,"[53] but his support for the work never wavered, even when Whitman went so far as to emblazon the spine of the 1856 edition with Emerson's words in gilt lettering: "I greet you at the beginning of a great career."

The Boston Stereotype Foundry was not the sort of place Emerson usually frequented. Even on a cold Saturday morning it radiated heat, and even on this St. Patrick's Day in Irish Boston the factory was in full swing. Typesetters in shirtsleeves on the top floor set text in movable type; among them Whitman recorded a black man "working at case" with "no distinction made between him and the white compositors."[54] When a page was complete, sample sheets were pulled from the proof presses for Whitman to approve. He had been given the use of a shabby little office on that floor, furnished with little more than a desk and a pair of chairs.[55] Once he signed off on the proof, the trays of type were sent downstairs to be cast as electrotype forms, which in turn were filled with hot lead in the basement foundry. The heat of the furnaces and the stench of molten lead made the rooms inside the foundry stifling.

When Eldridge and Emerson found Whitman here, the poet suggested that Emerson join him on a walk. Whitman told one correspondent that Emerson "kept possession of me all day," including during "a bully dinner."[56] More than likely it was on this day that Whitman showed Emerson the letter from Thayer & Eldridge, to which he was supposed to have remarked that "there was hope for freedom of thought and a free press when such a publishing house . . . had its home in Boston."[57] It may also have been on that day that Whitman and Emerson strolled together, arm in arm, on Boston Common and Emerson attempted to dissuade Whitman from publishing certain sexually explicit passages in *Leaves of Grass:*

> During those two hours he was the talker and I the listener. It was an argument-statement, reconnoitring, review, attack, and pressing home, (like an army corps in order, artillery, cavalry, infantry,) of all that could be said against that part (and a main part) in the construction of my poems, "Children of Adam." More precious than gold to me that dissertation—it afforded me, ever after, this strange and paradoxical lesson; each point of E.'s statement was unanswerable, no judge's charge ever more complete or convincing, I could never hear the points better put—and then I felt down in my soul the clear and unmistakable conviction to disobey all, and pursue my own way. "What have you to say then to such things?" said E., pausing in conclusion. "Only that while I can't answer them at all, I feel more settled than ever to adhere to my own theory, and exemplify it," was my candid response. Whereupon we went and had a good dinner at the American House.[58]

The conversation could have taken place that day, as Emerson introduced "W. Whitman, Brooklyn, N.Y." at the Boston Athenaeum on the eastern edge of Boston Common and secured him reading privileges. But it just as easily may have happened any number of times in March and April of that year. Whitman later recalled that he and Emerson "would occasionally meet" for dinner at the American House or the Parker House.[59] Charles Eldridge, too, remembered that "Emerson frequently came down from Concord to see [Whitman], and that they had many walks and talks together, these conferences usually ending with a dinner at the American House." These meetings were fixed clearly in Eldridge's memory because Whitman and Emerson "met by appointment in our counting room."

On whatever particular day the conversation occurred, Eldridge later attributed it to "the largeness of Whitman's charity" that he did not publish Emerson's arguments for dropping the poems. But Eldridge felt no such compunction, especially because Emerson's objections were not on artistic grounds:

> I cannot forget Walt said to me at the time that Emerson's principal arguments were directed to showing that if the objectionable passages were retained it would interfere with the general circulation of the book, and thereby impede, if not wholly prevent, his early recognition as a poet. That men would not buy the book and give it to women, and that it would scarcely be allowed under the conditions place on parlor center tables. Walt frankly acknowledged that he was saddened to find such temporal considerations the chief arguments offered by so great a man as Ralph Waldo Emerson.[60]

But Whitman did not seem at all troubled. He told his friend Abby Price that Emerson "treated me with the greatest courtesy" and not only wrote Fred Vaughan, one of Whitman's early lovers, that Emerson was "very kind" but recommended that Vaughan attend Emerson's upcoming lecture in New York.[61]

Indeed, many years later Whitman warmly recalled the conversation to Horace Traubel, emphasizing that Emerson was not concerned about "small fry moralities" but was "only putting up a worldy argument" for cutting certain poems. "He wanted my book to sell," Whitman remembered. "I said: 'You think that if I cut the book there would be a book left?' He said: 'Yes.' Then I asked: 'But would there be as good a book left?' He looked grave: this seemed to disturb him just a bit. Then he smiled at me and said: 'I did not say as good a book—I said a good book.' That's where he left it."[62] Whitman believed that Emerson knew he would not settle for this: "[He] liked me better for not accepting his advice."

Henry Clapp agreed with Whitman's response to Emerson. "I think you would have done well to follow Mr. Emerson's advice," he told Whitman, "but you may have done better as it is. At any rate, the book is bound to sell."[63] He had reason to be optimistic. Not only were Thayer & Eldridge proving to be devoted promoters of Whitman's work—willing even to publish poems too racy for Emerson—but they had shown a willingness to bail out Clapp's ever-struggling *Saturday Press*.

At the end of March Clapp wrote to Whitman asking if the young publishers might be willing "to do a good thing for me":

> To wit, advance me say one hundred dollars on advertising account—that is if they mean to advertise with me. Or if they don't to let me act for them here as a kind of N.Y. agent to push the book, and advance me the money on that score.
>
> I must have one hundred dollars before Saturday night or be in a scrape the horror of which keeps me awake o' nights. I could if necessary give my note at three mos. for the amount and it is a good note since we have never been protested.
>
> Of course I know how extremely improbable it is that Messrs. T. & E. to whom I am an entire stranger will do anything of the kind: but in suggesting it, I have done only my duty to the Sat. Press, and, as I think, to the cause of sound literature.[64]

The threat of bankruptcy was real enough. Whitman told Horace Traubel in later years, "Henry was always in financial difficulties: the Press never had anything but a hand to mouth existence: it was always at the point of passing in its checks."[65] William Winter, a coeditor of the *Press* in those months of 1860, later remembered bolting the doors of the office "to prevent the probable access of creditors." They had no money to pay their writers or the printer. One day they were "engaged in serious and rather melancholy conference as to the obtainment of money," Winter wrote. "Suddenly there came a loud, impatient knocking upon the outer door, and my senior, by a warning gesture, enjoined silence.

The sound of a grumbling voice was then audible, and, after a while, the sound of footsteps retreating down the stairs." The caller was Richard Henry Stoddard, a regular contributor come to collect his check, but Clapp sat steadfastly silent, smoking his pipe and listening for several minutes, until he was sure that Stoddard was safely gone. Such were "the embarrassing circumstances under which the paper struggled."[66]

Clapp told Whitman that he was "up to my eyes" in unpaid bills and mounting debts, "and over my eyes even to blindness." Friends, he said, had offered their "cheering words," but "the printer will not be paid in words."[67] He feared that he would be unable to publish any more issues of the *Saturday Press*, and all "for the want of a paltry two or three hundred dollars which would take the thing to a paying point, and make it worth ten thousand dollars as a transferable piece of property."[68]

Whitman refused to ask Thayer & Eldridge on Clapp's behalf for money, so Clapp wrote to them directly. Still flush from the sales of the Brown biography and eager to try a new venture, Thayer & Eldridge sent a check for two hundred dollars. In return Clapp would advertise *Leaves of Grass* for six months in the *Press* and insert as many mentions of the book as he prudently could. Whitman disliked being "the solicitor and medium of pecuniary aid" for Clapp's paper, but when pressed he conceded that the *Press* was an "original" and that, though Clapp himself was often reckless with money, Thayer & Eldridge's outlay had been "well enough invested."[69]

· · ·

Franklin B. Sanborn, one of the "Secret Six" who financed John Brown's raid, was upstairs at his desk when he heard a knock at the door of his house in Concord, Massachusetts. It was after nine o'clock on April 3. Sanborn had just returned from dinner at a friend's home, and he was already in his slippers. He put on a robe and went down to answer the door; there, outside in the darkness, were two men. "Does Mr. Sanborn live here?" one demanded. When he identified himself, Sanborn was grabbed and told he was under arrest. "I am from the U.S. Marshal's office," said the other man and began reading from a warrant issued by the Mason Committee. Before Sanborn knew what was happening, two more men were upon him, handcuffing him, and a fifth rode up with a carriage to whisk him away. Sanborn called to his sister to run to the neighbors and began screaming for help, struggling and kicking against the side of the carriage to keep from being thrown inside.

In no time Sanborn's neighbors had come to the rescue. They blocked the path of the carriage, and one, a lawyer, shouted to ask Sanborn if he wished to demand a writ of habeas corpus. When Sanborn replied that he did, the neighbor took off running for Judge Ebenezar Hoar's house. In the meantime Emerson, newly returned from Boston, arrived on the scene and petitioned for calm until the judge returned. Not long after, Judge Hoar approached with the writ held high for all to see. The marshals uncuffed Sanborn and were jeered out of town by the assembled crowd, but a ruling on the validity of the writ was scheduled for just the next day in Boston before Massachusetts Chief Justice Lemuel Shaw. While Henry David Thoreau slept at the Sanborn home to guard it against further invasion, Sanborn and his sister spent that restless night with friends.

Best known to literary scholars as Herman Melville's father-in-law, Judge Shaw was a cantankerous octogenarian with a reputation for strict adherence to the letter of the law. Sanborn knew he was no friend to the abolitionist cause; he had outraged the antislavery movement—and drawn public scorn from Emerson—a decade earlier when he upheld Mason's Fugitive Slave Law in a Massachusetts court. There was every reason to expect him to submit to Mason's authority again. But Sanborn had the best possible legal representation in John Andrew and Samuel Sewall. (Within a year of the proceedings, Andrew would be the governor of Massachusetts and Sewall its second chief justice, succeeding Shaw.) Nevertheless, Sanborn's radical friends were not willing to take the chance that he might again fall into the hands of federal marshals.

Summoned from Ohio, James Redpath slipped into Boston covertly late on April 3. He and William Thayer quickly agreed to attend Sanborn's hearing with concealed pistols, despite the obvious risk that Redpath himself would be arrested. Thayer (under the alias William Handy) wrote to Higginson to inform him:

> Mr Redpath has got home from the West. In case of arrest by U.S. authorities he will place himself under jurisdiction of our State court and thoroughly exhaust all legal test of power between the General and State Gov'ts and then he *wont* go to Washington— provided that at the outset a body of friends will help him personally if the decision goes against him.
>
> Now we propose if his case is tried in Boston, to have in the court room during the trial 25 men *well armed* under a competent leader. If the judge decrees that he must go to Washn, we will encircle and defend him against the Sergeant or U.S. Marshall.[70]

The following afternoon, as the courtroom was readied, Thayer and Redpath loaded their revolvers in the counting room at Thayer & Eldridge. Their plan was simple. If Shaw ruled that the marshals could take custody of Sanborn, then Redpath and Thayer, seated at the back railing of the courtroom on either side of the aisle, would "leap over, draw [their] revolvers, rush to Sanborn and drag him away."[71] Joining them were Eldridge, Hinton, William D. O'Connor (then at work on his novel for Thayer & Eldridge), John Le Barnes (whom Whitman had befriended at the Boston Water Works), and Whitman himself—though Thayer, when recalling the scene decades later, did not list Whitman among those armed. Seated at the front of the courtroom, the first four were responsible for overtaking the marshals, while Whitman, seated at the rear, was supposed to usher out Sanborn and his rescuers and then guard the door. As he listened to Andrew and Sewall argue his case, Sanborn remembered seeing Whitman: "He sat on a high seat near the door, wearing his loose jacket and open shirt collar, over which poured the fullness of his beard, while above that the large and singular blue eyes, under heavy arching brows, wandered over the assembly, as some stately creature of the fields turns his eyes slowly about him in the presence of many men."[72]

Whitman was not the only one scanning the room for trouble. While the court was in recess for Shaw's deliberation, one of the marshals recognized Redpath and started across the courtroom toward him. Redpath was alerted by Thayer, but he had wearied of running from federal agents. "Damn him, let him come on," he told Thayer. "I'll fix him."[73] But before the courtroom could erupt into violence, Shaw returned to deliver his ruling.

He found that the Mason Committee had the authority to issue an arrest warrant and that it could be served anywhere in the United States. However, the Committee's warrant specifically authorized the sergeant-at-arms of the Senate to make the arrest, and Shaw ruled that the sergeant-at-arms had no authority to "deputize his power to others out of the District of Columbia."[74] He ordered Sanborn's release, and the courtroom burst into applause. In the wake of the jubilation, *Vanity Fair* proposed a change to Webster's dictionary, such that henceforth "Concord" would be a synonym, not an antonym, of "discord."[75]

Despite the victory, Thayer worried that pro-slavery elements might still attempt to kidnap Redpath. He gathered his group of radical abolitionists in the counting room at Thayer & Eldridge on April 5 and called another meeting for the following night "to decide upon some plan." He told Higginson, "None but *fighters* are eligible. We are now fourteen in number who are willing to shoot or be shot at at five minutes notice in the caus[e] of the United States vs. Sanborn or Redpath or any other man who represents a principle of right—liberty."[76] No record exists identifying these fourteen men or whether Thayer expected that Whitman would join the fight if called upon.

After his narrow escape from the Sanborn courtroom, Redpath returned to Malden, Massachusetts, and holed up at home. Thayer & Eldridge were typesetting the pages of *Echoes of Harper's Ferry* and began to advertise the book along with a reissue of Redpath's interviews with southern slaves. But the Sanborn incident had driven Redpath into a paranoid exile. Despite Judge Shaw's explicit ruling that U.S. marshals could not legally arrest men called before the Mason Committee, Redpath braced himself for their imminent arrival. "I shall stay at Home & fire at the first intrusion on my premeses," he told Higginson. "I have thought the whole matter carefully over & believe that this course will be best & most effective in advancing the cause. That the body of a U.S. Marshal is not impervious to a bullet well directed, is a lesson which I think now needs to be demonstrated—and the times are ripe for it."[77]

Redpath was still in hiding when *Echoes of Harper's Ferry* was released at the beginning of May, but the book was already another success for Thayer & Eldridge; they had received more than ten thousand advance orders. Less than two weeks later *The Liberator* estimated that the book had sold more than thirty thousand copies. "It should be read," the paper proclaimed, "not by tens of thousands only, but by hundreds of thousands. Buy it, read it, lend it, talk of it."[78]

Even with this second success Thayer & Eldridge were frustrated by the delayed release of *Leaves of Grass*. A frontispiece portrait engraved by Stephen Alonzo Schoff from a painting by Charles Hine was blocking publication, and the reading public in Boston, who by now had taken notice of Whitman's presence in the Hub, were growing eager to see the book. A reporter for the *Boston Saturday Evening Gazette* wrote:

> The poet of "Leaves of Grass," (who hails from New York,) has been spending the last four weeks in Boston, busy in the overseeing of a much larger and superior collection of his tantalizing 'Leaves,' which, after running the gantlet of the United States and Great Britain, and receiving divers specimens of about the tallest kind of indignant as well as favorable criticism, seem to have arrived at a position where they can be read, their title clear to be considered *something*, at any rate. Whether good, better, or best,—or bad, worse, or worst—we shall be better able to tell when we get the new volume.[79]

Thayer & Eldridge were forced to issue a statement on May 5 that the book, originally announced for May 1, would "not be published until next week on account of some delay in finishing the steel portrait of the author which is to accompany the volume" and published another announcement the following week that the release would "be delayed until the 1st of June, in consequence of the Engraver being unable to finish the Portrait in season."[80] But Whitman, too, was growing impatient. "We are just now in 'suspenders' on account of the engraving," he wrote his brother Jeff. He decided to have a thousand copies printed from the incomplete plate and to let Schoff finish his work for use in successive printings.[81]

Even with the incomplete engraving, the results were impressive. The book weighed in at a hefty 456 pages, the poems were set in a daring combination of decorative display faces and an elite body text, and die-cut illustrations decorated blank spaces—all undertaken at Whitman's personal direction, as he designed each page and read proof at Rand and Avery through most of April. Everything about the book was meant to emphasize its extravagant elegance. Even Whitman acknowledged, "The printers and foremen thought I was crazy, and there were all sorts of supercilious squints (about the typography I ordered, I mean)." But everyone was delighted with the results. Whitman told his brother Jeff, "The foreman of the press-room . . . pronounced it, in plain terms, the freshest and handsomest piece of typography that had ever passed through his mill."[82]

But the cost to Thayer & Eldridge was dangerously high. Striking the stereotype plates alone tallied eight hundred dollars—for a book that sold for only $1.25.[83] The young publishers considered the book an investment, "increasing by months and years," Whitman wrote, "not going off in a rocket way, (like 'Uncle Tom's Cabin.')"[84] Still, after the cost of paper, binding, and printing, Whitman would have to make good on his promise of selling "copious thousands of copies" just for Thayer & Eldridge to break even.

On May 12 Henry Clapp received several copies of the book and became the first person in Whitman's New York circle to render judgment. He offered "high praise" to Thayer & Eldridge "for the superb manner in which they have done their work" but withheld comment on the poems for the review he planned to write for the *Saturday Press*, teasing Whitman, "The poet . . . shall hear from me next week." Clapp also instructed, "You should send copies at once to Vanity Fair, Momus, The Albion, The Day Book, The Journal of Commerce, Crayon—also to Mrs. Juliette H. Beach, Albion, N.Y., who will do you great justice in the S.P. (for we shall have a series of articles)—to Charles D. Gardette Esq, No 910 Walnut Street, Philadelphia, to Evening Journal, Philadelphia, and also some dozen copies to me to be distributed at discretion."[85]

At least two of the copies sent to Clapp were passed along to William Dean Howells in Ohio and Bret Harte in San Francisco. Whitman had Thayer & Eldridge send additional copies to the *New York Times*, the *New York Herald*, the *New York Illustrated News*, the *Herald of Progress*, *Frank Leslie's Illustrated Newspaper*, and the *New York Evening Post*, as well as to Pfaffians Ada Clare and Ned Wilkins. Thayer & Eldridge also peppered various Boston publications, including the *Atlantic Monthly*, the *Banner of Light*, the *Liberator*, the *Cosmopolite*, and the *Boston Post*.

Whitman asked all the reviewers to publish their notices on the new official date of the book's release: May 19, 1860. The publication date of *Leaves of Grass*, a Saturday in the middle of the month, might at first seem an odd choice, but Thayer & Eldridge had selected it strategically. It was the same day they would publish Richard Hinton's biography of William Henry Seward, a release timed to coincide with Seward's presumed nomination as the Republican candidate for president.

Late in the evening of May 14, 1860, John E. Howard Jr., a reporter for the *New York Times* (known to his contemporaries simply as "Howard of the *Times*") arrived in Chicago via the Southern Lake Shore Railroad from Buffalo. The train carried the eastern delegates to the 1860 Republican Convention, and a brass band was on hand to greet the train at the station. A parade of twenty thousand enthusiastic onlookers followed the delegates down brightly illuminated Lake Street to the heart of the city, where an enormous convention hall, dubbed "the Wigwam," had been erected especially for the gathering.[86]

Chicago was electric with anticipation. Fabric stores had sold out across the city as the organizers draped the Wigwam with banners and bunting; the keepers of hotels, boardinghouses, and restaurants had been readying for the influx for weeks; and the *Chicago Press and Tribune* warned visitors that the "light fingered fraternity" of pickpockets had sent their own delegation to the convention.[87] Inside the Wigwam the Young Men's Republican Club of New York had strung a banner over the west end of the stage, emblazoned with stars and two blanks following the lines "For President" and "For Vice President." "These blanks were eloquent with a purpose," wrote the *Tribune*, "the purpose of the entire Convention, all ready for the campaign but waiting for *the names.*"[88]

As Howard of the *Times* surveyed the scene just three nights before the Convention officially began, he tried to read the mood of the crowd. The feeling was strong for William Henry Seward of New York, he wrote, but "the main question seems to be who can be elected? Can Mr. Seward?" As the torches burned late into the night, Howard polled the wire-pullers and campaign insiders: "The Seward men are very confident. The Chase and Wade men work together. The Banks men are quiet, but expect a rally will be made in his favor at an early period." As an afterthought he added, "Illinois alone works hard for Lincoln."[89]

But Howard, like many of Lincoln's opponents, underestimated the advantage Lincoln enjoyed in Chicago. Strong with supporters in the area, he was able to dispatch men to spend days lobbying delegates from the lower North—especially Pennsylvania, Maryland, Indiana, and Missouri—making the argument that Seward could not carry their states in a general election. When the first ballot was cast on the night of May 17, Seward was short of the required 233 votes, with 173½, but Lincoln polled a surprising 102 votes, putting him firmly in second place. His campaign had packed the galleries by distributing counterfeit tickets to ten thousand bellowing Lincoln boosters, hooting their approval.

On the second ballot only a dozen delegates defected to Seward, bringing his total to 185, but in response to the crowd's voluble support scores of delegates switched their votes to Lincoln, bringing him nearly even at

181. When the second results were announced, a reporter for the *Chicago Press and Tribune* wrote that the roar "was positively awful": "Imagine all the hogs ever slaughtered in Cincinnati giving their death squeals together, a score of big steam whistles going together . . . with a stamping that made every plank and pillar in the building quiver."[90]

By the third ballot Lincoln had gained a kind of raw momentum as delegate after delegate was swept up by the excitement. Six defected from Vermont and Massachusetts, eight from New Jersey, nine from Maryland, four from Kentucky, and fifteen from Ohio.[91] Lincoln now had 231½ votes as the crowd waited breathlessly for the announcement of the final four votes from the chairman of the Ohio delegation. At last he stood. "I rise Mr. Chairman," he said, "to announce the change of four votes of Ohio from Mr. Seward to Mr. Lincoln."[92] Suddenly, the *Tribune* reported, "there were thousands cheering with the energy of insanity. . . . The Lincoln *yawp* swelled into a wild hosanna of victory."[93]

No one was more surprised—or exulted—by the outcome than Howard of the *Times*. "The work of the Convention is ended," he wired back to New York. "The youngster who, with ragged trousers, used barefoot to drive his father's oxen and spend his days in splitting rails, has risen to high eminence, and Abram Lincoln, of Illinois, is declared its candidate for President by the National Republican Convention."[94] The fact that the top political reporter at the *Times* did not know the correct name of the new candidate underscores what a surprise Lincoln's win was.

Thayer and Eldridge, however, were dismayed. Their carefully researched biography of Seward—timed for release on May 19, when newspapers were expected to carry news of his nomination—was suddenly a dead title. They hastily withdrew all advertising for the book (not a single review is known to have appeared) and turned their attention to Lincoln. Today fewer than ten copies of the Seward biography survive, including the personal copies retained by Hinton and Seward themselves. Whitman's new edition of *Leaves of Grass*, rushed through the press to be shipped to stores on the same day, suddenly had to carry its own weight—indeed, the full weight of Thayer & Eldridge. While Hinton set to work on a biography of Lincoln, Whitman's book would have to sell well enough to carry his publishers through a lean month.

Unfortunately Whitman had urged his friends to run their reviews as near to May 19 as possible. At the *New York Times* John Swinton, probably distracted by hurriedly gathering information on Lincoln, commissioned the review rather than write it himself and apparently had it sent to typesetting without reading it. Thus, on the day that the 1860 edition of *Leaves of Grass* finally appeared, the newspaper managed by Swinton—the man who had set the book's publication in motion—ran the first damning review. The reviewer has never been identified, but it was certainly not Swinton himself because the column not only condemned *Leaves of Grass* as "pretentious" with a "tendency to fall into the vulgar" but, in an accompanying review, also lambasted Swinton's old friend James Redpath's anthology *Echoes of Harper's Ferry*, singling out Redpath's contributions to the volume as "wretched trash" and denouncing him personally as "arrogant," "egotistic," and "flippant."

By comparison, the review of Whitman seemed almost temperate, allowing that the poet occasionally upturned a "handful of gold" by "throwing filth . . . from his moral cesspool." Thus the reviewer gave voice to a complaint that would soon grow into a chorus. *Leaves of Grass* was not only vulgar, it was obscene, gross, repulsive: "He seems to delight in contemplation of scenes that ordinary men do not love, or which they are content to regard as irremediable evils, about which it is needless to repine. Mr. Whitman sees nothing vulgar in that which is generally regarded as the grossest obscenity; rejects the laws of conventionality so completely as to become repulsive; gloats over coarse images with the gusto of a Rabelais, but lacks the genius or grace of Rabelais."[95]

Luckily Henry Clapp published his anonymous review of Whitman on the same evening in the *Saturday Press*. The unabashed puff was worthy of Whitman himself, and some have occasionally suspected Whitman's own hand in writing it, though Clapp's letters suggest otherwise. He began with grand pronouncements:

> We announce a great Philosopher—perhaps a great Poet—in every
> way an original man. It is Walt Whitman. The proof of his greatness
> is in his book; and there is proof enough.
>
> The intellectual attitude expressed in these Leaves of Grass, is
> grand with the grandeur of independent strength, and beautiful with
> the beauty of serene repose. It is the attitude of a proud, noble, vig-
> orous life. A human heart is here in these pages—large, wild,
> comprehensive—beating with all throbs of passion—enjoying all of
> bliss—suffering all of sorrow that is possible to humanity.[96]

The review proceeded along these lines for nearly two full columns,
heaping the praise on Whitman himself ("No man could utter himself
more fully and truly"), his book ("No book exists anywhere more beau-
tifully in earnest than this"), and even his eccentric poetics ("It rises and
melts into sweet and thrilling music whenever impelled by the beautiful
impulse of a grand thought or emotion").

At the close of the review, however, probably in an effort to temper his
praise, Clapp quoted Edward Everett Hale's sole disappointment in *Leaves
of Grass* when it first appeared in 1855: that it contained "one or two lines
which he would not address to a woman." From the time that Emerson
first voiced his reservation that "men would not buy the book and give it
to women," Thayer & Eldridge had feared this sort of criticism more than
any other. And rightly so. In the coming months the discussion of *Leaves
of Grass* would be dominated by allegations of obscenity that would so con-
sume both the *Saturday Press* and Thayer & Eldridge that neither would
survive.

CHAPTER TWO

The Representative Man
of the North

The smart scribblers who compose the better part of the
Northern literati, are all becoming infected with the new
leprosy—Whitmansy. This latest "representative man" of the
North has his imitators by the hundred, admirers by the thou-
sand, and an organ—the slang-whanging paper called *The
Saturday Press.*

Southern Literary Messenger, July 1860

On May 24, 1860, Whitman returned to New York via the Shore Line
Railway, a new express train from Boston that left at eleven o'clock each
morning and continued straight through, arriving in Manhattan at half
past seven. "I like that route better than the old one," he wrote Thayer
and Eldridge, "no dust that day, and fine view of the water, half the time."
But the serenity of his return trip wouldn't last. Back in Brooklyn he
found a package of forty copies of *Leaves of Grass* waiting for him—and a
minor furor over the book already brewing. Henry Clapp had divulged
Thayer & Eldridge's worst fear, that the book would be tarred as too sexually explicit for women, and the criticism had already been picked up by
the weekly magazines in New York.

In an unsigned review written for the *New York Illustrated News* George Searle Phillips hailed Whitman as a "devout and prophetic son of America, born of the people and the soil," and declared, "True as the needle to the North is he true to his country, to the brave mother language, and to the American people." Though his hosannas for Whitman's innovation and importance, his original blend of Eastern philosophy and rugged Americanism, continued paragraph after paragraph, even Phillips felt he could not give "unqualified praise" to this new edition: "We honestly think that he has written many things which, considering that women also and young girls go to make up the world, he might far better have left unwritten. We have no faith in Priapus, nor in the Phallic Symbolism. All that kind of worship and literature is long since dead for all good purposes—and needs no revival. And it seems sad to us—speaking from the common platform of the sexes—that so admirable a book should be marred by passages which put a taint upon its general purity."[1] Phillips had draped his disapproval in classical reference to Priapus, the Greek god of fertility and male genitalia, but it was clear that he balked at Whitman's sexual frankness for fear that the book might fall into the hands of women or even "young girls."

The point was seconded, more derisively, by William Young, the editor of the New York–based weekly *The Albion*, in a long parody written to accompany a brief, condemnatory review. One passage read:

> I luxuriate in Women.
> They look at me, and my eyes start out of my head; they speak to me, and I yell with delight; they touch me, and the flesh crawls off my bones.
> Women lay in wait for me, they do. Yes, Sir.
> They rush upon me, seven women laying hold of one man; and the divine efflux that thrilled all living things before the nuptials of the saurious overflows, surrounds, and interpenetrates their souls, and they say, Walt, why don't you come and see us? You knew we'd be happy to have you.[2]

Thayer and Eldridge wrote to complain to Clapp, but he had already provided them with a solution. More than a week earlier he had recommended that they send a copy to Juliette H. Beach. Beach was a regular contributor of poetry and reviews who would do Whitman "great justice in the Saturday Press" and attest to the appropriateness of *Leaves of Grass* for women.[3]

Clapp was certain that Beach would praise the book because in her recent review of Harriet Prescott's *Sir Rohan's Ghost* she had favorably mentioned Whitman. In Beach's estimation Prescott's novel wore "the garb of prose" but was actually an exquisite poem reminiscent of Whitman's "grand simplicity of expression and Eastern style." To prove her point, Beach told readers that she had "amused" herself by turning some of the descriptive passages from Prescott into Whitmanic stanzas. She offered examples, such as:

> The three graves, the long slope, and the sea behind;
> And before,—between the gaps of the cliffs reddening with
>   morning,—
> The cross-roads, and sunrise boiling wildly
> Athwart low inland plains.[4]

Clapp believed a review from Beach would help quell the outcry of lewdness and impropriety. Thayer & Eldridge sent the book, and Clapp wrote to Beach to urge a swift response.

Meanwhile, back in Boston, both Thayer and Eldridge attended the first meeting of the Political Anti-Slavery Convention at Mercantile Hall. They, along with Redpath, Hinton, and several other of Brown's men, had called the convention and invited such prominent abolitionists as Frederick Douglass and Susan B. Anthony, in hopes of nominating Gerritt Smith for president. But the party, like much of the nation, was shocked and divided by Abraham Lincoln's unexpected selection in Chicago. Redpath, still in hiding, did not attend the meeting in person but sent a letter to be read to the assembly. To the surprise of many, he declared his devotion to the Republican Party and his intention to vote for Lincoln. "There is no help for slavery in the hair-splitting New England, but only in the railsplitting North-west," he wrote. He felt that Lincoln, as a westerner like John Brown, was more apt to institute abolition, bringing about civil war, and Redpath was now solely "pledged to the work of inciting an armed insurrection among the slaves of the South." Stephen S. Foster, the organizer of the convention, pronounced himself "astounded" and decried Redpath's letter. Hinton, however, rose to defend Redpath—and, by extension, Lincoln—explaining to the assembly that New Englanders could not understand men of the great West. "In New England, men think and deliberate," he told them, "but the West reduces to practice."[5] In a matter of weeks Hinton would complete a rushed biography of Lincoln—the nation's first—to be published by Thayer & Eldridge. The publishers also issued a large, elaborately detailed portrait of Lincoln for sale to an eager public that would scarcely recognize the face of the one-term congressman from Illinois, who had not held elective office in more than a decade and whose chief fame rested on his high-flown oratory in his debates en route to losing to Stephen A. Douglas.

For his part, Clapp was less sold on the unknown Lincoln than were his Boston kinsman. While the New York newspapers were still scrambling for the correct spelling of his first name—was it Abram or Abraham?—Clapp said he had consulted "the best authorities" without success, but he had ascertained that Lincoln "is sixteen feet high, and fifty-one years long; that he is thin and angular as a split-rail; that he was born a Hoosier, but finally became a Sucker; that he has been in turn a farm-laborer, a top-sawyer, a flat-boatsman, a counter-jumper, a militia captain, a lawyer, a Presbyterian, and a politician; that he beat Douglas over the left in Illinois, and drove him into the U.S. Senate; that his favorite motto is, 'two shillings are better than one'; and that he is spotless in everything but his linen."[6] Clapp then joked that, immediately after Lincoln's nomination, "about a dozen of the leading publishers in the country offered, each, a large reward for his Life,"[7] apparently unaware that Thayer & Eldridge were among those who had commissioned hasty biographies.

On the evening of June 1, Juliette Beach's review arrived at the offices of the *Saturday Press.* According to legend, in the rush of production Clapp sent the review to the typesetter without reading its contents, but this is clearly untrue. He opened the letter, read the review, and had enough time to compose a brief editorial justification that appeared beneath it in the same column: "It will be seen by an article in to-day's issue that our esteemed and accomplished correspondent, Mrs. Juliette H. Beach, having glanced at Walt Whitman's '*Leaves of Grass,*' is disposed, upon the whole, to take a somewhat unfavorable view of them. It always gives us pleasure to print every variety of opinion upon such subjects, especially when, as in this case, the careful reader can have no reasonable doubt as to the writer's meaning."[8]

If Clapp thought his statement would somehow soften the review's impact, he was wrong. It was not only a blistering condemnation but, worst of all, it went much further than any previous critique in denying Whitman's suitability for women readers. Beach scoffed at the notion that Whitman was simply depicting physical love with poetic frankness. "Walt Whitman's poems are not amorous; they are only beastly. They express far more truthfully the feelings of brute nature than the sentiments of human love."[9] She insisted that the book was wholly inappropriate for women because Whitman had so little real affection for women: "Walt Whitman assumes to regard woman only as an instrument for the gratification of his desires, and the propagation of the species. To him all women are the same, with but this difference, the more sensual have the preference, as they promise greater indulgence. His exposition of his thoughts shows conclusively that with him the congress of the sexes is a purely animal affair, and with his ridiculous egotism he vaunts his prowess as a stock-breeder might that of the pick of his herd."

Two positive notices of the book appeared on the same day, in the Boston *Banner of Light* and in the *New York Illustrated News,* but both were totally eclipsed by Beach's rant. Not only did she deride Whitman's poetry; she openly suggested that Whitman himself was immoral—and irredeemable. "I doubt if, when the Judgment-Day comes, Walt Whitman's name will be called," she pronounced. "He certainly has not enough soul to be saved. I hardly think he has enough to be damned." She concluded by calling on Whitman to commit suicide.

Thayer and Eldridge were outraged. "*I* think that Mrs. Beach's criticism is just about the damndest piece of scolding ever written by a woman who does not know what she is talking about," Thayer wrote Whitman. "My wife was *indignant,* and I should not wonder if she writes a reply to it."[10] For the publishers, however, this was more than a mere matter of honor. They had unveiled Hinton's biography of Lincoln on the same day as the appearance of Beach's review. The back cover of the Lincoln book was boldly emblazoned with an advertisement for *Leaves of Grass,* and the book was formally announced in a purchased notice in the *Saturday Press* that had run on the same page as Beach's review. Hinton even likened the vice presidential candidate Hannibal Hamlin to Whitman. "He is careless, and almost slovenly in his dress," Hinton wrote of Hamlin. "He is none of your kid-glove gentry, but is large handed and open palmed to every member of the free, unwashed democracy. A traveler through the town of his residence may see him any summer, about haying-time, in the fields in his shirt-sleeves, like the commonest laborer, and in his social intercourse with men he pays but little regard to the conventionalities of so-called polite society. He is 'free, fresh, savage,' as Walt. Whitman says, and thinks just as much of you, in shabby attire, as if you were faultlessly clad in shining broadcloth."[11] Thayer and Eldridge had gone out of their way to yoke their Lincoln biography to *Leaves of Grass,* and now Henry Clapp, the very person who had championed Whitman's work and sought their financial support for the *Saturday Press,* threatened to derail both books and endanger the future of Thayer & Eldridge itself.

Within days portions of the review began to appear in large-circulation newspapers and magazines, such as the *New York Tribune* and the *Saturday Evening Post* in Philadelphia. Beach wrote excitedly to

Clapp with a strange confession: the review was not hers at all but the work of her husband, who was angered that the book had been sent to her. "I like Leaves of Grass!" Beach insisted. "I have the greatest faith in the book. Its egotism delights me—that defiant ever recurring *I*, is so ir-resistably strong and good."[12] Yet she felt that she could not endorse Whitman now that her husband had so publicly condemned him. "I re-gret extremely that I have been obliged to deny myself the pleasure of writing at length and for publication, my view of 'Leaves of Grass.' . . . I could have reviewed the book in a manner worthy of it, and yet have been not misunderstood myself." She also lamented the lost chance to argue against selecting certain passages from *Leaves of Grass* as examples of las-civiousness. "It is useless in judging this book to draw dividing lines and say this is good, and this is bad," she told Clapp. "It is to be accepted and pronounced upon en masse."[13]

Clapp quickly composed a retraction for the next issue of the *Satur-day Press*, explaining, "The error arose from the fact that we were ex-pecting an article from Mrs. Beach on the book (it having been for-warded to her by the publishers of our particular request), and that when the looked-for MS. arrived we sent it directly to the printer, with the usual instructions to sign the name of the author—concerning which we had not the slightest doubt—in full."[14] To further reinforce his point, Clapp also ran a series of endorsements by women readers of *Leaves of Grass*, beginning on the same page as his retraction with a letter by Mary A. Chilton of Islip, Long Island.

Though their exact relationship is unknown, Chilton and Whitman were acquainted enough for her name to have appeared in Whitman's ad-dress books twice prior to 1860, the first time in a list that included two other early feminists, Ernestine L. Rose and Abby Price.[15] Chilton de-fended *Leaves of Grass*; it was not filth but reached beyond the simple con-fines of social constructions of morality: "In his refusal to recognize such distractions as 'decent and indecent' in the human structure—though, in the opinion of another critic, this is 'monstrous beyond precedent'—I see the sweetest simplicity and child-like innocence."[16]

But Chilton was no ordinary defender of Whitman. Though she listed her address simply as "Islip, Long Island," *Saturday Press* readers would have known that she made her home at the Modern Times commune, a free-love experimental community on Long Island. During this same summer of 1860, Moncure Conway, the disciple of Emerson and among Whitman's earliest champions, visited Islip and declared Chilton the "Queen of Modern Times," who had come to "sum up all the wrongs of society in the one word 'marriage.' "[17]

The editors of the *Springfield Daily Republican* were aghast at Chilton's suggestion that *Leaves of Grass* was anything but "smut" and declared her defense of the book evidence of "how far into degradation certain new lights are ready to be led." But they were even more alarmed to find these notions discussed openly in respectable publications:

> A professedly obscene book carries with it its own condemnation among decent people, and finds its own market among the vicious and unclean. Besides, there are laws against its promulgation; and appeal can be made to them if it is openly exposed for sale, or adver-tised, or sold more secretly. This literature is not unfrequently stuck in one's face at steamboat landings by lousy scoundrels who peddle filth for a living, but one can always cry "police" if he will, and stop it. Here, however, is a book with many respectable associations—respectable publishers—the author a writer for the Atlantic Monthly—"for sale everywhere" on respectable book-shelves—in very respectable type and binding—advertised in respectable papers—and yet it has page after page that no man could read aloud to a decent assembly without being hooted out of it, and that could not be published in the columns of a daily newspaper without dis-gusting and outraging a virtuous community.[18]

The writer concluded by asserting that *Leaves of Grass* was "more scan-dalous" than any book he had ever seen and warned his readers that the naturalism advocated by Whitman would lead to polygamy of the sort embraced by the Mormons or "promiscuous intercourse of the sexes" as espoused by various Messianic cults. "Spiritualism, whenever it has cut loose from the Bible as the only authoritative revelation from heaven," he reminded his readers, "has gone just as naturally into free-love as water runs down hill." He viewed *Leaves of Grass* as nothing less than a threat to the institution of marriage.

Whitman received far kinder notice from his fellow Pfaffian Adah Isaacs Mencken Heenan, who wrote an article for the *New York Sunday Mercury* in praise of those who "swim against the current." She produced a long, motley list of such men but focused on Whitman:

> Look at Walter Whitman, the American philosopher who is centuries ahead of his contemporaries, who, in smiling carelessness, analyzes the elements of which society is composed, compares them with the history of past events, and ascertains the results which the same causes always produced, and must produce. . . . He hears the Divine voice calling him to caution mankind against this or that evil, and wields his pen, exerts his energies, for the cause of liberty and humanity!
>
> But he is too far ahead of his contemporaries; they cannot comprehend him yet; he swims against the stream and finds me company. The passengers, in their floating boats, call him a fanatic, a visionary, a demagogue, a good-natured fool, etc., etc. Still he heeds them not: his mental conviction will not permit him to heed them.[19]

Whitman was pleased by the acknowledgment. "Did you see what Mrs. Heenan says about me in last 'Sunday Mercury'—first page?"[20] he asked Thayer and Eldridge. But her praise was hardly likely to win Whitman readers among respectable middle-class women.

Mencken was a famed stage actress in New York's bowery and the child of a French Creole woman and the prominent New Orleans free Negro Auguste Theodore. At a young age she had married the Jewish musician Alexander Isaac Mencken but left him when she became pregnant by the world-champion prizefighter John C. Heenan—or so she claimed. In January she announced that she and Heenan were secretly married, but he denied her claim. By April it was reported that she had never divorced her first husband, and allegations of her "polygamy" circulated nationally.[21] When her endorsement of Whitman appeared in June, Mencken was eight months pregnant and the public was bandying about various theories of the identity of the child's father—including the possibility of Robert H. Newell, editor of the *Sunday Mercury*. In fact, Newell and Mencken married two years later, and in his memoirs he recalled (referring to himself in the third person) that he "detested Whitman's poetry, but loved Menken, and she was able to beguile the editor into running her tribute."[22] The backing of a "mulatto" actress accused of bigamy who was about to bear the child of an unknown father was not exactly the sanction Thayer and Eldridge had been hoping for. Thayer wrote Whitman that they had read the review and considered it "a good indication that the book is reaching the lower strata."[23]

On June 23 Clapp ran two final commentaries by anonymous women reviewers. The first, by "C. C. P.," seemed to offer further difficulty for Whitman by association with those who defended him. She argued, "While we truckle to our bodies, trying to cheat ourselves and one another into oblivion of the potent physical facts, while we feed with exciting novels and amorous poetry those passions we dare not own, we are shocked, for sooth, when a great, earnest, sorrowful man gives us the facts which, gilded over with poor art, we accept readily enough." But C. C. P. went on to praise Whitman's "manly courage" for admitting that he had "sinned with prostitutes and felons, (and who has not?)."

The second review, signed simply "A Woman," finally defended Whitman's "deeply religious nature." Hoping to prove more than Whitman's purity, she quoted selectively from "Walt Whitman" (later retitled "Song of Myself"): "I find letters from God dropped in the street, / And every one is signed by God's name." He emerges as a minor religious prophet:

> If all others could find letters from God in the street, those who now
> see in Walt Whitman nothing but beastliness, would be glad to take
> him by the hand and pray to be forgiven. Nay, more, they would
> ask to sit at his feet that they might the better learn to read these
> heaven-dropped messages.

These bold and truthful pages will inevitably form the standard book of poems in the future of America. . . . God bless him. I know that through "Leaves of Grass," Walt Whitman on earth is immortal as well as beyond it.[24]

This, at last, appears to have been the review Thayer & Eldridge had been hoping for in order to settle the whole issue of Whitman and women. They quoted this defense at the head of all their advertisements in the *Saturday Press* for months to come.

For his part, Whitman seems to have wearied of the controversy. In midsummer he received a letter from a thirty-two-year-old working-woman, Susan Garnet Smith, from Hartford, Connecticut, who wrote to tell him that one of her friends at work had loaned her a copy of *Leaves of Grass*. She took it with her on a walk, while "stealing an hour from labor," and responded to the poems precisely as so many puritanical critics had feared women readers might. She not only proclaimed her love for Whitman but called on him to conceive a child with her: "My womb is clean and pure. It is ready for thy child my love. Angels guard the vestibule until thou comest to deposit our and the world's precious treasure. Then Oh! how tenderly, oh! how lovingly will I cherish and guard it, our child my love."[25] She added, almost as an afterthought, that the child—a son, she was sure—"must be begotten on a mountain top, in the open air." Whitman flipped the envelope over, inscribed it "? insane asylum" in pencil, and tucked it away with his papers, evidently without ever penning a reply.

The fact that Whitman ignored Smith seems not to have affected his popularity with the female readers of Hartford. Barely a month later he received a letter from Wilhelmina Walton (unpublished until now), also from Hartford. After reading about *Leaves of Grass*, she told Whitman, she decided to try the book for herself:

I understood the Poet!—I too had felt my heart beat against the broad bosom of the earth, and kissed the dewy tears from her face.— talked with the stars, and dallied with the ocean;—embraced the rough old scragly oak, and in return hear an anthem wail from his hoar branches:—had lain upon a mossy bed within the quiet, dusky dingle;—through [*sic*] my arms above my head to catch the stray sunbeams;—hugged it to my bosom transported with extatic emotion;—yet never came before my vision sensual forms or thought found place in my imagination;—Was I passionless?—Did I not love the sun and stars, the birds and flowers, rocks and trees and man, the laborer, broad chested, sun burnt, vigorous man! and woman—*my sister*—gentle, lovely woman. . . .

Why did you not drape your poems with a *fig leaf* brother Walt?—Not for me—it would have roused me from my dream of bliss. . . .

I have read your poem and pronounce it "good" as you merge from behind the screen and stand boldly forward—*I give you my hand*, and return your kindly greeting.—*God bless* you for the "Leaves of Grass" which you have gleaned from the meadow; on the highway;—by the seashore on the camp ground, wet with the dews of heaven and "tears of angels."[26]

As with the letter from Susan Garnet Smith, there is no evidence that Whitman ever replied to Wilhelmina Walton.

Whitman rebuffed even his most ardent and serious women readers. Katharine Brooks Yale, whose novel *Abbie Nott and Other Knots* (published under the pseudonym Katinka) was the first book to carry an epigraph from *Leaves of Grass*, received no response to repeated overtures. She wrote an envious letter to Abby Price, the one woman who seemed able to penetrate the poet's inner circle:

I congratulate you on your rare good fortune in knowing that magnificent *outlaw*, Walt Whitman. I am always looking in the streets, on the Omnibus driver's seats, and about the wharves, for the monstrous genius, but although I am sure I should know his face, I never have seen it. Wise, witty, sad man! few know him, infinite tenderness, docile as a child, defiant, a moral torpedo, shocking by his electrical nature everybody that touches him—a perpetual surprise! What a friend to know! I have sent word to him several times to come and see this place and us. If he only knew Mr. Yale, a being as genius as himself, and myself, as disrespectable a person as he could to find, I am sure he would come.[27]

But Whitman seems never to have answered those letters and never visited.

. . .

Perhaps in an attempt to deflect attention from persistent criticisms of obscenity, Whitman prevailed upon John Swinton to afford him a full column of the *New York Times* for a new poem. Whitman had attended the June 16 parade down Broadway for envoys from Japan who had come to sign a trade agreement with the United States. He recorded the event in verse whose message was wholly philosophical, wholly metaphysical. And didn't Swinton owe him this space after the negative review of the month before and the firestorm that followed? "The Errand-Bearers" appeared on page 2 of the *New York Times* on June 27 and is at its dizzying best when Whitman describes the thronging crowd and the pageantry of the scene:

> When million-footed Manhattan, unpent, descends to her
>   pavements;
> When the thunder-cracking guns arouse me with the proud roar I
>   love;
> When the round-mouth'd guns, out of the smoke and smell I love,
>   spit their salutes;
> When the fire-flashing guns have fully alerted me—when heaven-
>   clouds canopy my city with a delicate thin haze;
> When, gorgeous, the countless straight stems, the forests at the
>   wharves, thicken with colors;
> When every ship, richly drest, carries her flag at the peak;
> When pennants trail, and street-festoons hang from the windows;
> When Broadway is entirely given up to foot-passengers and foot-
>   standers—when the mass is densest;
> When the façades of the houses are alive with people—when eyes
>   gaze, riveted, tens of thousands at a time;
> When the guests from the islands advance—when the pageant moves
>   forward, visible;

When the summons is made—when the answer that waited
 thousands of years, answers;
I too, arising, answering, descend to the pavements, merge with the
 crowd, and gaze with them.[28]

While reveling in the Broadway spectacle, the majority of the poem shows surprisingly little interest in the Japanese envoys and their stated diplomatic purpose, instead focusing on the grand symbolism of "the Orient" meeting with the democratic promise of the New World. As Gay Wilson Allen observed, "The circle is complete: past and present, East and West are now joined, their cultures and people mingle. The poet foresees American commerce and political influence threading the islands and archipelagoes of the globe."[29] Thus the poem devolves into a vague exultation of manifest destiny and fails to achieve any real rhetorical force as Whitman becomes mired in generalizations and abstraction, punctuated by occasional exclamations of "Libertad!"

Intended as a chant of optimism, Whitman's grand pronouncements instead opened him to justified criticism, even ridicule. "It seems the bad enough that the poor Japs should be beset by politicians, dowagers, alderman, billiard makers, Peter Funks and stock brokers," quipped the *Milwaukee Daily Sentinel*, "but all this is endurable in comparison with the atrocious climax which the New Yorkers have allowed to cap their cruelty. They have allowed the notorious Walt Whitman (whose jangles would be the death of an insane Malay) to write one of his soul seething poems at them. This is too horrible for belief. . . . We could never have believed before that human nature was so depraved."[30]

The *Portland Transcript* in Maine referred to Whitman as "the riproarer" and "a filibuster on Parnassus" and generally mocked "The Errand-Bearers": "He saw the Japanese in the streets of New York and immediately went into a 'fine frenzy,' in which he shouts 'Libertad' at stated intervals, and sees a great deal more than common folks in the moon-eyed Japanese. He sees Paradise, Caucasus, Brahma, 'enveloped mysteries,' Polynesia, Confucius himself—all these, Libertad, and more, in the pageant procession. In fact, he falls into an ecstatic vision, not without a certain sweep of grandeur, but ridiculous from the rant and egotism which accompanies it."[31]

This complaint was seconded by George William Curtis, the editor of *Harper's New Monthly Magazine*. He objected to the poem, not on the usual grounds of Whitman's radical form or his iconoclastic beliefs, but because the poem was a cascade of language without musical framework to structure it: "In the kaleidoscopic lines of Mr. Whitman—in the profuse lines of many and gorgeous adjectives, of highly-colored words—there is not music, although there is description. The Muse will not ride on a corduroy road. . . . The spectator says fine and striking things, often with cadence, never with the essential melody of song."[32]

Whitman's friends at Pfaff's were not nearly so sensitive in their insights. They quickly turned out a pair of parodies. Listed as "Not by Walt Whitman," the poem "The Song of the Barbecue," published in *Vanity Fair*, lampooned "The Errand-Bearers" in lines such as "Libertad! Redad! Whitead! Bluead!" The other parody, titled "The Torch-Bearer," which appeared in both the *Saturday Press* and *Vanity Fair*, was an unusually astute satire, whose author clearly had more than a fleeting acquaintance with Whitman's work. Whitman's lines are transformed thus:

When, terrible in the midnight, begins the wild roar of cannon;
When the ear-cracking cracker awakes me with its continual cracks;
When punch and confusion are in the house and the "morning call"
  is brought to me in a tumbler;
When the stars and stripes hang round in a very miscellaneous
  manner;
When Broadway is entirely given up to patriotic youth—then Young
  America bristles;
When the police are in a state of mind and the Alderman in a state
  of body;
When in point of fact there is the devil to pay generally;—
Then is the Fourth of July, and I, rising, behold it.

> I descend to the pavement, I swerve with the crowd, I roar exultant, I
> am an American citizen, I feel that every man I meet owes me
> twenty-five cents.

Despite the artistic failings of Whitman's poem, it had succeeded bril-
liantly on another count. It brought Whitman again before the public
and, however briefly, turned the discussion away from the indecency of
Leaves of Grass to focus on this new metaphysical poem. It turned commentary from his obsession with the flesh to criticism of his grandiose vision of the meeting of East and West. In the hands of more experienced
publishers this national publicity might have been a boon to Whitman,
but the green young men of Thayer & Eldridge were still learning the
business.

William Thayer and Charles Eldridge had spent only a few years in the
book trade as clerks for Dayton and Wentworth before founding their
own publishing firm. But even for two novices their marketing schemes
ranged from the ill-conceived to the absurd. One advertisement, head-
lined "Watches Given Away!," promised "A gift valued from two dollars
to one hundred dollars given with every Book sold at retail prices. At
least one Watch is guaranteed to every twelve Books!"[33] For a publisher
whose books all sold for $1.50 or less, it's difficult to see how giving away
expensive premiums would have turned a profit.

In June, after sluggish requests for the pamphlet of reviews they called
Leaves of Grass Imprints, they wrote Whitman, "[We have] concocted a
plan by which we hope to give the Imprints a very wide and telling circulation."[34] They began running a series of anonymous advertisements
in *Frank Leslie's Illustrated Newspaper* under the heading "A Good Book
Free" and went so far as to obtain a post office box so that no reader could
guess their identity. One such classified read, "One of the most interesting and spicy Books ever published, containing 64 pages of excellent
reading matter, will be sent FREE to any address, on application to box
3263, Boston Post Office. This is no advertisement of a patent medicine

or other humbug. All you have to do is to send your address as above, and you will receive by return of mail, without expense, a handsome and well-printed book, which will both amuse and instruct you."[35] In no time they were receiving three hundred requests per day—far more than they could fill—but "the orders [for *Leaves of Grass*] by mail do not seem to come in much yet."[36]

When they did advertise *Leaves of Grass* by name it was in an odd hodgepodge of publications. Display ads ran on a regular basis in expected venues, such as the *Saturday Press*, the *Times, Tribune, Herald, Frank Leslie's Illustrated Newspaper,* and the *New York Illustrated News*, but they also placed notices in papers far from the East Coast. In the *Daily Cleveland Herald* they announced that the book was available at Hawk & Brother on Superior Street; in the *Chicago Press and Tribune* they advertised that the book was for sale at McNally's on Dearborn; in the *Cedar Valley Times* in Iowa they encouraged readers to order by mail; and in the *Daily Evening Express* they told readers that *Leaves of Grass* was in stock at Roman's in the Montgomery Block of San Francisco.

The scattershot approach was partly a response to difficulty circulating the book to mainstream bookstores. Brown and Taggard, the largest distributor to bookstores in Boston, refused to offer the book. Likewise, D. W. Evans & Co., the publisher and major bookshop on Broadway in New York, initially advertised and carried the book but abruptly stopped in the middle of June. Reviews questioning the morality of *Leaves of Grass* were having a chilling effect on bookstore orders.

In response Thayer & Eldridge began an ambitious campaign of sending puff editorials to newspapers. The plan was to build mail orders and create "an overwhelming demand among the mass public" that bookstores would be forced to meet.[37] One such piece in the *New York Illustrated News*, however, seemed to praise Thayer & Eldridge as much as Whitman:

Thayer & Eldridge, of Boston, have made a hit, and achieved what Barnum calls "immense success," by the publication of the "Leaves of Grass"—which, if we may judge by the conflicting reports of it in the newspapers, is the true modern Sphynx, imitating the Antique Sphynx, in that it propounds questions to all passers-by, which they cannot, for the life of them, answer. . . . It is superbly printed, on the finest paper, as if the publishers want it to remain amongst us, as permanent literature—which we, for one, have no doubt it will. Thayer & Eldridge are a young and rising firm in the Modern Athens, and are not only plucky and enterprizing, but men of discernment and intellectual ability—things which publishers get on very well for the most part, without, all the world over. May Thayer & Eldridge prosper abundantly![38]

Whether because of the obscenity uproar or in spite of it, by mid June the first printing was nearly sold out and Thayer & Eldridge wrote Whitman to inform him that "the second is all printed and ready for binding."[39] They did not think, however, that "this Summer is the time to commence a rigorous and systematic course of advertising." They feared that as the cities emptied for the summer, their announcements would reach fewer readers. "As soon as cooler weather comes," they assured Whitman, "we intend to advertise largely both by circular, porters, and the press." But they did run a series of advertisements in June, which they hoped would "touch the pleasure travelers in all the principle [*sic*] cities."[40] One such ad asked, "Are you going into the country?" and guaranteed readers, "*This*, out of all the countless volumes in the stores, is *the* one to take with you, and run over in the field, in the shade of the woods, or on the mountains, or by the sea-shore."[41] They also addressed a special message to the trade. Where previous advertisements had promised the finest "type, casting, paper, presswork, ink, binding, etc.,"[42] they now exhorted, "Book-dealers! this is no lumbering stock that when you invest in it, will remain on your shelves. You can depend on a quick sale for every copy."[43]

Another reason for Thayer & Eldridge's unconventional marketing was their near-total inability to sell books in the South. Laws banning the sale of Hinton R. Helper's *The Impending Crisis* had expanded to encompass any book construed as antislavery. In January one of Thayer & Eldridge's book agents in Alabama had been arrested for soliciting advance orders of their edition of Fleetwood's *Life of Christ*, a condensed New Testament with abolitionist commentaries disguised as textual notes. The local vigilance committee reviewed the case and reported, "We find no evidence to convict him of tampering with slaves, but as he is from the North, engaged in selling a book published in the North, we have a right to suspect him as being an Abolitionist, and we therefore recommend, in order to guard ourselves against possible danger, that he be immediately conducted by the military out of this county into the next adjoining."[44] If Thayer & Eldridge book agents had been suspected of being abolitionists in January, before the publication of Redpath's biography of John Brown and his anthology *Echoes of Harper's Ferry*, there could be no doubt now. And the consequences were growing more and more dire.

A book agent selling the *Cottage Bible* in Henderson, Texas, had been forced to refund money and was run out of town after the notes accompanying the text, like those in Fleetwood's edition, wherever they could be "made to bear on the slavery question," were judged to be "not fitted for the south."[45] Henry A. Marsh's bookstore in Camden, Arkansas, was burned by a vigilante mob and Marsh narrowly escaped hanging after "he was examined by a Vigilance Committee on a charge of being an Abolitionist from Texas."[46]

Even in Washington, those intent on silencing antislavery sentiment grew increasingly bold. After Charles W. Sumner delivered his impassioned four-hour speech "The Barbarism of Slavery" on the Senate floor in early June, he received death threats and intimidating letters. In mid-June, when Thayer & Eldridge's pamphlet edition of Sumner's speech was already on press, the senator was visited at his apartment in Washington by a stranger who said he would soon return with friends to hold Sumner "accountable" for his words. When the threat was reported in the northern press, Thayer & Eldridge wrote Sumner immediately: "If you need assistance in defending yourself against the ruffians of the Slave Power, please telegraph us *at once*, or to some of your friends here who will notify us. There is a strong feeling here, and we can raise a small body of men, who will join with your Washington friends, or will alone defend you."[47]

In this overheated environment Thayer & Eldridge had very few, if any, book agents remaining in the South by May 1860, and none were selling *Leaves of Grass*. The *New Orleans Sunday Delta* complained that they had been forced to review Whitman's book sight unseen, based on nothing more than the few poems that had appeared in the *Saturday Press*, because "his publishers have not sent the lately published volume to the South."[48]

The *Southern Field and Fireside* in Augusta, Georgia, also reviewed the book sight unseen, though the writer artfully concealed his ignorance of the new volume. The review, titled "A New American Poem," focused on every detail of the 1855 edition—the size of the page, the presswork, the steel-engraved frontispiece—but made no mention of the appearance of the new edition, saying only that the book "is again brought before the public, enlarged, altered and rendered, if possible, more disgusting and abominable than in its pristine shape." The reviewer worried that this new edition "may find its way into respectable bookstores and even pure households, by reason of the attention it has received. To save the latter from moral contamination and the necessity of using disinfectants, we feel bound to say so much by way of caution as will enable them to learn the true character of the volume. Not that we would pollute our columns with quoting any of its vilest passages."[49] The few passages that were quoted were extracts from the same passages published in Henry Clapp's earlier review in the *Saturday Press*.

Apparently aware that Whitman's work was reaching the South almost exclusively through his pages, Clapp selected two poems from the Thayer & Eldridge book for his June 9 edition, "Mannahatta" and "Longings for Home." These two poems, Clapp must have guessed, would be received with anger in the South. "Mannahatta" (misspelled by Clapp as "Manahatta") is largely a paean to urban New York, but in praising the freedoms of his beloved city Whitman explicitly mentions slavery near the poem's close:

A million people—manners free and superb—open voices—
    hospitality—the most courageous and friendly young men;
The free city! no slaves! no owners of slaves!

In San Francisco *The Golden Era* reprinted the poem from the *Saturday Press* (complete with misspelled title), accompanied by a parody entitled "San Francisco," which portrayed the western city according to Whitman's structure but with a jaundiced eye. Looking on the city, the parodist imagines "The pipes of Otard, the vast quantity of Bourbon, the stupendous seas of lager, / The cigars smoked, the many thousands of feet of plug annually masticated, and the Atlantic oceans of saliva expectorated." In San Francisco, where freedom from slavery had been declared a decade earlier over the objections of the city's wealthy gold interests, he sees "The free city. No slaves sir! No Octoroons, / The immaculate nigger."[50]

The *New Orleans Sunday Delta* also reprinted "Mannahatta" but confronted it more directly. The editor bristled at claims of Whitman's "Parnassian honors" based on his "lusty naturalness": "We will only say . . . that an alligator floundering in a slough, a hog wallowing in the mire, a buzzard plunging its beak into carrion, and many other objects of similar disgust, may all be lusty and natural, but not particularly sublime, beautiful, captivating, or even pleasant."[51]

"Longings for Home," on the other hand, was an extended poem urging the South to return to the fold of the United States, exhorting, "O magnet-South! O glistening perfumed South! My South!" Clapp must have known that southern editorialists would rankle at Whitman's claim that he longed to be a son of the South:

An Arkansas prairie—a sleeping lake, or still bayou;
O my heart! O tender and fierce pangs—I can stand them not—
    I will depart;
O to be a Virginian, where I grew up! O to be a Carolinian!
O longings irrepressible! O I will go back to old Tennessee, and
    never wander more!

The *Southern Literary Messenger* reprinted the full text of "Longings for Home" with an introduction by the editor, George William Bagby, who called the poem a "sample of [Whitman's] obnubilate, incoherent, convulsive flub-drub." He warned readers, "It culminates in the spasmodic idiocy of Walt Whitman. The smart scribblers who compose the better part of the Northern literati, are all becoming infected with the new leprosy—Whitmansy."[52] Bagby took exception to the final passage, in which "Whitman says he 'grew up' in Virginia. We should feel mean if this statement were anything else than a Whitmaniacal license, accent on the first vowel of license." When one of the *Messenger*'s readers from New York wrote to defend Whitman, arguing that "Ossian's poetry is something in the style of Whitman's," Bagby responded deridingly, "The Bible, also, is 'something in the style of the Book of Mormon.' "[53]

The *Virginia Free Press* in Charlestown—where John Brown had been hanged only six months earlier—was the only Virginia paper to weigh in directly on Whitman. They afforded *Leaves of Grass* only a few lines, just enough to condemn the book as "incomprehensible and nonsensical" and to praise Juliette Beach's "candid opinion" and (borrowing a phrase from the *New York Tribune*) her "frank avowals," apparently unaware that they had been retracted almost immediately.[54] This fact alone suggests that the editors had never seen the book or the *Saturday Press* itself, just selective reprintings and accounts of what the book contained.

Less than a hundred miles away in the nation's capital, however, the book was readily available to book buyers. Taylor & Maury's Washington Bookstore on Pennsylvania Avenue had advertised *Leaves of Grass* even before its publication in May. By late summer the book was most easily available at Philp & Solomons Metropolitan Bookstore, directly next door to Taylor & Maury's. A review published in the *Daily National Intelligencer* in August specifically directed readers there and praised the book in hand for its "exquisite typography, imprinted on paper of irreproachable quality." A reviewer for the *Intelligencer* had delivered a long and thoughtful, if somewhat mixed, review of *Leaves of Grass* in 1856, but after the expansion of the book by nearly one hundred poems, the same reviewer seems to have lost patience with Whitman.[55] Four years earlier he had written:

> Without, perhaps, ever having read Spinoza, he is a Spinozist. . . . With-out knowing how to chop the formal logic of the schools, he is a necessitarian and fatalist, with whom "whatever is is right." The world as he finds it, and man as he is, good or bad, high or low, igno-rant or learned, holy or vicious, are all alike good enough for Walter Whitman, who is in himself a "kosmos," and whose emotional nature is at once the sensorium of humanity and the sounding board which catches up and intones each note of joy or sorrow in the "gamut of human feeling."[56]

After the publication of the new edition, the reviewer continued to com-pare Whitman to Spinoza but no longer viewed him as a proponent of the unity of all things but as an indiscriminate praiser whose work was less pantheistic than it was a mere auctioneer's catalogue:

> Unique in his literary style, Walt is, like a genuine disciple of Spin-oza, perfectly indifferent with regard to the matter that enters into the composition of his book. Things good and things bad, things de-cent and things indecent, things pretty to the eye and things ugly, things sweet to the taste and things bitter, things fragrant to the nos-trils and things noisome, things smooth to the touch and things rough, are to him one and the same. Accordingly the reader will find in this "poem" an inventory (expressed in a style something like a cross between Butler's Hudibras and an auctioneer's advertisement) of all things good and bad, decent and indecent, pretty and ugly, sweet and bitter, fragrant and noisome, smooth and rough, enumer-ated in categories designed to exhaust the sensations of humanity and hold a mirror up to the universe at large.[57]

The negative review, however, is far less surprising than the fact that the book was carried by Philp & Solomons. They were far from aboli-tionist booksellers; in fact, they were one of Washington's leading pur-veyors of pro-slavery books. At the time of the *National Intelligencer* review, the only title featured in their advertisements was *The Nachash Origin of the Black and Mixed Races*, a biblical justification for enslaving Africans by C. Blancher Thompson. The ad prominently proclaimed, "Negroes are not the children of Adam; their status by creation is that of subjects."[58]

The advertisement would no doubt have incensed Whitman more than another mixed review of the book. He had placed as the centerpiece of the cluster "Enfans d'Adam" the untitled poem we now know as "I Sing the Body Electric," with its concluding scene of "The slave's body for sale—I, sternly, with harsh voice, auctioneering, / The divine list, for myself or you, or for any one, making":

> Gentlemen, look on this wonder!
> Whatever the bids of the bidders, they cannot be high enough for it,
> For it the globe lay preparing quintillions of years, without one
>   animal or plant,
> For it the revolving cycles truly and steadily rolled.
>
> In this head the all-baffling brain,
> In it and below it, the making of the attributes of heroes.[59]

No single paper summarized the southern rejection of Whitman better than the *Houston Telegraph*. After voicing the usual dislike for the book's reputed sexual content—supposedly so pervasive that its pages "literally stink with obscenity"—the reviewer drew a clear geographic line dividing the book's reception. Although Whitman's poetry was "meeting with much favor in the North," the writer reported, he was "happy to say that the literary taste of the South has not been sufficiently cultivated to enable it to assimilate such foods as these 'Leaves of Grass.'"[60]

. . .

Nowhere was the chasm between the advocates and detractors of *Leaves of Grass* more distinct, or more physical, than in the Ohio Valley, between Kentucky to the south and Ohio and Indiana to the north. A writer for the *Louisville Daily Journal*, for example, attacked the book based solely on the reviews. "A good deal is said in the papers about a new edition of a rather notorious book," he began. "The thing is beneath contempt. Decent folks would sooner batten, like neat cattle, upon the 'grass' of the meadows than, like unclean ones, upon that of Walt. Whitman's book."[61] Meanwhile, in abolitionist Columbus, just two hundred miles to the northeast, Whitman enjoyed a comparatively warm response from William Dean Howells, under the influence of his father and the fugitive followers of John Brown.

Whitman was encouraged by his reception in Ohio and was convinced that his book would find a foothold in the West. In early June he sent Clapp an impassioned article, originally published in the Philadelphia *City Item*, by young Henry P. Leland. He told Clapp, "[Leland's words have] certain little grains of salt that I wish to see put in[,] a way of 'leavening' the lump of _____ you know what."[62] It is easy to see why Whitman liked the review. Leland wrote, "He sings very little for the opera, but for oyster-men and clam-diggers, and Western hunters and raftsmen, and farmers and red-cheeked matrons, and omnibus-drivers and mechanics; and for all true Americans, he whistles like an oriole of a warm May morning. He sits down by you familiarly, but not 'famillioniarely,' and tells you of Rocky Mountains, primeval forests, Southern bayoux, Northern lakes, Western prairies, Eastern rock-bound sea-shores, far-stretching prairies, scenes of sunlight, and fresh blowing air."[63] Apart from the flattery, Leland suggested that *Leaves of Grass* would find its true readership not just among the omnibus drivers and mechanics Whitman already so desperately courted in Manhattan, but also among hunters in the West and boatmen along the Ohio River.

Ironically, it was not one of the western roughs that first championed Whitman from the north bank of the Ohio but a transplanted Virginian who had studied Transcendentalism under Emerson. Moncure D. Conway was no stranger to Whitman; in fact, in September 1855 he became the first reader of *Leaves of Grass* to seek out Whitman in Brooklyn and deliver the good news of Emerson's approval. A minister at the First Unitarian Church in Washington at the time, Conway at first seemed an unlikely devotee, but in his way he was no less radical than Whitman. After he lost his ministry in 1856 when his congregation became disgruntled over his antislavery sermons, he was invited to the First Unitarian Church of Cincinnati, where his ideas were more acceptable. But even in the West his hard-line views were divisive. At the meeting of the Western Unitarian Conference in 1857 he insisted on an antislavery resolution even though William Greenleaf Eliot of St. Louis, one of the conference's founders, left the organization as a result. Indeed, two years later half of Conway's congregation in Cincinnati left to form a new church in objection to his sermons. In 1860, to push his ideas on literature and politics, Conway founded a new monthly, *The Dial*—borrowing its name from the defunct Transcendentalist periodical edited by Emerson—in part because he saw a unique opportunity in Cincinnati.

"Cincinnati is separated from Kentucky only by the narrow Ohio," he wrote. At the time, Cincinnati and Covington, Kentucky, were like one town split by the river, some of the same roads even continuing on both sides, but it was possible to look from the bluffs of Cincinnati into Kentucky and "see the slaves at their work."[64] Conway abhorred the institution of slavery, but he disavowed the methods of John Brown. In his review of Redpath's biography in *The Dial* he decried the use of morality to justify war: "John Brown's method of dealing with slavery was apiece with his false theology and his uncultured mind." He cautioned his readers, "Look not at the arrow, but the path."[65] Three months later, in reviewing *Echoes of Harper's Ferry*, he explained, "Every nation must write its own Bible. America has written its Genesis: Concord and Bunker Hill are chapters in it. John Brown has opened the Book of Exodus."[66] What remained to be seen was who would write our Leviticus, our book of holy laws for America to live by.

In Columbus William Dean Howells, writing for the *Ohio State Journal*, praised Conway's new magazine. He may not have agreed with Conway on all points—especially on the topic of John Brown, whom he felt had acted righteously—but Howells admired Conway's ambition. Boston had long been "the only place in the land where the inalienable right to think what you please has been practiced and upheld," he wrote, but Conway sought to place Cincinnati on that same "serene eminence." Conway, in turn, sought out Howells and soon pronounced his "confidence in the genius and promise" of his poetry in the pages of *The Dial*. Not long after, Howells went to Cincinnati to visit Conway. The two men talked at length about slavery, Lincoln, and literature. "Howells seemed to have read everything," Conway remembered later. "At least, whenever I mentioned any writer or work I found he had been searching the same."[67]

Among the authors who dominated their conversation was Whitman. Conway soon after praised Whitman lavishly in the pages of *The Dial:*

> The Leaves of Grass has been our companion out in the wild outlooks of Newport and Nahant, we have read it at night after following the throngs of New York by day, we have conversed with its music when the obligato was the whizz and scream of the locomotive which bore us across the continent, and have turned to it from the calm rush of the Father of Waters, from the loading here and there on its shores by the glare of pine-knot fires, from the eager crowd of men and women chatting, singing, gaming in the saloon, and we confidently announce that Walt Whitman has set the pulses of America to music. Here are the incomplete but real utterances of New York city, of the prairies, of the Ohio and Mississippi,—the volume of American autographs.[68]

Howells remained intrigued by Whitman, particularly his frequent appearances in the *Saturday Press*. Clapp's weekly "was a power," Howells remembered later, and "young writers throughout the country were ambitious to be seen in it." He knew well. Howells had published his poetry more than fifteen times in the *Press* by the summer of 1860. But he was conflicted. On the one hand, he disagreed with those who declared Whitman immoral but, on the other hand, he considered Whitman's work too undisciplined to be considered poetry.

At the end of June, after spending the first half of the year in Columbus, Howells took the train home to Jefferson in Ashtabula County, the first leg on a cross-country trip to seek work in Boston and New York. In recounting for the *Ohio State Journal* the outset of his journey in the wee hours of the morning, Howells began:

> I believe I am not singular in the lothness I have sometimes felt to be called up at three o'clock in the morning to go away upon the cars.
>
>> You are the same as I,
>> You are no different from me,
>
> says Walt Whitman. So it is you I celebrate as much as myself. And it is you have retired with the dreadful consciousness that you are to be roused at three in the morning.[69]

He spent two weeks in Jefferson preparing for his trip eastward and, in the meantime, contributed articles to the *Ashtabula Sentinel*, edited by his father.

In a review of *Leaves of Grass* written for the paper, Howells gave voice to his ambivalent feelings toward the book and humorously recounted for Jefferson's uninformed readers how Whitman had risen to such strange notoriety:

> Nearly a year ago, the bull put his head through the New York Saturday Press enclosure, and bellowed loud, long, and unintelligibly.
>
> The mystery of the thing made it all the more appalling.
>
> The Misses Nancy of criticism hastened to scramble over the fence, and on the other side, stood shaking their fans and parasols at the wretch, and shrieking, "Beast! Beast!"
>
> Some courageous wits attempted to frighten the animal away by mimicry, and made a noise as from infant bulls.
>
> The people in the china-shop shut and bolted their doors.
>
> Several critics petted and patted the bull; but it was agreed that while his eyes had a beautiful expression, and his breath was fragrant with all the meadow-sweetness of the world, he was not at all clean, and in general, smelt of the stables, and like a bull.[70]

In anticipation of seeing Henry Clapp in a few weeks, Howells sent one copy of the review on to New York and gave the other to his father to print in the *Sentinel*.

When Howells arrived in New York in August he went to meet Clapp for the first time at Pfaff's. Howells reported that he thought as a contributor and "at least a brevet bohemian" he would be welcomed at "the famous place."[71] But he found the bandying jests more unnerving than exhilarating. When Howells told Clapp that he had newly arrived from Boston, where he had met Nathaniel Hawthorne, the editor asked what he thought of the man behind *The Scarlet Letter*. Howells told Clapp that Hawthorne was shy, but he forgave this because he was shy himself. Clapp pulled out his pipe and shouted, "Oh, a couple of shysters!" to the roaring delight of all those assembled at the long table. Howells sat down, ordered a pancake, and listened to "the whirling words of my commensals." By eleven o'clock he was exhausted and decided to leave.[72]

On his way out, passing a table near the stairs, someone stopped him to introduce him to Walt Whitman, seated at the table's head. Whitman did not stand but leaned back in his chair and extended his hand to Howells, "as if he were going to give it me for good and all." Howells was stunned into silence at the sight of the bard of Manhattan: "He had a fine head, with a cloud of Jovian hair upon it, and a branching beard and mustache, and gentle eyes that looked most kindly into mine, and seemed to wish the liking which I instantly gave him, though we hardly passed a word, and our acquaintance was summed up in that glance and the grasp of his mighty fist upon my hand."[73]

Despite the warm meeting with Whitman, Howells left New York the next day without seeing any more of the city. "The bohemians were the beginning and the end of the story for me," he later wrote, "and to tell the truth I did not like the story."[74]

As the summer wore on and copies of *Leaves of Grass* reached England, negative reviews began to pour in from the other side of the Atlantic, including from the *Leader and Saturday Analyst,* the *Literary Gazette,* the *Saturday Review,* the *London Critic,* and *The Spectator.* Whitman's old enemies at the *Brooklyn Eagle* dutifully reprinted the worst of these to assure they did not go unnoticed in New York and ran a broad parody that began, "Look here, Walt Whitman, what made you write this book, these Leaves of Grass, full of good thoughts, bad thoughts, naughty thoughts, noble thoughts?"[75] For Whitman, however, the most stinging of these critiques came from the English *Saturday Review:* "It is a book evidently intended to lie on the tables of the wealthy. No poor man could afford it, and it is too bulky for its possessor to get into his pocket or to hide away in a corner. . . . The odd thing is, that it irresistibly suggests its being intended for the luxurious and cultivated of both sexes. We are almost ashamed to ask the question—but do American ladies read Mr. Whitman?"[76]

By now Whitman was accustomed to the insistence that the book was unsuitable for women, but he worried over the characterization of the book as "luxurious" and affordable only to the fine men and women who would place it on their parlor tables. Taking the criticism to heart, he suggested to Thayer and Eldridge that the next printing should have paper covers and its price dropped from $1.25 to $1. "This would afford a splendid living American Vol.," Whitman wrote. After the response from Ohio he felt confident that it would "go like the devil through the West, and among the young men everywhere."[77]

Earlier in the spring Whitman had written his brother Jeff, "[Thayer & Eldridge] think every thing I do is the right thing,"[78] and this time was no different. "We approve heartily of your idea in regard to a change in this respect," Eldridge wrote, but they were reluctant to use paper covers for a dollar book, "nor paper covers for any kind."[79] Instead, they proposed a dollar edition with flexible cloth covers and a new $1.50 edition bound in cloth over boards that would include an addendum of new poems. They expected to be out of the second printing by the end of August, so Whitman would have to work fast.

Before Thayer & Eldridge could proceed with the expanded edition of *Leaves of Grass*, they racked up still more debt, again at Whitman's suggestion. The *Saturday Press* had been struggling financially since the early spring and the publishers were considering buying it. When they wrote to ask Whitman's opinion, he apparently endorsed the idea. Thayer wrote on August 17 to thank Whitman for his advice and informed him that they expected to assume financial responsibility for the paper on September 1.

Blame for this decision cannot be placed entirely on Whitman, however; as early as the spring Thayer and Eldridge had discussed the possibility of starting a new Boston-based magazine with William O'Connor as its editor. Intending to compete with the *Atlantic Monthly*, Thayer envisioned a journal that "shall sustain with great ability radical views on the reformatory questions of the day, and combine these with the highest literary character."[80] He expected contributions from Emerson, Higginson, and O'Connor himself. The prospect of combining that effort with the *Saturday Press*'s New York readership and established writers—including Whitman, Clapp, Ada Clare, George Arnold, and Fitz-James O'Brien—must have seemed a sure thing.

Moreover, Thayer and Eldridge were both true believers in Whitman's work—admirers more than mere publishers and bordering on the devout. They steadfastly believed they could make money selling his work and supporting the newspaper that championed him. When Whitman wrote to say that he missed their warmth and wished he could be with them again, Thayer wrote reassuringly:

> *We* too wish you could be with us in Boston for we have *so* much to say; and our "fanatic" wants to get under the refreshing shelter of Walt's spirit; he does not ask Walt to talk, but only for the privilege of looking into those eyes of calm; and through them to enter into that Soul, so deep in its emotions, so majestic in all its thought-movements, and yet so simple and childlike. Yes, Walt. Whitman; though men of the world and arch-critics do not *understand* thee, yet

some there be among men and women who *love* thee and hold thy
spirit close by their own.

In response to Howells's claim that the "Misses Nancy of criticism" had
fled in fear of Whitman, shrieking, "Beast! Beast!," Thayer insisted, "We
do not care one single damn for the Miss Nancys of Bookdom but shall
continue to publish and *sell* Leaves of Grass 'so long' as Walt. will have
us."[81] But they felt that Whitman should answer the charges directly before they issued a new edition of *Leaves of Grass*.

Instead, Whitman composed an anonymous item that purported to be
a review of *Leaves of Grass Imprints*, the promotional pamphlet of reviews
mailed free by Thayer & Eldridge to all who requested it. The review,
published in the *Brooklyn City News*, was actually an opportunity for
Whitman to answer his critics and to plainly state his poetic mission. The
remarkable, full-column statement of purpose is a singular document—
which, strangely, has been almost entirely ignored by scholars.

Whitman first set out to explain that "the egotistical outset, 'I celebrate myself,'" was not meant to voice the feelings solely of the poet but
to speak "for him or her reading it precisely the same as for the author."
It is telling that Whitman not only maintained that he was merely a
stand-in for the reader but that his readers might as easily be women as
men. The poem "Walt Whitman" should be thought of as "the Song of
the sovereignty of One's self," he wrote, both presaging and explicating
the title by which the poem is today best known, "Song of Myself," as
well as making a broad, national claim for his book. "The book is a gospel
of self-assertion and self-reliance for every American reader," he continued, "which is the same as saying it is the gospel of Democracy."[82]

Whitman saw himself as "devoting his life to the experiment of
singing the New World in a New Song—not only new in spirit, but new
in letter, new in form." This not only explained but justified his unusual
meters, his unruly and wildly associative style; it also explained "the general *howl*" of disapproval that the book had received "both in America and

in Europe." The book established "new canons" and had to be judged by
them "just the same as America":

> Neither can the song of Leaves of Grass ever be judged by the
> intellect—nor suffice to be read merely once or so, for amusement.
> This strange song (often offensive to the intellect) is to be felt, ab-
> sorbed by the soul. It is to be dwelt upon—returned to, again and
> again. It wants a broad space to turn in, like a big ship. Many readers,
> perhaps the majority, will be perplexed and baffled by it at first; but
> in frequent cases those who liked the book least at first will take it
> closest to their hearts upon a second or third perusal.[83]

The difficulty came from his poetry's "peculiar idiomatic flavor," which
Whitman freely admitted he had taken from the "celebrated New York
'rough,' full of muscular and excessively virile energy, full of animal blood,
masterful, striding to the front rank, allowing none to walk before him,
full of rudeness and recklessness, talking and acting his own way, utterly
regardless of other people's ways."

It was this very rudeness that led many reviewers to mistake the new
American voice of *Leaves of Grass* for vulgarity, and it was old world standards of propriety that had blinded them to the divine possibilities:

> The cry of indecency against Leaves of Grass amounts, when plainly
> stated, about to this: Other writers assume the sexual relations are
> shameful in themselves, and not to be put in poems. But our new
> bard, walking right straight through all that, assumes that those very
> relations are the most beautiful and pure and divine of any—and in
> that way he "celebrates" them. No wonder he confounds the ortho-
> dox. Yet his indecency is the ever-recurring indecency of the inspired
> Biblical writers—and is that of innocent youth, and of the natural
> and untainted man in all ages.
>
> In other words, the only explanation the reader needs to bear in
> mind to clear up the whole matter is this: The subjects (amativeness,
> &c.) about which such a storm has been raised, are treated by Walt
> Whitman with unprecedented boldness and candor, but always in the
> very highest religious and esthetic spirit. Filthy to others, *to him* they
> are *not* filthy, but "illustrious." While his "critics," (carefully minding

never to state the foregoing fact, though it is stamped all over the book,) consider those subjects in Leaves of Grass, from the point of view of persons standing on the lowest animal and infidelistic platform. Which, then, is really the "beast"?[84]

Whitman's response is striking, but it was published anonymously and only in a local newspaper that was already avowedly sympathetic to him and his work.

Despite their fervent enthusiasm for Whitman's work, Thayer and Eldridge could no longer deny that the sales of *Leaves of Grass* had stalled. As the anxiety of the nation pushed the economy into a stock panic and recession, the publishers feared for their prospects of survival if they continued to broaden their financial risk. Thus they suggested that, rather than issue two editions of an expanded *Leaves of Grass*, they would run another printing of the previous edition as planned and also issue a new book by Whitman—a book impossible to criticize as lewd, as it would instead highlight Whitman's ardent nationalism and would be published in time for the presidential election.

In typical fashion, Thayer & Eldridge advertised heavily, running announcements in the *Saturday Press, Vanity Fair,* the *Atlantic Monthly, The Liberator,* and the *American Publishers' Circle and Literary Gazette.* In October Whitman sent his publishers the text for a full-page announcement for the book he was by then calling *The Banner At Day-Break,* to appear at the back of O'Connor's *Harrington.* He also asked for an advance against future royalties. Thayer acknowledged receipt of the advertisement and had it inserted, but warned Whitman to be patient. They were financially overextended and needed to delay the release of his book:

> We cannot however stereotype your little book now, as we have so much already underway. We shall hardly be ready for it under two months, but shall certainly commence on it by the first of January.
>
> In regard to money matters, we are very short ourselves and it is quite impossible to send you the sum you name. We would if we could. Business will be stagnant with us till after the Presidential election when with our new books we shall get up a rush. . . . We

shall let you know when we are ready for the Banner at Daybreak, so as to give you ample time to make preparations to come on.[85]

Whitman was no doubt disappointed that his hymns to American unity would not be available in time for the election, but the book was still provisional at best and the added time would help him fill in the gaps. He believed, as did most in the North, that with the passing of the election season all would return to normal.

Whitman didn't know, however, that a correspondent for the *Charleston Mercury*, at almost exactly that moment, was sniping angrily about this very tendency among New Yorkers. "The Stock panic is now nearly over," he wrote. "They cannot realize, in the first place, that the South, or any single Southern State, will secede in the event of Lincoln's election; and, in the second place, that Lincoln will be rash enough to provoke secession by an overt act." The stock market was rebounding, he believed, on the strength of little more than a blithe belief in "the 'patriotism' and 'good sense' of the American people." A truer indicator of northern uncertainty was the reduced lists of nearly every American publisher for November and December. "The publishers," he wrote, "promise nothing until after the Presidential election. Nothing of importance is now in press." By his count, only six titles of interest had been announced for the remainder of the year, all of which were issuing from Boston and four of which were Thayer & Eldridge titles. New Yorkers as a whole, the *Mercury* correspondent worried, did not recognize the importance of such indicators. "They have lived through so many crises that they expect the 'impending crisis' to pass away like a light cloud on a summer sky."[86]

CHAPTER THREE

The Volcanic Upheaval
of the Nation

The volcanic upheaval of the nation, after that firing on the
flag at Charleston, proved for certain something which had
been previously in great doubt, and at once substantially settled
the question of disunion. In my judgment it will remain as the
grandest and most encouraging spectacle yet vouchsafed in any
age, old or new, to political progress and democracy.
     Walt Whitman, *Memoranda During the War*, 1876

All afternoon, on Saturday, November 3, 1860, New York was pelted by
a driving rain. The wind turned umbrellas inside out; rain glutted gutters
and topped the brims of overshoes. By five o'clock the streetcars and stages
were crowded with those who could no longer brave the storm. Then,
about eight, the wind picked up and "for nearly two hours blew with the
force of a hurricane."[1] Wind sheared the limbs from some trees, lifted
other trees by their roots; it tore off awnings and blew down signs. Flood-
water filled the streets. In Brooklyn the Hamilton and Donaldson Paper
Factory on Carroll Street was struck by lightning; fire spread from the
straw-bedded hayloft to the timber frame, and the structure burned
swiftly to the ground.[2] A gable from a brick building under construction
at Myrtle and Nostrand was ripped off, and the wall underneath collapsed

and crushed the cottage next door.[3] By the next morning Brooklyn was wrecked. Tree limbs lay scattered around Fort Greene Park, near Whitman's home; the sound of hammers tacking down shingles and clapboard siding filled the air; the fire department had to be called out to extinguish the still smoldering ruins of the paper factory.[4] The *New York Times* joked sardonically that at least the "streets were never in a cleaner condition."[5]

It was easy to make light of the downpour, because, amazingly, no deaths were reported in New York, Brooklyn, or Long Island. The city had weathered safely what the *New York Evangelist* described as "one of the most terrific storms that we have ever witnessed," and the writer hoped that "in the political world, as in nature, after the storm there shall be a great calm."[6] But to almost anyone who had been watching congressional debates grow increasingly tumultuous in recent months while grassroots support for Lincoln swelled, it seemed an obviously vain hope.

As early as July Congressman Laurence M. Keitt publicly advocated secession for South Carolina should Lincoln win election, citing what he considered to be the ongoing erosion of his state's rights. "He concedes the certainty of a Republican victory," wrote the *New York Times*. "He acknowledges fully and frankly that the Democracy is utterly demoralized and broken,—that the South can no longer rely upon it,—and that, unless all political symptoms are deceptive and false, Mr. Lincoln is to be our next President. Under these circumstances he thinks the South can do nothing else but secede."[7] Keitt was soon followed by other prominent South Carolinians, including former speaker of the House James Lawrence Orr, former senator Robert Barnwell Rhett, and Congressman William W. Boyce.

In a stinging editorial Horace Greeley ridiculed these calls for secession and mocked the idea that the distinguished gentlemen of South Carolina were worried about constitutional infringements on states' rights. Instead, he insisted, they feared that "a Republican ascendancy at Washington will strongly tend to hasten the exodus of Slavery from Delaware, Maryland, Missouri, and all the Border Slave States. They aim to bully the Free States out of their choice for President; or, that failing, to drag the border Slave States into a rebellion which, however it may result directly, will have the effect of chaining those States more completely to the car of Slavery. The game is a bold one; but it will not win."[8]

By September, however, the rhetoric had turned from political gamesmanship to outright threats of civil war. In a widely circulated public letter, Orr claimed that Lincoln would not be able to enforce laws in the South, "unless at the point of the bayonet and over the dead bodies of her slain sons."[9] In a public response Amos Kendall, postmaster general under Andrew Jackson, reminded Orr that South Carolina had tried a similar challenge to President Jackson in 1832. When Jackson's own vice president, John C. Calhoun of South Carolina, supported his home state's right to nullify any federal law with which it disagreed, Jackson replied that such laws would be enforced by the federal military if necessary: "150,000 men tendered their services to the President to aid him if necessary in executing the laws of the United States; the time will be when 200,000 will volunteer for a like purpose, should resistance be made to his legitimate authority."[10]

Thus on Tuesday, November 6, when the polls opened in New York, the storm of the weekend may have passed, but it was apparent that the political storm was only beginning. Anxiety was running so high across the city that crowds surrounded the offices of every newspaper early in the evening, eagerly awaiting the returns from each ward and county. A writer for the *New York Times* reported that men climbed on each other's shoulders to try to see into the second-story windows and "flattened their noses painfully against the panes—one would have imagined that they thought to smell out the returns." To satisfy the throng results were called out as they arrived over the telegraph: "There were cheers and groans and huzzas and hisses. And until the night had grown old and morning was born, the clamorous crowd demanded more news and later intelligence."[11]

A similar scene played out at the offices of the *New York Herald*, where a crowd of three to four thousand gathered. As night fell and ward returns began to come in, the *Herald* wrote the results on transparency paper and hung the sheets from their second-floor window. They had mounted a high-powered limelight on a building across the street to il- luminate the returns well into the night. Whenever the writer of the re- sults appeared again at the window, a commotion went up and brought the mixed crowd ever closer to rioting. Looking upon the motley masses, the *Herald* writer was reminded of Whitman: "Gentlemen with opera glasses, and 'roughs' without, were together in a 'glorious jam,' " a phrase Whitman had used during his newspaper days to describe the crowded streets of the city.[12]

Indeed, the returns from heavily Democratic New York City and Brooklyn would be crucial. Without sufficient Republican ballots there, Lincoln would not be able to carry New York State and would fall seven electoral votes short of a majority. In far distant Springfield, Illinois, Lin- coln, too, was anxiously awaiting word to come over the wires, fearing the worst. But the New York political boss Thurlow Weed had turned out Re- publican voters, and not long after midnight the results were announced. Even before Lincoln himself received the dispatch those crowded in the streets of New York knew the name of their new president—and greeted the news ominously.[13]

When a transparency was hung outside the offices of the *Herald* an- nouncing "Abraham Lincoln is elected President," a shout went up: "Three cheers for the Union!" Many from the crowd quickly joined in with "Hip, hip, hooray! Hip, hip, hooray!" But soon a countercheer came swelling from the crowd: "One, two, three, four, five, six—nigger, nig- ger, nigga-ar!" The calm after the storm had ended, and the cacophony in the streets of New York, said the *Herald*, sounded like the "rumbling of distant thunder."[14]

But the spectacle that night signaled more than the political trouble ahead; it also revealed the newfound power of the telegraphic dispatch. "If any one doubted . . . that the telegraph wires were big with the fate of this glorious Union," wrote the *Times*, "a walk in the vicinity of the dif- ferent newspaper offices would have speedily convinced him to the con- trary." The people of New York had "demanded to know the fate of the

Union before daybreak," and the newspapers had delivered.[15] The *Times* reporter predicted that in the coming years readers would rely on "the information supplied by their party newspaper" for word of "whether the country were saved or lost."[16]

Thayer & Eldridge began advertising William D. O'Connor's *Harrington* almost as soon as election results were received. They serialized the novel in *The Liberator* and offered "liberal terms" for book agents "to sell . . . the most brilliant Anti-Slavery Novel yet written."[17] They had reason to press for sales. The book had failed to meet expectations for advance orders at the New York Book Publishers' Association, and many of their agents, even in the North, were unwilling to sell an abolitionist novel on commission after Lincoln's election. As bound books began to arrive, Thayer held out hope that *Harrington* would sell in the same way the John Brown books had only months before—on the strength of public interest and word of mouth.

For Whitman the arrival of the book was cause for excitement. For several months Thayer & Eldridge had advertised "A New Volume of Poems by Walt Whitman," but on the last page of advertisements at the back of *Harrington*, the title and table of contents of Whitman's new book were revealed. *The Banner At Day-Break* would be "a handsome volume of about 200 pages," including the new poems "Banner At Day-Break," "Washington's First Battle," "Errand-Bearers," "Pictures," "Quadrel," "The Ox-Tamer," "Poemet," "Mannahatta," "The Days," and "Sonnets," plus a "supplement containing criticism, &c."[18] Much in this proposed table of contents was still filler; "Poemet" and "Mannahatta," for example, had already appeared in *Leaves of Grass*. But the first few poems listed were ready, and they collectively represented Whitman's artistic attempt to dramatize the crisis of the union and the urgency of its preservation— even if its preservation came at the cost of civil war.

Whitman intended the title poem, in particular, to dramatize the threat of secession by lending each view its own voice: the voice of the poet, the voices of father and son, and the voices of the banner of America and the pennant of war. At this tense moment in history the banner and pennant speak as one, as a kind of Greek chorus, exhorting the "Bard, out of Manhattan" to speak to the children of the North and West, "Where our factories hum, where our miners delve the ground / Where our hoarse Niagara rumbles, where our prairie-plows are plowing." And Whitman the poet responds appropriately, urging the child to look on the banner and pennant. "I hear and see not strips of cloth alone," he writes. "I hear the tramp of armies, I hear the challenging sentry; / I hear the jubilant shouts of millions of men—I hear LIBERTY!" The father urges his son not to be entranced by the flapping banner and words of the poet but to

> Look at these dazzling things in the houses, and see you the
>   money-shops opening;
> And see you the vehicles preparing to crawl along the streets with
>   goods:
> These! ah, these! how valued and toil'd for, these!
> How envied by all the earth![19]

But the son is not swayed by the father's talk of prosperity and accommodation in the name of peace. If war is the only path to liberty, then he chooses war:

> O my father, I like not the houses;
> They will never to me be anything—nor do I like money;
> But to mount up there I would like, O father dear—that
>   banner I like;
> That pennant I would be, and must be.[20]

The poem is unusually conventional in its structure and its simplistic system of symbols, especially when contrasted with "A Child's Reminiscence" and "Bardic Symbols" of less than a year before. Nevertheless, the strongly pro-war stance of the poem was strikingly radical. Perhaps half a year spent in the constant presence of Thayer, Eldridge, Redpath, Hinton, and O'Connor had convinced Whitman of the purgative power of war. Speaking in his own voice, the voice of the poet, Whitman declares his allegiance to the banner and pennant and his willingness to join with the child:

> Out of reach—an idea only—yet furiously fought for, risking bloody
>   death—loved by me!
> So loved! O you banner leading the day, with stars brought from
>   the night!
> Valueless, object of eyes, over all and demanding all—O banner
>   and pennant!
> I too leave the rest—great as it is, it is nothing—house, machines are
>   nothing—I see them not;
> I see but you, O warlike pennant! O banner so broad, with stripes, I
>   sing you only,
> Flapping up there in the wind.[21]

This overtly nationalistic and militaristic poem was followed by a historical narrative but with an implied contemporary lesson. "Washington's First Battle" (later revised to become "The Centenarian's Story") was narrated by a Revolutionary War veteran and intended as a reminder that America's greatest victories had often arisen from moments that appeared to be devastating losses. The poem chronicles the Battle of Brooklyn, the first pitched battle in which Washington engaged, where the general's men, including Whitman's own great-uncle, were savagely defeated by Cornwallis on the battlefield:

> Jauntily forward they went with quick step toward Gowanus' waters;
> Till of a sudden, unlook'd for, by defiles through the woods,
>   gain'd at night,
> The British advancing, wedging in from the east, fiercely playing
>   their guns,
> That brigade of the youngest was cut off, and at the enemy's mercy.
> The General watch'd them from this hill;
> They made repeated desperate attempts to burst their environment;
> Then drew close together, very compact, their flag flying
>   in the middle;
> But O from the hills how the cannon were thinning and
>   thinning them![22]

This scene was clearly iconic for Whitman, as he returned to it again and again in his writings. In the 1855 edition, in the poem later retitled "The Sleepers," Whitman had described Washington "on the entrenched hills amid a crowd of officers," watching "the slaughter of the southern braves confided to him by their parents." But, on reflection, Whitman saw significance less in the sacrifice of the common men than in the decision that General Washington made in the battle's aftermath.

"The more I have thought it over," Whitman wrote in an unpublished manuscript from this period, "the more I am convinced that the few days, perhaps the few hours, following this battle, held the most momentous and weighty consequences of any in the life of Washington and in the destinies of These States." Washington's brilliance in this moment was his flexibility, his unwillingness to sacrifice more men to a hopeless cause. Instead, he executed a precise retreat under the cover of darkness that allowed his army to recoup and fight under more favorable conditions on another day:

> In dismay, in the toils in the hours of rain and darkness—He planned the retreat to Manhattan Island—he saved the American cause.— Alert, sleepless, stern, impassive, he decided upon this step, took the practical means for it, and his own vigilant eyes overlooked the final performance of it.—He stood at the ferry landing (now Fulton ferry, Brooklyn side) sending orders, receiving intelligence, encouraging the despondent.—What grander moments were there, even in the life of George Washington than they?—He stood at the landing all that critical night—he was still there at day-break, and more than an hour afterward.—He was one of the last to leave the Brooklyn shore.—[23]

Washington had refused to lead the "brigade of Virginia and Maryland" into slaughter simply to preserve his sense of honor. It was his willingness to retreat that "saved the American cause." The poem is a parable for southern readers, urging them to withdraw from the prospect of war to once again save the lives of their "southern braves." After all, Washington's most glorious moment arose from the decision to withdraw from battle, not a stubborn determination to fight that ultimately would have doomed the young nation.

After Lincoln's election Whitman began drafting additional new poems for the collection. In one notebook entry he imagined a poem for two voices "as of a Dialogue A. L—n and W"; he imagined the exchange as if spoken in a dream, then jotted as a potential title "Lessons for a President elect," subtitled "Dialogue between WW. and 'President elect.'"[24] In another poem, "Ship of Libertad," he wrote:

> Why now I shall know whether there is any thing in you, Libertad,
> I shall see how much you can stand
> perhaps I shall see the crash—is all then lost?
> Welcome the storm—welcome the trial—let the waves
> Why now I shall see what the old ship is made of
> Any body can sail with a fair wind, or a smooth sea[25]

Thayer & Eldridge were less exuberant. Hinton's biography of Lincoln had gone through three editions, but it sold for only twenty-five cents and returned barely any financial gain. Lincoln's election not only set the country lurching toward war, it also spelled an absolute end to book sales in the South. Thayer & Eldridge began advertising *Leaves of Grass* in the *Saturday Press* as "Chants of the Prairies," quoting from "A Word Out of the Sea" in the head of the column ad ("Solitary, singing in the West, / I strike up for a New World") and emphasizing the positive reviews the book had received in Ohio.

Ironically, as the dual failures of *Leaves of Grass* and *Harrington* were threatening the future of the publishers, a wave of positive reviews for *Harrington* began to appear. At the end of November Whitman, too, received an unexpected dose of praise. In a review of John Greenleaf Whittier's new book of poems, George Searle Phillips of the *New York Illustrated News* disparaged Whittier's detachment. Instead, it was Whitman that he commended "to all thinkers and believers in America, as the first rude, but intrinsically great example, of what is in store for us. He is our John the Baptist, and heralds a greater than he, as the future will abundantly prove."[26] Unfortunately Whitman could no longer take solace in predictions of coming fame. By December the news from Thayer & Eldridge was dire.

They wrote O'Connor at the end of November to inform him that the "sale is dull at present," but they remained cautiously hopeful: "If the country does not all go to smash we have no doubt as to a successful future for the work."[27] It was not to be. On the first of December Thayer wrote Whitman, "Things look immensely dubious today. Cant tell you anything encouraging at present. We are working *hard*."[28] Four days later he wrote, "We go by the boards tomorrow." Friends of theirs would normally have bailed them out, he explained, but the sale of books in fall 1860, by Thayer's own admission, had been "stagnant . . . till after the Presidential election."[29] Now many feared civil war and "the prospect of bad business for the next six to twelve months to come." Their supporters advised them "to stop immediately and wind up and begin again" after the conflict subsided.[30] Thayer later remembered, "We were caught with all sails spread, without warning of the storm. Merchants at once began to retrench and reduce liabilities. Capital hid itself. Banks were distrustful. No one knew how the war would end. Books being a luxury, there was no demand. All book firms were 'shaky.' . . . Anti-slavery people were interested in keeping us up, but they were forced to call in their funds and most reluctantly let us go down."[31] He instructed Whitman to return the advance check for *The Banner At Day-Break*; the book would not appear. But he promised that Whitman's accounts with Thayer & Eldridge had been fixed; the poet would owe his publishers only "a nominal sum."[32]

As Christmas drew near and winter settled across Manhattan, a pall seemed to hang over the city, a spreading darkness that swallowed everything. On December 20 South Carolina officially announced its secession from the Union, and other southern states were threatening to follow. William Henry Seward, already selected by Lincoln to serve as his secretary of state, attended the New-England Dinner in New York two days after South Carolina's withdrawal and was called to stand and address the crowd. He told those assembled he was "opposed to any compromises" with the South, but there was no need to worry.[33] "Sixty days' more suns will give you a much brighter and more cheerful atmosphere," he said. Whitman recalled many years later that "folks generally believed the prediction."[34]

. . .

The year 1861 couldn't have begun much worse for Whitman. The first weekend of the new year came and went without an issue of Henry Clapp's *Saturday Press;* Thayer & Eldridge publicly declared bankruptcy; and, worst of all, Seward's prediction of a "more cheerful atmosphere" never came to pass. Instead, as the month wore on South Carolina was joined in secession by Mississippi, Florida, Alabama, Georgia, and Louisiana. For the poet who had declared barely five years earlier, "The United States themselves are essentially the greatest poem," the swift dissolution of the Union must have been especially difficult to accept.

Ironically, the withdrawal of the pro-slavery southern states meant that long-contested Kansas was finally admitted to the shaky Union as a free-soil state on January 29. The *New York Times* hailed the news in a brief item in the evening edition. "Kansas has been kept out of the Union because she was *not* a Slave State," the paper reported, but now, without opposition in Congress, "she is at last a member of the Federal Union."[35] Whitman, however, greeted the word out of Washington as an ill portent rather than a victory. He composed the short poem "Rise, lurid stars" to voice his misgivings about the entrance of the thirty-fourth state:

> Rise, lurid stars, wooly white no more;
> Change, angry cloth—weft of the silver stars no more;
> Orbs blushing scarlet—thirty four stars, red as flame,
>   On the blue bunting this day we sew.
>
> World take good notice, silver stars have vanished;
> Orbs now of scarlet—mortal coals, all aglow,

> Dots of molten iron, wakeful and ominous,
>   On the blue bunting henceforth appear.[36]

The flag's silver stars had turned to "mortal coals" glowing "red as flame," but Whitman remained insistent that the stars still numbered thirty-four. Despite the secessions, despite the upcoming Alabama convention to select a president of the newly formed Confederacy, despite the pending vote in the Texas Senate on a resolution of secession, Whitman remained unwilling to concede the fracture of the nation. Perhaps this defiant viewpoint had difficulty finding favor with newspaper editors; perhaps Whitman himself had misgivings about the poem. Either way, it never appeared in print.

In the meantime Whitman was contacted by Marshall "Harvey" Jewell, a Boston lawyer, acting on behalf of Rice Kendall and Co., the primary supplier of Thayer & Eldridge's paper. Jewell wrote to inform Whitman that he owed $20.24. William Thayer had warned Whitman that his account would show a debt to Thayer & Eldridge but assured him it would be "a nominal sum."[37] Nominal or not, Whitman couldn't pay. Soon after, Thayer & Eldridge turned over the plates of *Leaves of Grass* as compensation to their creditor and former boss, Horace Wentworth.

Some Thayer & Eldridge authors managed to raise the money to buy back their plates from Wentworth. Lydia Maria Child, for example, the editor of Harriet Jacobs's *Incidents in the Life of a Slave Girl*, one of the other books on Thayer & Eldridge's schedule for spring 1861, scraped together enough to acquire the plates of her book and have it privately printed at the end of January. James Redpath, too, purchased the plates for his *Guide to Hayti* and self-published the book. Most were not so lucky. Ada Clare's novel *Asphodel*, advertised for publication in December 1860, was never published and appears to be lost. Thomas Wentworth Higginson's history of slave revolts remained unpublished for nearly another thirty years.[38] And, though many of the poems appeared in print later, Whitman's planned volume *The Banner At Day-Break* never became a reality, a victim of an industry stricken by panic at the election of a president still so unknown to most Americans that they couldn't pick him out in a crowd.

It was nearly half past four on February 19 when Abraham Lincoln's line of carriages turned down Broadway's wide avenue toward the Astor House. Flags flew from every roof and storefronts were strung with banners. "Welcome to the President elect. Prosperity to his Administration and to our Union," read the sign over the headquarters of the Republican Party. Another hanging from the balcony of *Putnam's Monthly* quoted Lincoln's Cooper Union address, "Right makes right!" and the banner draped over Isador Bernhard and Son urged, "Welcome, Abraham Lincoln, we beg for compromise."

In early February Lincoln had received a series of invitations to stop and speak as he made his way from Springfield, Illinois, to his inauguration in Washington. He spent a week dotting the country—giving major speeches in Indianapolis, Cincinnati, Columbus, Pittsburgh, Cleveland, Buffalo, and Albany, before finally arriving at the 30th Street Station in New York City. Mary Todd Lincoln smoothed down her husband's wild mop of hair, gave him a kiss, and mounted her carriage for a wives' reception, while Lincoln joined an entourage of eleven closed carriages bound for the Astor House. It took almost an hour and a half for the procession to wend through the crowd of a quarter-million onlookers.

Among them, Whitman sat atop an omnibus, parked against the curbstone, opposite the Astor House at the south end of City Hall Park. He enjoyed, by his own estimation, "a capital view of it all." More than a decade later, he still remembered the scene in vivid detail: "The broad spaces, sidewalks, and street in the neighborhood, and for some distance, were crowded with solid masses of people, many thousands."

> The omnibuses and other vehicles had all been turn'd off, leaving an unusual hush in that busy part of the city. Presently two or three shabby hack barouches made their way with some difficulty through the crowd, and drew up at the Astor House entrance. A tall figure

step'd out of the centre of these barouches, paus'd leisurely on the
sidewalk, look'd up at the granite walls and looming architecture of
the grand old hotel—then, after a relieving stretch of arms and legs,
turn'd round for over a minute to slowly and good-humoredly scan
the appearance of the vast and silent crowds.[39]

The lanky president-elect impressed Whitman with "his look and gait—
his perfect composure and coolness," and his "dark-brown complexion,
seam'd and wrinkled yet canny-looking face." Even in his twilight years,
Whitman remained haunted by that visage. "Of technical beauty it had
nothing," he wrote, "but to the eye of a great artist it furnished a rare
study, a feast and fascination."[40]

Lincoln declined to make any formal remarks to the crowd, saying, "I
could not be heard by any but a very small fraction of you at best; but what
is still worse than that is, that I have nothing just now to say worth your
hearing."[41] Those close to the Astor House steps laughed appreciatively,
but from across the street where Whitman sat he could hear nothing but
the hushed silence of the crowd straining to hear, a silence he perceived
not as a show of respect but a collective held breath, waiting to see if something more would occur. There were thirty thousand people gathered
around the Astor House and Whitman guessed that "not a single one [was
Lincoln's] personal friend." Even before the crowd gathered, many had
"fear'd some mark'd insult or indignity to the President-elect—for he
possess'd no personal popularity at all in New York city, and very little political. But it was evidently tacitly agreed that if the few political supporters of Mr. Lincoln present would entirely abstain from any demonstration
on their side, the immense majority, who were any thing but supporters,
would abstain on their side also."[42] New York was so fraught with radical
Democrats that Whitman had "no doubt" that "many an assassin's knife
and pistol lurk'd in hip or breast-pocket there, ready, soon as break and
riot came." But no one said a word, and Lincoln turned and entered the
Astor House to deliver his speech as planned. "The result," wrote Whitman, "was a sulky, unbroken silence, such as certainly never before char-
acterized so great a New York crowd."

The incident seemed to crystallize the weeks preceding Lincoln's inauguration. All were eager—and anxious—to learn what the new president would do about the rampant rebellion already on his hands. At several stops along his eastward journey, he was asked for the text of his inaugural address, but he always demurred. He was still working on it, still adding and striking passages. The public would have to wait until he was sworn in.

In the early hours of morning, drum and fife bands could be heard going up and down the streets of Washington, D.C. Enormous American flags flew over all the official buildings in the capital, as well as every school, business, and many private homes. The thirty-four-star flag envisioned by Whitman in "Rise, lurid stars" would not be official until July 4, but they had been readied ahead of time for that day—March 4, Inauguration Day. The overcast skies threatened rain but never produced more than a brief shower and did nothing to dampen the enthusiasm of the throng pushing up the mall toward the Capitol building, its dome still incomplete and caged by scaffolding. "For four hours the crowd poured on," reported the *New York Times*, "in one continuous stream of old and young, male and female—staid old Quakers from Pennsylvania, going to see friend Abraham—and lengthy Suckers, Hoosiers and Wolverines, desirous of a peep at Mr. Lincoln—Buckeyes and Yankee men from California and Oregon, from the Northeast, Northwest, and a few from the Border States. The large majority, however, were Northern men, and but few Southerners."[43]

Fearful of an assassination attempt, officials had erected a wooden barricade around the stage, and General Winfield Scott's troops patrolled the area around the Capitol. Though Whitman was in New York, far from the proceedings, he noted that every newspaper reported the tense and militarized atmosphere. Lincoln was to take his oath "amid armed cavalry, and sharpshooters at every point," Whitman remarked. "[It is] the first instance of the kind in our history—and I hope it will be the last."[44]

Despite all fears, the president-elect was led to the stage and introduced by Senator Edward Dickinson Baker of Oregon without any ruckus or commotion, so Lincoln stepped to the podium, unfolded the manuscript of his speech, and began in a clear, steady voice: "In compliance with a custom as old as the Government itself, I appear before you to address you briefly." Unlike most orators of his day, Lincoln *was* brief, but his carefully crafted speech was a masterpiece of forceful rhetoric. He did not avoid the urgent crisis facing the nation, nor sidestep its most pressing issue. "One section of our country believes Slavery is right, and ought to be extended," he said, "while the other believes it is wrong and ought not to be extended." Despite this fundamental disagreement, he warned that the problem would only increase if the one country was divided into two. "Physically speaking, we cannot separate," he explained; the two sections would still lie contiguous but would no longer share common national goals—and the result could be violence.

But Lincoln insisted that this was not a war of northern aggression, as southerners complained. "The Government will not assail you. You can have no conflict without being yourselves the aggressors." He cautioned both sides that civil war would not resolve their fundamental differences. "Suppose you go to war," he said, "you cannot fight always, and when, after much loss on both sides and no gain on either, you cease fighting, the identical questions as to terms of intercourse are again upon you." He called on the country—the *whole* country, North and South—to "think calmly and well upon this whole subject," rather than acting in the frenzy of heated emotion. The fate of the Union, "the momentous issue of civil war," he told the people of the South, "[is] in your hands . . . and not in mine." In the famous closing lines of his speech, Lincoln reminded his "dissatisfied fellow-countrymen," "We are not enemies, but friends. We must not be enemies. Though passion may have strained, it must not break our bonds of affection. The mystic chords of memory, stretching from every battlefield, and patriot grave, to every living heart and hearthstone, all over this broad land, will yet swell the chorus of the Union, when again touched, as surely they will be, by the better angels of our nature."[45]

To the roar of the crowd's approval Lincoln was sworn in by Chief Justice Roger B. Taney. The newly inaugurated president then repaired to the Senate chamber and awaited the carriage to take him and his wife to the White House, where the rest of the day and long into the night was occupied by the inaugural ball.

By the next morning, when the president arrived at his office for the first time, the festive glow had faded. Waiting on his desk Lincoln found an urgent dispatch from Major Robert Anderson, commander of federal troops at Fort Sumter. Rebel forces had cut the fort's supply lines earlier that spring, and Anderson wrote to report that in six weeks his provisions would run out. As his first task in office, Lincoln had to decide whether to withdraw Anderson's troops and risk giving the appearance of federal acquiescence to the new Confederacy or to supply them by force and risk starting a civil war.[46]

In an effort to shore up majority support as president-elect, Lincoln had filled his cabinet with old political adversaries; already at least one of his cabinet members, now known to be Seward, had turned on him and was feeding the newspapers information from inside the cabinet room. General Winfield Scott, reported the *New York Evangelist*, "is understood to hold the opinion that reinforcements could not now throw into Sumter without an immense loss of life." The newspaper ran a cable received from Washington on March 12 that claimed, "It is now positively ascertained that Major Anderson will almost immediately receive orders to withdraw from Fort Sumter."[47] The *Evangelist* was not the only paper receiving such wires, and the intelligence was having a dramatic impact. "The news of the probable withdrawal of the United States troops from Fort Sumter, flashing by telegraph all over the land," wrote *The Independent*, "has profoundly affected the public mind of the country." That paper's editorialist, like many others in the North, considered such a move tantamount to a "conspicuous and undeniable confession of defeat by the National Government."[48]

There is no direct record of Whitman during this tense time, though he occasionally appeared as the butt of jokes in the pages of *Vanity Fair*, virtually the house organ of Pfaff's after the demise of the *Saturday Press*. Where the *Saturday Press* had regaled its readers with praise for Whitman, in the pages of *Vanity Fair* he came in for regular (and often facile) ridicule. In the March 9 issue the editors mused, "What will Walt. Whitman's Leaves of Grass be when they are dried, and posterity has raked 'em—Hey?," a thin joke that was reprinted in numerous newspapers nationally.[49] At the close of another short piece on a bill before the New York legislature proposing to set a standard per-mile price for cab fare, the writer suggested that Whitman should be consulted since he "is said to understand long measures."[50] He suffered similar ridicule in the pages of *Frank Leslie's Budget of Fun* in a parody beginning:

> I see them all around me—the crowd rushing by daylight through
>   the fashionable house,
> Eager, avid of grasping at the patric life above them,
> Of seeing how folks live.
> I swear they are all lively—they are all norms,
> Envisaging objects. Such as
> Egyptian marble-topt dressing-tables, scagliola-slabbed etagéres,
> One Lombard bureau, two carved curled maple washstands,
> A black oak hat rack with deer horns and silver knobs,
> Six rosewood chairs covered with velvet, two large rocking chairs,
>   one easy ditto.[51]

And so it continues, cataloguing the contents of a house in minute detail for another thirty-three lines, before finally concluding: "So you might go on through all the goods and chattels of all humanity. That's the way to do it, Walter." While the joking class at Pfaff's poked fun at Whitman, however, more serious efforts were under way among their journalistic brethren, preparing for a war that now seemed to be in the offing.

Under a newly awarded federal contract, Western Union was working hastily on a transcontinental telegraph line, and individual newspapers were connecting to it from points considered likely to generate news. New York newspapers had formed the Associated Press a decade earlier, but in April they established a bureau in Washington with a staff of fifty agents. With the help of an efficient, well-disciplined corps of telegraph correspondents, word of cabinet meetings went directly from Seward's lips to the pages of the New York media.

At the same time the *New York Tribune* perfected a method of quickly and cheaply stereotyping plates by making papier-mâché molds of their handset type beds. Multiple presses running simultaneously meant that more copies could be produced and that extra editions with breaking news could be printed more cheaply, and therefore more often. The combined technology of instant communication and swift, mass printing allowed New York newspapers to cover an event within a day and distribute that news to ever larger numbers of readers.

As the weeks wore on and the roar of indignation grew louder, Lincoln, to his credit, recognized that Fort Sumter was no longer merely a tactical position; it was a political one. Abandoning the fort would mean abandoning his presidency—perhaps abandoning the Union—before he had even had a chance to organize his administration. But if face could be lost in the press, it could also be saved there. Lincoln had promised the South, "[The] Government will not assail you." He would send the military to Fort Sumter in unarmed boats to deliver "food for hungry men," and, he informed Governor Pickens of South Carolina, "no effort to throw in men, arms, or ammunition, will be made," except "in case of an attack on the Fort."[52]

Every daily and weekly newspaper dispatched a reporter to Charleston, with a view of Fort Sumter in the harbor, to await the outcome of the standoff. North and South, every edition filled with rumors of a last-minute pullout and speculation that both sides were planning secret attacks. The *New York Herald*, under the headline "The Impending War," carried multiple daily communiqués from Charleston, waiting for the southern response to the dispatch of federal supply ships.

Whitman remembered talking with Martin Kalbfleisch, the newly elected mayor of Brooklyn, onboard the Fulton ferryboat at about this time. Kalbfleisch lamented Lincoln's promise not to attack the South unless they attacked first and told Whitman that he "hoped the Southern fire-eaters would commit some overt act of resistance, as they would then be at once so effectually squelch'd, we would never hear of secession again."[53]

It was shortly after midnight on April 13, 1861. The performance of Verdi's *Masked Ball* had just let out on Fourteenth Street, and Whitman was walking down Broadway toward Brooklyn. Newsboys darted from one side of the street to the other, shouting out the headlines of the extras rushed from the presses. At Prince Street Whitman stopped, bought a copy, and crossed over to the Metropolitan Hotel, where the gaslights still burned and people were gathered to read the news. As the crowd grew, one person read aloud the telegram from Charleston. The dispatch in the *New York Times* began, "The ball has opened. War is inaugurated."[54]

In the morning edition the *Times* recounted, "Through all our streets last evening at a late hour the news spread with electrical rapidity that the great contest had at last commenced."[55] The latest dispatch reported that three war vessels had arrived from New York to support the troops at Fort Sumter but had not yet entered the mouth of the harbor, and the reporter felt it was "fair to conjecture" that the troops aboard must by then have been ashore and returning rebel artillery fire in order to create cover for the fleet and force passage of supplies. "We have full confidence," the report concluded, "that nothing will be left undone to make the rebel chiefs of the great conspiracy bitterly repent."

The *Times* and other northern newspapers would learn not to print conjecture and assumptions. By midafternoon, as many New Yorkers settled into the belief that the rebellion had been suppressed, federal troops surrendered Fort Sumter, and overrunning rebel forces hoisted a Confederate flag over the shell-battered ramparts. When word traveled north, Whitman sketched out another flag poem. It began:

Peace no more but flag of war,
No more soft and courteous folds, weft vindictive,
Now the ordeal is come and the destinies are waiting—stern and dim
    the two stand a-waiting.[56]

But the waiting didn't last long. Within days Lincoln had issued a call for seventy-five thousand troops, and the war excitement was "daily increasing in Brooklyn."[57]

Vigilantism ran rampant, as the most ardent factions of Unionism now sought to solidify public support by any means necessary. An angry mob encircled the *Eagle*'s offices because the editors had refused to display the American flag as a show of loyalty to the Union; the postmaster general ordered its New York office not to accept the *Eagle* for mailing on the grounds that they were inciting disloyalty, encouraging the enemy, and urging concessions to the demands of the South; and a grand jury was convened to investigate whether the *Eagle* was guilty of stirring traitorous sympathies.[58] Even so, Whitman later recalled that "the gravity of the revolt, and the power and will of the slave States for a strong and continued military resistance to national authority, were not at all realized at the North, except by a few. Nine-tenths of the people of the free States look'd upon the rebellion, as started in South Carolina, from a feeling one-half of contempt, and the other half composed of anger and incredulity. It was not thought it would be join'd in by Virginia."[59] On April 18, however, New York papers carried the news that the Virginia State Convention, at a meeting in Richmond the day before, had indeed voted in favor of secession. The Convention also urged the governor to muster volunteers to defend the state against northern encroachment.

In response, New York erupted into a show of patriotism, and the flag that Whitman saw woven of "weft vindictive" became an object of communal pride. "Every hotel, every public building, almost every store, and ten thousand private dwellings in this city are at this moment enlivened with a display of flags," reported *The Independent*. "The star-spangled banner everywhere flutters in the wind."[60] Whitman's younger brother George was swept up in the patriotic fervor and signed a hundred-day commitment with the 13th Regiment of the New York State Militia, known familiarly as the Brooklyn Grays for their gray uniforms.[61]

The same day, Thayer, writing to Whitman from Massachusetts, confessed that his mind, too, had strayed from all thoughts of literature into "war fever." "My soul swells as I contemplate the mighty issues involved in this contest," he told Whitman. He saw the war as a final battle to settle slavery, not a philosophical struggle over rights and freedoms the southern states thought were guaranteed to them. "The Abolition of Slavery," all by itself, he wrote, "[will] send this nation to a most glorious destiny. Either under one confederacy or two, we shall have no peace until slavery is crushed out."[62]

Thayer lamented only that his small children and sick wife prevented him from making "a speedy offering of myself to the Government as a soldier." He believed that his skills would be of little use to the army, but his enthusiasm for the cause was real and he would gladly make himself cannon fodder for the Confederate Army: "I *could* fire my gun once and die for my country." The sentiment was shared by many across the North, and even New York, long a hotbed of southern sympathy, had swung hard toward Union at all costs.

In Brooklyn, after just a few days of drilling in the city parks and marching up and down the streets, Brigadier General Crooke issued orders for all members of the 13th New York to report for inspection at the arsenal on Portland Avenue.[63] That night the 13th received its marching orders. Even as they prepared to depart, many of the troops remained dangerously undersupplied. More than two hundred of the newly enlisted men had no cross-body belts, jackets, or even blankets. The *Eagle* reported, "The regiment is composed of the flower of Brooklyn—young men who know their duty and will do it under any circumstances. The great majority are raw recruits, and many of them leave families and some parents, who are in a measure dependent upon them for support. Most of these are in want of necessaries for the campaign."[64]

Nevertheless, on the afternoon of April 23 the 13th New York State Militia started from the Henry Street Armory and crossed over to Manhattan for official review. They marched down Broadway, past buildings hung with bunting and streamers, the sidewalks jammed with well-wishers shouting encouragement. Whitman captured the scene in jottings for a poem titled "Broadway, 1861," composed amid the swirl and thrill of those early days of the war:

> The sights now there
> The splendid flags flying over all the stores
> (The wind sets from the west—the flags are out stiff and broad—you
>   can count every star of the thirty-four—you can count the
>   thirteen stripes.)
> The regiments arriving and departing,
> The Barracks—the soldiers lounging around,
> The recruiting band, preceded by the fifer—
> The ceaseless din
>
> I too am drawn:
> Come, since it must be so—away from all parlors and offices!
> Form the camp—plant the flag-staff in the middle—run up the flag
>   on the halyards!
> Unlimber the cannon—but not for mere salutes, for courtesy,
> We will want something, henceforth, besides powder and wadding.[65]

Later, in revising this poem (and retitling it "Drum-Taps"), Whitman added to the panoramic tableau of Broadway a small, poignant vignette of a mother and son:

> The blood of the city up—arm'd! arm'd! the cry everywhere;
> The flags flung out from the steeples of churches, and from all the
>   public buildings and stores;
> The tearful parting—the mother kisses her son—the son kisses his
>   mother;
> (Loth is the mother to part—yet not a word does she speak to detain
>   him;)
> The tumultuous escort—the ranks of policemen preceding, clearing
>   the way;
> The unpent enthusiasm—the wild cheers of the crowd for their
>   favorites;
> The artillery—the silent cannons, bright as gold, drawn along,
>   rumble lightly over the stones;
> (Silent cannons—soon to cease your silence!
> Soon, unlimber'd, to begin the red business).[66]

Despite this note of tenderness, Whitman, too, was caught up in the war euphoria enveloping the city. "War!" he exulted near the poem's close, "be it weeks, months, or years—an arm'd race is advancing to welcome it."

He later recalled that George and other members of the 13th were "provided with pieces of rope, conspicuously tied to their musket-barrels, with which to bring back each man a prisoner from the audacious South, to be led in a noose." The 13th marched to the wharves, boarded the steamship *Marion* at six o'clock, and soon after departed, accompanied by the *James Adger* and the brig *Perry*, for Annapolis, Maryland, to the cheers and waves of the adoring crowd. Everyone expected "our men's early and triumphant return," Whitman later remembered, but the "events of '61 amazed everybody north and south, and burst all prophecies and calculations like bubbles."[67]

． ． ．

Despite the war excitement, Whitman remained focused on his desire to publish an expanded 1861 edition of *Leaves of Grass;* with George now absent, the financial need was more urgent than ever. Walt's eldest brother, Jesse, was also engaged in the war effort at the Brooklyn Navy Yard, where, Whitman recorded, he was "employed in the store-house, where they are continually busy preparing stores, provisions, to send off in the different vessels."[68] Walt publicly described his brother as "a steady industrious man," but privately Jesse wrestled with violent mental illness and had trouble holding his job, forcing him to live at home.[69] Of Walt's other brothers, Andrew was married with two children but was most likely an alcoholic and rarely worked due to poor health; Jeff had a reliable job at the Brooklyn Water Works but was recently married and had an infant daughter; and Edward was mentally disabled and probably had a mild form of cerebral palsy. Only Andrew had his own home; the others were crowded into their mother's modest house on Portland Avenue with only Jeff's income as a reliable means of support.

George had earned a good living as a carpenter, but now the family would be without his wages for over three months. Walt took the new responsibility seriously, entering a vow in his notebook foreswearing alcohol and fat meats, resolving instead to foster "a great body—a purged, cleansed, spiritualised invigorated body."[70] He also wrote to Thayer to ask about Horace Wentworth, hoping that he might be willing to bring out a new edition of *Leaves of Grass*, using the Thayer & Eldridge plates now in his possession and appending a sheaf of the new poems that Whitman had completed in the intervening year and intended for *The Banner At Day-Break*. But Thayer doubted Wentworth's interest in an addendum for a new edition: "As Wentworth is an illiterate man and knows not *real* merit in literature I think he will not be inclined to go to expense extra to make additions to L of G and yet he may—can't tell. You had best write him. He is a man who loves to be wiley sometimes & therefore may defer giving you a definite answer to your questions of him & especially in view of the present unsettled condition of the Country."[71]

Undeterred, Whitman sent a letter to Wentworth and went so far as to compose a preface for the new edition, which he apparently imagined appearing in June, shortly after his birthday. "I commenced Leaves of Grass in my thirty-sixth year, by publishing their first issue," he wrote. "Twice have I issued them since, with successive increase, the present being the Fourth Issue, with the latest increase. I am to-day (May 31, 1861) just forty-two years old; for I write this introduction on my birthday—after having looked over the poem, as far as accomplished. So far, so well; but the most and best of it, I perceive remains to be written—the work of my life ahead, which I will yet do."[72] In stirring fashion, he concluded, "In short, the book will not serve as books serve—But as the rude air, the salt sea, the burning fire, and the rocky ground—sharp, full of danger, full of contradictions and offense. . . . Those silent old suggestions! Can you, perusing them, and never understanding them, yet dwell upon them with profit and joy? Then try these chants."[73]

But Wentworth had no interest in investing in *Leaves of Grass*. He was operating out of the old Thayer & Eldridge storefront, reprinting their out-of-stock titles from plates and offering them for sale. At first he had gone to the trouble of altering the Thayer & Eldridge title pages. The

1861 edition of O'Connor's *Harrington*, for instance, was recast to read "Wentworth, Boston, 1861," and he even printed a pamphlet of reviews—similar to Whitman's *Imprints*—in an attempt to interest book agents. Soon, however, Wentworth gave up on legitimate promotion of Thayer & Eldridge authors and decided to reprint their editions unaltered, making it difficult for authors to prove that these new editions were not part of the original stock Wentworth had purchased. For a few of his own better selling titles, Wentworth went so far as to produce 1861 editions with the imprint of Thayer & Eldridge added to the title pages.[74] All of his plans appear to have been designed to produce books without payment to their authors. For Whitman, the realization that his "new American bible" was now in the hands of an unscrupulous miser must have come as a crushing blow.

What he could not have known was that these were merely the first tremors of a tectonic shift that was about to rock the entire American publishing industry. As each new state seceded from the Union, northern publishers steadily lost the ability to collect on sales, as well as potential customers for new books. Now that the war itself had arrived, the industry was further shaken by entirely new trends in readership, as Americans virtually abandoned literary works, especially poetry, in favor of news of the day.

No industrywide statistics exist to document the near collapse of American book publishing in 1861, but a number of important bellwethers provide some hint of the suddenness with which the industry changed after the outbreak of the Civil War. The list of publications received for review, as published in two major magazines, is one such telling barometer. The *North American Review* listed seventy-seven books received for the quarter from July to October 1860 but only fifty-eight books received for the same period in 1861, a decline of 25 percent. More dramatically, the *Atlantic Monthly* received an average of thirty-eight books per month for review in the second half of 1860, but in the first half of 1861 received an average of only twenty-two per month, a 42 percent decline.[75]

Such a swift and dramatic drop in the number of new books published in the North can be explained partially by the unique dependence of northern publishers on southern readers. Hinton R. Helper, in the *Impending Crisis of the South* (1857), pointed out that of more than three hundred American publishers at that time, fewer than thirty were headquartered in the South. To exploit this potential market, northern publishers throughout the 1850s offered deep discounts and attractive return policies to southern booksellers. Ticknor and Fields, the pioneer of these practices, increased its profits from less than one thousand dollars in sales in the South in 1850 to more than ten thousand dollars by 1859.[76] However, by often extending their standard four-month period for payment to as long as six months or even a year, publishers recorded many profits from southern booksellers—and counted on them to cover the publication of new books—long before those debts were collected. Thus when the fighting broke out at Fort Sumter, it not only signaled the loss of future orders but left many northern publishers with no way to collect outstanding balances. Ticknor and Fields recorded that half the accounts due in the southern states for late 1860 and 1861 went uncollected. As a result, not only were their orders for 1861 62 percent lower than in the previous year, but the company also recorded a real loss of $4,701.17.[77]

Many publishers, including Thayer & Eldridge, could not withstand such losses and went out of business in late 1860 and 1861. As early as July 1860 Lydia Maria Child wrote that the market was "glutted with plates sold by booksellers that have failed."[78] But the situation soon got much worse. The *Atlantic Monthly*, the *North American Review,* and the *American Publishers' Circular and Literary Gazette* listed twenty-eight northern publishers who announced literary books for fall 1860.[79] Of these, nine—nearly a third—had ceased publication by the end of 1861. The publishers that did continue to issue new books drastically cut back their lists, especially their literary titles. By June 1861 the situation had become so dire that the weekly *American Publishers' Circular and Literary Gazette* announced, "Hereafter, and until the revival of the Book Trade, we shall issue but one edition of this Journal per month. The entire absorption of public interest by current events has caused a nearly complete cessation in the demand for new books, and publishers have in consequence discontinued their usual issues."[80]

Even if Whitman had found a publisher who wanted to issue *Leaves of Grass* in 1861, it is unlikely the book actually would have appeared. As the market for literary texts showed signs of faltering, even James T. Fields, the editor of Ticknor and Fields, wrote to Bayard Taylor to delay publication of *The Poets' Journal* with the excuse "The Times are so shaky." To Thomas Wentworth Higginson—who, like Whitman, had already seen one of his books scheduled for 1861 lost to the collapse of Thayer & Eldridge—Fields wrote that publication would have to be postponed until they knew "how McClellan is doing." In the end a mere thirteen poetry titles were published in 1861.[81]

Many publishers abandoned their literary lists altogether in favor of titles designed to satisfy the new market of Union soldiers. T. B. Peterson and Brothers of Philadelphia, which in 1860 had specialized in publishing Dickens (more than a half-dozen of his novels) and Alexandre Dumas, in May and June 1861 published *The Zouave Drill, The Soldier's Guide, The Soldier's Companion*, and *The Volunteer's Text-Book*. Beadle and Company of New York, which had focused on short biographies of frontier heroes and dime adventure stories, between May and July issued the *Dime Squad Drill Book, Dime Songs for the War, Dime Union Song Book, Dime Union Song Book No. 2, Dime Military Song Book*, and dime biographies of the Union commanders Winfield Scott and George B. McClellan. Nearly every northern publisher—including Lippincott, Putnam, and Scribner—published similar titles, so that by July 1861 eight of the eighteen titles received by the *Atlantic Monthly* were handbooks aimed at Union soldiers.[82]

Many books—and their authors with them—were left orphaned. But they weren't out of work for long. Most, like Whitman, turned to the very market that was pushing them out of the book trade: newspapers. George William Curtis in *Harper's Monthly* complained, "The street corners, at which their offices usually are, are surrounded by eager people, and a few brief words at noon or night are the kernel of the abundant fullness of news which the morning papers bring."[83] Oliver Wendell Holmes reported that the newspaper had gained the same sudden preeminence in the literary circles of Boston. "It will be had, and it will be read," he wrote. "To this all else must give place. If we must go out at unusual hours to get it, we shall go."[84]

As dailies became hugely popular, weekly newspapers were even more endangered than books. While large publications such as *Harper's Weekly* competed by adding ever more intricate illustrations to draw readers, smaller weeklies were forced to make a decision: they could either go over to daily publication, or they could focus their content on areas ignored by daily papers, especially literary content. Whitman's Brooklyn provides an especially good microcosm of the pressure placed on such publications. Produced in the shadow of New York publishing giants like the *Times, Tribune*, and *Herald*, Brooklyn newspapers—aside from the well-established *Eagle*, which published two editions daily—were poorly equipped to cover the war. Weeklies such as the *Long Island Star* and the *Brooklyn City News* failed to survive the Civil War, and the *Brooklyn Union* and *Brooklyn Standard* stayed afloat only by combining their operations in 1863. First, however, the *Union* and *Standard* engaged in a two-year bitter rivalry, in which both newspapers, for a time, went over to daily publication. To fill that additional space, the *Union* ran a weekly column of Brooklyn history, and in May the *Standard* hired Whitman to compose a competing series.

Early advertisements announced that the *Standard* would become a daily on June 3, though it would continue "in the independent and indomitable spirit that has characterised the weekly." As added features of the daily, the *Standard* would offer more war coverage and a series of articles about old Brooklyn. "The Standard has several correspondents at the seat of war," read one advertisement, "and by the aid of special messengers and the telegraph will be able to give graphic and early accounts of whatever may occur there." The column-length ad promised that " 'Brooklyniana,' written expressly for the Standard by a distinguished

literary gentleman," would be the "most interesting series of local reminiscences of the Past ever published."[85] Another ad, headed "Brooklyn
Men, Brooklyn Women, Old and Young, Married or Single, are invited
to peruse the articles entitled Brooklyniana!," provided a detailed list of
all the articles that would appear in the series—all the people, places, and
historical events that would receive attention. The "distinguished literary gentleman," of course, was Whitman.

Critics have tended either to dismiss or look harshly on the "Brooklyniana" essays, seeing them in retrospect as evidence of Whitman's political disengagement in the early months of the Civil War or, worse still,
as confirmation of "an arresting set of blinders" worn as a result of
"Whitman's amnesia for the spreading Civil War."[86] But this interpreta-
tion ignores a number of important historical factors. First, as previously
mentioned, Whitman accepted the assignment in order to earn income
in the absence of his brother George. Second, the series was commissioned as a result of shifting patterns of readership and newspaper publishing in summer 1861. In short, the series would never have been undertaken were it not for the financial pressures the war placed on both
Whitman and the *Brooklyn Standard*. Third, there is ample evidence to
suggest that the overwhelming majority of the material in "Brooklyniana" was recycled from a book of Brooklyn history that Whitman was
planning and drafting in the early 1850s, during his stint as editor of the
Brooklyn Freemen. No surviving copies of the *Freemen* are known to exist,
but it is entirely possible that whole articles in the early sequence were
simply republished, as Whitman did later, in 1862, with a series of short
essays, "Letters from a Travelling Bachelor," that he wrote for the *New
York Sunday Dispatch* between 1849 and 1850 under the pen name "Paumanok." Finally, and perhaps most important, the articles were published
anonymously, and the strong possibility exists that there are numerous
other articles, yet to be identified as Whitman's, when he was accepting
any writing assignment that offered an attractive fee. The chance that he
wrote about the war in other articles is at least as likely as not.

Thus the primary value of "Brooklyniana" is not what the series reveals about Whitman's pattern of authorship, but what it suggests about the pattern of Brooklyn readership. When Whitman looks ahead to a time "in Brooklyn, and all over America, when nothing will be of more interest than authentic reminiscences of the past," he is speaking to some need to imagine a time beyond war, a time when "all over America" once again encompasses a single, unified nation. Such a desire is not mere escapism; it is a counterbalance, ballast against the storm. Every front page was dominated by news of hardship and suffering on the war front. These off-handed, conversational histories provided a palliative and a reminder that the city had weathered similarly trying periods along the path to becoming the community its citizens now shared.

There was certainly no shortage of bad news to be reported in the dailies. The pro-Democrat *Brooklyn Eagle*, Whitman believed, in particular "makes the worst of it, every day, to stop men from enlisting."[87] As early as May the *Eagle* had reported that the "main portion" of the 13th was in "a bad condition as regards clothing and other requisites." The paper reminded readers that the young men had left Brooklyn on three hours' notice, many before they had been issued uniforms or were even afforded time to pack their own clothing. "They have done hard duty," the writer told readers and insisted that "they should be attended to, and that as speedily as possible."[88] Mother Whitman, naturally, was worried at this news and sent an anxious letter to George, but before she received a reply, the reports from Camp Brooklyn grew worse.

On June 20 Charles Kelsey, a civilian from Washington, accompanied by three Brooklynites, visited the 13th in camp. Kelsey was shocked by the conditions he found there and wrote a letter to a Brooklyn friend, who in turn handed the letter over to the editors at the *Eagle*. Kelsey reported that every man in the regiment despised Colonel Abel Smith, at whose hands "they are treated like dogs." As an example, Kelsey described the torrential rains that had fallen on the night they arrived at their present ground and how "the Colonel took shelter in the nearest house, and left his regiment in the drenching rain 36 hours without a mouthful to eat."[89]

Copies of the *Eagle* and other Brooklyn papers were being delivered to the camp and circulating hand to hand among the troops there. When George Whitman read this latest article he wrote to reassure his mother and to dispute the reports. "I see some very foolish articles in the papers about sutch as not haveing any thing to eat for 36 hours and being almost naked," he wrote her, "but you must not believe any thing of the kind as we are all as well off as we could expect."[90] His mother's health had been poor for some time, but she was suffering especially in the summer heat. She went every other day to Henry R. Piercy's sulfur vapor baths on Willoughby, which Walt thought were "rather agreeable," to ease the arthritis in her shoulders and wrists.[91] George did not want her, in her already weakened condition, to trouble herself over how he was getting by. "I am not in want of anything and I don't believe we shal see any fighting at all," he told her and promised, "I shall soon be with you again."[92]

When George's letter arrived on July 12 Walt responded immediately to thank him for the welcome news: "There have been so many accounts of shameful negligence, or worse, in the commissariat of your reg't. that there must be *something* in it—notwithstanding you speak very lightly of the complaints in your letters." But George's company was due for removal on July 21 and would be back in Brooklyn by August, so everyone in the Whitman household was feeling relieved. "We are all very glad the 13th is coming home—mother especially," Walt wrote. At the very end of his letter he added, "All of us here think the rebellion as good as broke—no matter if the war does continue for months yet."[93]

CHAPTER FOUR

War-Suggesting Trumpets, I Heard You

War-suggesting trumpets, I heard you;
And you I heard beating, you chorus of small and large drums.
Discarded lines from "Little Bells Last
Night," October 1861

At half past three on July 21, 1861, the *New York Herald* correspondent
William Shaw wired an urgent dispatch from a telegraph office near Manassas, Virginia. The battle that had been brewing there for weeks had finally taken place, and Shaw was jubilant with the news. "We have carried
the day," he cabled. "The rebels accepted battle in strength but are totally
routed."[1] The *Herald* rushed out an extra with the headline "Heroism of
the Union Forces . . . They Know No Such Word as Fail!" that newsboys
eagerly hawked in the streets. The *Tribune* issued a similar extra edition,
informing readers that rebel troops had been "forced back inch by inch,
until they were driven from Bull's Run, leaving their dead on the field and
the National troops undisputed victors." Henry Raymond of the *Times*
concluded his report by exhorting, "Now on to Richmond!" When Shaw
reached Washington at about six o'clock he expanded and embellished his
earlier report with a fanciful description of the Confederate retreat. The

Herald's morning edition arrived on doorsteps and newsstands with his account under the headline "The Great Union Victory at Bull's Run—How Brightly Breaks the Morning!"[2]

In fact, at that very moment, as Whitman recorded later, defeated federal troops "commenced pouring into Washington over the Long Bridge at daylight on Monday, 22d—day drizzling all through with rain." Of all those reporting from Manassas only the *World* got the story right, on the strength of the reporting of Edmund Clarence Stedman, who, after leaving the staff of the *Saturday Press*, had joined the *World* in 1860 and volunteered as a war correspondent in the first months of the war. As the other dailies were running accounts of glorious victory, Stedman described the late afternoon rout and the humiliating terror-ridden flight to Washington. "The retreat, the panic, the hideous head-long confusion, were now beyond a hope," he wrote. "I saw officers with leaves and eagles on their shoulder-straps, majors and colonels, who had deserted their commands, pass me galloping as if for dear life."[3]

Stedman's dispatch from the scene—and later his personal account at Pfaff's—fueled the dislike Whitman already harbored for federal officers. "There you are, shoulder-straps!" he wrote later, "but where are your companies? where are your men? Incompetents! never tell me of chances of battle, of getting stray'd, and the like. I think this is your work, this retreat, after all." But he felt equally betrayed by the soldiers. The strong young men who had paraded their confidence down Broadway with nooses affixed to their bayonets were now "recoiling back, pouring over the Long Bridge—a horrible march of twenty miles, returning to Washington baffled, humiliated, panic-struck. Where are the vaunts, and the proud boasts with which you went forth? Where are your banners, and your bands of music, and your ropes to bring back your prisoners?"[4]

Stedman's account was so singular among New York papers that the *World* reported on July 23, "The demand for this authentic and clear narrative was so great that our ten-cylinder press running from morning til night was unable fully to supply it." They reissued the story in the semiweekly and weekly editions and finally as a separate edition, issued by Rudd & Carleton on August 1, to meet the demand.[5]

The mood across the city had swung from elation to feelings of deep betrayal and mistrust. "There isn't a band playing," Whitman wrote, "and there isn't a flag but clings ashamed and lank to its staff."[6] This personified flag appeared again in Whitman's post–Bull Run revision of "Rise, lurid stars," now retitled "Up, lurid stars!":

> Up, lurid stars! martial constellation!
> Change, tattered cloth—your silver group withdrawing;
> Bring we threads of scarlet, in vacant spots resetting,
> Thirty-four stars, red as blood.
>
> World, take good notice! the silver group has vanished;
> Notice clustering now, as coals of molten iron,
> Timely, warning baleful, off these western shores,
> Thirty-fours stars, red as blood.[7]

The American flag had transformed from an "angry cloth" to a "tattered cloth." On July 4, the new American flag of thirty-four stars had become official, but less than a month later, the stars, which had earlier appeared "red as flame," were now "red as blood."

To make up for their errors in reporting, the editors of the New York dailies competed to show their determination in the face of a northern defeat. The *Herald*, in particular, felt the weight of its burden. Many still accused the staff of pro-southern leanings, so much so that in the coming days the editors removed all disparaging judgments of how the soldiers behaved on the retreat. If their own reporters had not been on the field, then they were in no position to criticize. Instead, the paper ran rousing editorials, one after another, encouraging support for the war. "Those magnificent editorials!" Whitman would recall years later. "They never flagg'd for a fortnight. The *Herald* commenced them—I remember the articles well. The *Tribune* was equally cogent and inspiriting—and the *Times, Evening Post,* and other principal papers, were not a whit behind. They came in good time, for they were needed. And there is no denying that these loud cheerful clarion tones of the *Herald* and the rest, coming on the instant gave the key-note to what followed, on the National side, and soon restored the Union energies with determination five times magnified."[8] But even if the papers succeeded in rallying public sentiment, they failed to secure the public trust.

By August the *Herald* was contemplating the suspension of its Sunday edition, which it had begun in case of significant developments over weekends. Rumors that the *Times* might do the same were in such wide circulation that the editors issued a statement from their own pages: "We commenced the publication of a Sunday morning edition simply because of the intense excitement concerning the war, and the consequent eagerness to know the news at the earliest moment, rendered it necessary. When the necessity ceases we shall suspend the Sunday issue; but we cannot before."[9]

The *Times* editors further explained that the prospect of a protracted war after Bull Run had prompted many businesses to stop advertising, for fear that an economic downturn might leave them with bills they couldn't pay. The loss of advertising cut the New York dailies deeply. The budgetary strategy at most papers, explained the *Times*, always had been "to receive from sales just enough to pay for white paper and ink,— leaving all other expenses, type-setting, correspondence, telegraphic news, reporting and editorials to be paid for by advertisers. While advertising was good this was easily done; but now it is quite another thing,—and most of the papers are consequently more or less crippled."[10]

The *Herald* began running all of its classifieds in large type in an effort to woo advertisers and fill column inches. They proposed a unified price increase for all city papers, from one cent to three, and the sharing of costs such as time on the telegraph wires.[11] The *Times* switched from the more expensive bleached white paper to cheaper gray paper, a move that eventually became the paper's signature and earned it the nickname "the Old Gray Lady."[12] These moves may have saved their respective newspapers, but they did nothing to repair their reputations. By August readership was swelling for the longer, more in-depth reporting and the increasingly lavish illustrations of the weekly publications.

On August 6, 1861, George Whitman arrived in New York City and was mustered out of the 13th New York State Militia. Along with the other early volunteers of the 13th, George had left Virginia on July 20, just before the beginning of Bull Run, where George's former comrades, particularly members of the all-Irish 69th New York, had suffered heavy casualties. Though their military obligation was satisfied, many among the ranks of the 13th could not stomach the losses suffered and began joining new units then forming in the city.

After more than a month back in Brooklyn and a half-hearted attempt to return to normal life, George finally joined them. On September 18 he reenlisted in the Shepard Rifles (later the 51st New York) and the following day received a promotion to sergeant major. The *New York Times* announced that the regiment expected "to leave for the seat of war in about a week."[13] During those same few days Walt composed a new poem, "Beat! Beat! Drums!," a rousing call to arms, rife with the martial rhythms of the recruiting drums and the fervor of the daily newspapers:

> Beat! beat! drums!—Blow! bugles! blow!
> Through the windows—through doors—burst like a force of
>   ruthless men,
> Into the solemn church, and scatter the congregation;
> Into the school where the scholar is studying;
> Leave not the bridegroom quiet—no happiness must he have now
>   with his bride;
> Nor the peaceful farmer any peace plowing his field or gathering his
>   grain;
> So fierce you whirr and pound, you drums—so shrill you bugles
>   blow.
>
> Beat! beat! drums! Blow! bugles! blow!
> Over the traffic of cities—over the rumble of wheels in the streets;

Are beds prepared for sleepers at night in the houses? No sleepers
    must sleep in those beds;
No bargainers' bargains by day—no brokers or speculators. Would
    they continue?
Would the talkers be talking? would the singer attempt to sing?
Would the lawyer rise in the court to state his case before the judge?
Then rattle quicker, heavier drums—and bugles wilder blow.

Beat! beat! drums! Blow! bugles! blow!
Make no parley—stop for no expostulation;
Mind not the timid—mind not the weeper or prayer;
Mind not the old man beseeching the young man;
Let not the child's voice be heard, nor the mother's entreaties.
    Recruit! recruit!
Make the very trestles shake under the dead, where they lie in their
    shrouds awaiting the hearses.
So strong you thump, O terrible drums—so loud you bugles blow.[14]

The poem left little doubt as to Whitman's stance on the war and gathered the force of his rhetorical cataloguing around an urgent refrain, as if the poem were specifically composed to be read aloud to a sympathetic audience.

Indeed, one evening soon after, Whitman declaimed from the manuscript of the poem at Pfaff's.[15] Such impromptu readings were not unusual; Jay C. Goldsmith later recalled that the regulars at Pfaff's convened nightly at six o'clock, took their dinner, then broke out their clay pipes. "Whitman generally had a half-written 'yawp'—that's what he called a short poem—to submit to us," Goldsmith wrote.[16] The poem Whitman shared that night, however, did not solicit the like-minded accord he had expected. Instead it sparked an unusually heated debate around the table about whether the federal government should continue its war, now that nearly six months had passed without a resounding Union victory.

Just as the argument reached its peak, the poet George Arnold rose from his chair and lifted his wine glass. Twenty years later Whitman told William Sloane Kennedy that Arnold then "proposed the toast 'Success to the Southern Arms!'" In response Whitman "broke out into a fierce and indignant speech."[17] As Goldsmith remembered it, however, the disagreement did not end with Whitman's rant:

> Walt warned George to be more guarded in his sentiments. George fired up more and more. Walt passed his 'mawler' toward George's ear. George passed a bottle of claret toward the topknot of the poet's head. Pfaff made a jump and gave a yell of "Oh! mine gots, mens, what's you do for dis?" Clapp broke his black pipe while pulling at Arnold's coat-tail; Ned Wilkins lost the power of his lungs for five minutes after tugging at the brawny arm of Walt; and we all received a beautiful mixture of rum, claret, and coffee on the knees of our trousers. Everything was soon settled, and Walt and George shook hands, and wondered much that they were so foolish.[18]

Whitman later huffed that Goldsmith's version of events was the "silliest compound of nonsense, lies & rot," but Charles E. Hurd, an associate editor at the *Boston Daily Evening Transcript* who lived in New York, remembered that the argument did indeed turn physical.[19] As he recalled, though, "the only violent conduct on the occasion was that shown by George Arnold, who reached across the table, in the heat of a discussion on rebellion (in which he favoured secession), and seized Walt Whitman by the hair."[20]

Within days after the altercation, "Beat! Beat! Drums!" would be the most widely reprinted and circulated poem of Whitman's career; it was published in newspapers in New York City and Boston, then reprinted and parodied in the *Brooklyn Daily Eagle*, reaching from a utopian commune in Upstate New York to the goldfields of San Francisco.

On Saturday morning, September 21, 1861, the new issue of *Harper's Weekly* arrived on newsstands around New York City.[21] The cover, dated September 28, featured a dramatic full-page illustration of Captain William E. Strong, of the 2nd Wisconsin, firing his pistols into the chests of two Confederate soldiers who had attempted to disarm him.[22] Their arms were flung wide and their eyes turned toward the sky in despair, while Captain Strong looked on with steely indifference. Inside, Whitman's poem "Beat! Beat! Drums!" appeared for the first time, tucked unassumingly on the last text page of the issue.

Though *Harper's Weekly* normally ran poems on the second page of each sixteen-page issue (either at the head or foot of the first column),[23] "Beat! Beat! Drums!" appeared on the fifteenth page, between the latest installment of Sir E. Bulwer Lytton's serialized novel *A Strange Story* and the long captions printed at the back of each issue to accompany large illustrations. Nearly half the page was consumed by advertisements for everything from "Matrimony made Easy" to "Gardiner's Rheumatic and Neuralgic Compound."[24] This position suggests that the poem was inserted late into the issue. If this is the case, Whitman's motivation for publishing in *Harper's Weekly* might have been born, at least partly, from its short editorial schedule. That is, if "Beat! Beat! Drums!" were submitted on September 20, it would still have been possible to work it into the September 21 issue—if only in the very last available space.

However, Whitman's decision to submit "Beat! Beat! Drums!" to *Harper's Weekly* rather than its sister publication, *Harper's Monthly*, where he had submitted poems in 1860, also demonstrates a shift in his intended audience. The *Monthly* was indisputably the literary outlet of the Harper Brothers publishing firm; during 1861 the magazine was serializing Trollope's *Orley Farm* and Thackeray's *Adventures of Philip*, interspersed with poems by Elizabeth Barrett Browning, Charlotte Brontë, and Bayard Taylor, as well as a number of Whitman's friends from Pfaff's, including Thomas Bailey Aldrich, Fitz-James O'Brien, and George Arnold. During this same period, however, the magazine published almost no mention of the Civil War. Its first literary work addressing the war did not appear until August 1861, when the *Monthly* published O'Brien's "The Countersign," a poem about a tense night spent on guard duty at Camp Cameron, near Washington. The *Monthly*'s editor, George William Curtis, did not mention the war in his column, "The Editor's Easy Chair," until September, noting, "Newspapers, never so little profitable, were never in so great demand." Curtis admitted the necessity of

1.
Portrait of Walt Whitman used as the frontispiece to the 1860 edition of *Leaves of Grass*, engraved by Stephen Alonzo Schoff after a painting by Charles W. Hine. Walt Whitman Archive.

2.
James Redpath, posed with a copy of the *New York Tribune*, about 1858. Kansas State Historical Society.

3.
Henry Clapp, about 1860, from William Winter's memoir *Old Friends*.

4.
A lithograph of Abraham Lincoln by J. E. Baker, after a photograph taken by Charles A. Barry in Springfield, Illinois, June 1860. This print was published and distributed by Thayer & Eldridge. Library of Congress.

5.
A daguerreotype of William Douglas O'Connor, about 1855. Library of Congress.

6.
A drawing of Whitman meeting William Dean Howells at Pfaff's in 1860, from Howells's memoir *Literary Friends.*

7.
George Washington Whitman in a tintype taken between his promotion to sergeant major on September 19, 1861, and his field promotion to second lieutenant on April 16, 1862. Trent Collection, Duke University.

8.
Newspaper vendors selling near the front lines, as photographed by Alexander Gardner. Library of Congress.

9.
Walt Whitman in a portrait by Mathew Brady, taken between August and October 1861 at Brady's Broadway studio. Library of Congress.

10.
The dead of Antietam, as photographed by Alexander Gardner in September 1862. Library of Congress.

11.
Edwin Forbes's original drawing, "Fall in for Soup," with Whitman pictured third in line, December 1862. Library of Congress.

the war, but on the next page recommended that his readers pick up literary works from secondhand bookstores as a "retreat from the fierce sun and news of fiercer war."[25]

By contrast, *Harper's Weekly*, though it satisfied its readers' literary interests by serializing Dickens's *Great Expectations*, published numerous poems about the war.[26] Almost always without literary pretensions and universally anonymous, these poems responded to recent war news or were written on the spot with epigraphs and identifiers to tie them to their moment of composition. The poem "Fort Sumter," for example, carries the epigraph "An Impromptu, by a Virginian Lady Still in the Union," as well as the annotation "Baltimore, *April* 19, 1861."[27] Other poems were illustrated with lithographs, such as the elegy "Ellsworth, a Battle Hymn for Ellsworth's Zouaves," which appeared with a large woodcut of Colonel Ellsworth as well as a portrait of one of the sergeants under his command. Occasionally poems even appeared as direct companions to a news item; thus the poetry was fully integrated into the other war content provided by the *Weekly*.[28] In short, Whitman's publication of "Beat! Beat! Drums!" in *Harper's Weekly* assured that it would reach the "eager people" that Curtis described waiting for news on the street corner, rather than the typical *Harper's Monthly* subscriber, who enjoyed the literary content as a "retreat" from the war.

How exactly Whitman came to publish in *Harper's Weekly*, however, remains unclear. All of his publications to date had come through personal connections: in Clapp's *Saturday Press* during 1859 and 1860, in the *Atlantic Monthly* at the suggestion of Emerson and Edward Howard House, and in the *New York Times* at the behest of John Swinton. When Whitman submitted his work without such connections, his luck was considerably poorer: *Harper's Monthly* declined "A Chant of National Feuillage" in January 1860; the *New York Courier* passed on "Thoughts" that same month; Whitman indicated in his manuscripts that he had submitted his poem "Kentucky" to the *New York Tribune* in September 1861, but it never appeared; and the *Atlantic Monthly*, under a new editor, James T. Fields, rejected "1861" in October. Given this record of rejections, it seems likely that Whitman had some connection to one of *Harper's Weekly's* associate editors. This is partly borne out by the story of Whitman's scuffle with George Arnold. Jay C. Goldsmith asserts that Henry Clapp was in the midst of the fray, and Charles E. Hurd's description of the event also places him at Pfaff's that night. Both men featured "Beat! Beat! Drums!" in their respective publications within days of the fracas.

After the collapse of the *Saturday Press*, Clapp became the drama critic for the *New York Leader* in April; when its editor, Charles Graham Halpine, enlisted after Bull Run, Clapp was promoted to editor in September. In a matter of weeks he reprinted "Beat! Beat! Drums!" The poem appeared in the *Leader* only hours after its publication in *Harper's*, but ran with an attribution to its fellow weekly. More than likely this means that Clapp had the poem in hand (and knew of its pending publication) before its appearance on September 21. The *Leader* was a pro-Democrat weekly, but the poem appeared as part of a growing trend of pro-Union poetry published there after the defeat at Bull Run.

The *Boston Daily Evening Transcript*, under the editorship of Daniel N. Haskell, had supported Lincoln in the 1860 election and heralded his arrival to office in 1861, calling him "clear-headed, sound-hearted, good tempered, firm and thoroughly honest."[29] The *Transcript's* editorial voice, however, was set by the Reverend Thomas Bayley Fox, a Harvard graduate and Unitarian minister, who took over the job as full-time editorial page editor in 1858 and imbued his columns with Old Testament fervor.[30] Accused of bloodlust in the summer of 1861, Fox replied, "We are bloodthirsty and we do cry, Spare not the use of every weapon against treason, because in thus feeling and arguing we believe we are maintaining the cause of right, of peace and humanity."[31]

"Beat! Beat! Drums!" fit perfectly with the zealous pro-Unionist stance of the *Transcript*, which reserved daily space for such verse on page 2 under the masthead. Though the rest of the page consisted of foreign news and official reports brought in over the telegraph wire, the poem was almost always original work, selected by Charles E. Hurd. The poems sometimes ran anonymously (perhaps the work of Hurd himself, who was a would-be poet), but when they were reprinted from other sources they always ran with attributions. Interestingly, on September 24, 1861, Whitman's poem featured no indication that it had been reprinted from *Harper's Weekly*. There is also a significant typo ("his" repeated in line 5) and an exclamation point turned into a question mark in line 19 (which significantly alters the exhorting "Recruit! recruit!" to a hesitating "Recruit! recruit?"). Clapp's version, published in the *Leader*, also varies in several minor ways from the text of *Harper's Weekly*. These variants leave open the question of whether Clapp and Hurd received slightly different manuscript copies directly from Whitman, or the typesetter simply copied the text from *Harper's Weekly* imprecisely. Whatever the case, the primary common ground shared by Clapp and Hurd seems to be not their readerships or editorial stances, but the fact that both were on hand at Pfaff's the night of Whitman's reading.

However, none of the publications of "Beat! Beat! Drums!" in September 1861 is more surprising than its appearance, noted here for the first time, on the front page of the *Brooklyn Daily Eagle* on September 23. Whitman had suffered a strained relationship with the *Eagle* since 1848, when he was fired by the paper's financial backers, who described him as "slow, indolent, heavy, discourteous, and without steady principles" and accused him of being "a clog upon our success."[32] Afterward Whitman wrote for the paper intermittently but, as is apparent from his correspondence with George over the summer, he still disliked and distrusted the owners and editors. That the *Eagle* should choose to reprint "Beat! Beat! Drums!" is a testament to the poem's popularity.

But the *Eagle* could never pass on a chance to needle Whitman. Less than a week after running the original poem, the paper published "To the Wars," an undocumented parody of "Beat! Beat! Drums!" Identified as written by "Waller Quitman," the parody not only lampoons the lines reprinted in the *Eagle* five days earlier but also renews the image of Whitman as "lounging" and "loafing":

To the wars! to the fierce wars, away,
Ye Bummers and lazy, loafing men hanging 'round taverns;
Meanly, and ignobly waiting to be called to the bar—
By chance customers, whose footsteps are ever tending to the temple
    of Bachus!
Arise! arise! ye torpid set,
Hitch up the waist-band of your nether garments,
And away to the fierce war!
Ye can slake your rum-begotten thirst in the pellucid waters
    of the Potomac.

To the wars! to the fierce wars, away,
All ye prowling, sturdy hangers on the Hall of Justice,
And around the passages and purlieus thereof—
Craving for pap from immaculate office-holders and virtuous
    Aldermen!
Have ye no shame—no *vim*—ye lazy, lounging set of political
    beggars?
Too long have ye been fattening on the city flesh pots!
'Tis time ye do something for your eaten bread: your country calls—
Go ye to the fierce war, that may be even now raging on the banks of
    the Potomac!

To the wars! to the fierce wars, away,
Ye stump orators, ye nominating committee men;
Give one year's respite to the poor loaves and fishes.
Many of you, nay, most of you, have bone and muscle; the right stuff
    for soldiers!
In a crisis like this, everything belongs to your country!
Go! Let the old men—the ancients of the land—fill the offices
    'till ye return.
Gird up your loins, then, every mother's son of you!
Be not found in these diggins when General Draught come along,
    for then you must go—or, ingloriously find a substitute![33]

As a parody the humor is nearly completely oblique and faded by time.
The comedy seems to center on the irony of Whitman, the renowned
loafer behind *Leaves of Grass*, now calling the men of Brooklyn to action.
The first stanza, for example, conjures the nightly scene at Pfaff's, Whit-

man's most familiar environ but one whose regulars he did not include among the people who must set aside their daily activities for the cause of the Union. With debate raging about the imminence of a general draft, the poem also implies that Whitman is urging immediate volunteering for a three-month stint as a way of avoiding a general draft of indeterminate length. This very method of draft dodging had been discussed as recently as September 17 in the *Eagle*.[34] The success of this parody is extremely limited, but its most telling line may be the header "For the Brooklyn Eagle." Almost none of the poetry published in the *Eagle* appeared with this distinction; this was usually reserved for staff-authored editorials. This may imply that this parody was authored by one of the *Eagle*'s editors and thus may partially explain the *Eagle*'s purpose in publishing "Beat! Beat! Drums!" in the first place. Perhaps the staunchly antiwar editors considered the poem less a rousing call to volunteer than a hypocritical war cry from a lounger, and, in case readers had missed the point, followed up with a parody.

The reasons for the final two 1861 publications of "Beat! Beat! Drums!," both previously unnoted, are no less obscure, though apparently driven by entirely different motives. On October 3 the poem appeared in Upstate New York, in the four-page weekly Oneida *Circular*. The *Circular*, published and edited by John Humphrey Noyes, founder of the Oneida "free love" community, was intended to be "the exponent of the Bible Communism, advocating Religion of the Bible, and the Socialism of the Primitive Church."[35] Though the newspaper did carry occasional news of the war, its content was primarily focused on promoting the ideals of the Oneida community, which, though not specifically pacifist, included a nonviolent stance consistent with the New Testament. Noyes offered no clues to his motivation for reprinting the poem, noting only, "The following poem is finely descriptive of one of the phases of to-day's life."[36]

However, the version published in the *Circular* does contain one very telling variant from all previous printed versions. The second line reads, "Through the windows—through doors—burst like a force of armed men." All previous versions read "ruthless men." This is especially significant because, in the one extant manuscript of "Beat! Beat! Drums!," a nearly final version held at the Library of Congress, various lines differ from the version that eventually appeared in *Harper's*. The one textual variant in that manuscript matches the variant in the *Circular*; the second line ends "armed men." This suggests that the newspaper was not reprinting from *Harper's*, as were the other newspapers, but setting directly from one of Whitman's manuscripts or from a copy prepared by a third party acquainted with Whitman.

This latter possibility is especially intriguing because the most likely intermediary would be the artist Larkin Mead. In 1855, when Mead was apprenticing under Henry Kirke Brown in Brooklyn, the young man had written to his sister Elinor to ask, "Have you seen 'Leaves of Grass'? I suppose that it is one of the greatest books ever written in this country."[37] In fall 1861 Larkin was back in New York City with his sister and her fiancé, William Dean Howells. That these three young admirers should be gathered in New York in October 1861—awaiting passage to Venice, where Larkin would study art and Howells, appointed consul to Venice by Abraham Lincoln, would marry Elinor on New Year's Eve—is important because Larkin and Elinor were nephew and niece to the editor of the *Circular*, John Humphrey Noyes.

Howells remembered each of his meetings with Whitman so vividly that the absence of such an account seems to be evidence that neither he nor the Meads saw Whitman during this time. However, Whitman had maintained a close friendship with Henry Kirke Brown; thus it may be that Brown passed the manuscript to one of the Meads and they, in turn, passed it along to their uncle. Whatever the method of transmission, it seems apparent that an early manuscript version of "Beat! Beat! Drums!" was circulating among Whitman's circle in New York.

More than a month later, and as far removed culturally and geographically as one could be from the utopian communes of Upstate New York, "Beat! Beat! Drums!" appeared for the final time that year, on the back page of San Francisco's four-sheet *Daily Evening Bulletin*.[38] The editors es-

poused an ideology that sympathized with both the radical experimenta-
tion of Whitman's poems in general and with martial enthusiasm of his
great call to arms in particular. Started as a socially progressive newspaper
in 1855, the *Bulletin* hired James King as its first editor; he was shot dead
in the streets by a city supervisor who had been targeted in one of King's
anticorruption editorials. The extent of the *Bulletin*'s isolation is plain in its
early years from its limited reporting of national news, which had to be delivered by pony express from Carson City, Nevada. The paper didn't begin
receiving direct dispatches until October 24, 1861, after the completion of
the overland telegraph, just weeks before they published Whitman's
poem.[39] How the poem came into the hands of the editors remains a mystery. Perhaps it was given to them by Bret Harte, a former Pfaffian who had
come west to write for the *Golden Era* but occasionally contributed to the
Bulletin. Or perhaps the *Bulletin* simply exchanged with the *Circular;*
the telltale line in the *Daily Evening Bulletin* also reads, "Through the
windows—through doors—burst like a force of armed men."

· · ·

As "Beat! Beat! Drums!" enjoyed ever-wider circulation, Whitman was at
work on a new poem, titled "Kentucky." The surviving drafts celebrate the
decision by the legislature of Kentucky on September 11 to call on the governor to order all Confederate troops out of the state. For more than a
week before this action, Kentucky's neutrality was strongly challenged, and
which side the state would take in the mounting Civil War was very much
in question. Confederate troops under Gideon Pillow crossed the border
into Kentucky on September 3, moving toward Columbus, Ohio, with the
intention of trying to control the Mississippi River. Skirmishes followed at
Columbus and Hickman before Ulysses S. Grant seized control of Padu-
cah on September 6, effectively giving Union forces command of the Tennessee, Ohio, and Cumberland Rivers. Pro-Union feelings rapidly swelled
across Kentucky, convincing the legislature to abandon neutrality. Confederate troops did not withdraw from Kentucky—in fact, fighting inten-
sified across the state—but after September 11 Confederates were officially

enemy occupiers, effectively entering Kentucky into the war on the Union side.[40]

Word of Kentucky's decision appeared in the New York newspapers on September 13, and Whitman began drafting the poem almost immediately, thus placing its composition at exactly the same time as "Beat! Beat! Drums!" A clear, fair copy of the final poem is not currently known; however, numerous drafts in the Library of Congress can be pieced together into a near-final version:

> Son of hunters! Son of the pleasant valleys and sweet-tasting rivers!
> Son of Virginia! would that you knew our joy in you today reflecting America's joy!
> Would that you saw where anxiously waited, these million eyes of Manhattan!
> Would that you knew how we felt, when the answer came to America's listening ears—
> When she heard the sound of your sonorous cry as it rose clear and shrill, wafted across the Ohio;—
> When she saw you, advancing, with sinewy tendons, drest in your hunting shirt, with your rifle on your shoulder
> —And then, as to you Virginia, why will you strive against me, (we seem'd to hear America say,)
> For more than I can conquer you you have provided me to conquer yourself,
> For you provided me Washington, and have provided me these also.[41]

This version of the poem almost certainly predates October 1861 because several lines appear to have been reused in the poem "1861," submitted to the *Atlantic Monthly* at that time. Whitman writes in "Kentucky" that Manhattan "saw you, advancing, with sinewy tendons, drest in your hunting shirt, with your rifle on your shoulder." These lines are reworked in "1861" for the opening of the poem—"a strong man erect, clothed in blue clothes, advancing, carrying a rifle on your shoulder"—and the poem's closing: "Saw I your gait and saw I your sinewy limbs clothed in blue."

Even more of the lines resurface in "Virginia—The West" (first published in 1872), which also features the lines "The noble son on sinewy feet advancing" and "Drest in blue, bearing their trusty rifles on their shoulders." But lest it be suggested that these lines are merely recycled from "1861," compare "Kentucky":

> —And then, as to you Virginia, why will you strive against me, (we seem'd to hear America say.)
> For more than I can conquer you you have provided me to conquer yourself,
> For you provided me Washington, and have provided me these also.

to "Virginia—The West":

> Then the Mother of All with calm voice speaking,
> As to you Rebellious, (I seemed to hear her say,) why strive against me, and why seek my life?
> When you yourself forever provide to defend me?
> For you provided me Washington—and now these also.[42]

It appears that "Kentucky" is not an incomplete, uncollected poem, but rather an early draft of "Virginia—The West." In fact, the structure of the poem as it appeared in 1872 is identical to the poem in 1861, though the language became significantly more abstract and generalized by the later date. Kentucky assumed the allegorized form of "Rebellious" and America became the "Mother of All," but there was virtually no further elaboration on the theme put forth in the "Kentucky" manuscripts.

It is reasonable to assume, therefore, that Whitman may have submitted a finished form of "Kentucky" for publication. The head of one of the draft pages bears his canceled inscription, "If convenient set up in your larger type, put at the head of any column on 5th page, and do not put 'for the Tribune' over the head," suggesting that he originally intended the poem for publication in the *New York Tribune*, which had featured a number of war-related poems, including work by James Russell Lowell, John Greenleaf Whittier, and Bayard Taylor. Whitman's poetry never appeared there. However, the fact that the poem did not appear in print elsewhere during the Civil War in no way precludes the chance that a draft was completed and submitted for consideration. In fact, the possibility is bolstered by the documented record of Whitman's failed attempt to publish the poem "1861."

On October 1 Whitman submitted "1861," along with two unidentified poems the next day, to "J. R. Lowell / Atlantic Monthly."[43] James Russell Lowell was the editor of the *Atlantic* when Whitman published there in 1860. Unbeknown to Whitman, however, James T. Fields, a partner in the *Atlantic*'s publisher, Ticknor and Fields, took over the editorship of the magazine in May 1861 as a cost-saving measure.[44] The *Atlantic* did not publish a list of its editors, and Whitman was not the only writer to submit to Lowell in error. On October 8 Lowell wrote to Fields promising some of his own work soon and enclosing "an article by Mr. S. A. Eliot—and three [poems] from Walt Whitman. '1861' he says is $20. the others $8. each."[45] Two days later Whitman received an impersonal reply, signed only "Editors of the Atlantic Monthly": "[We are returning] the three poems with which you have favored us, but which we could not possibly use before their interest,—which is of the present,—would have passed."[46]

Fields seems to imply that he could not publish "1861" before the end of the title year; however, examination of his editorial correspondence at the time strongly suggests otherwise. For instance, David Atwood Wasson submitted the poem "Time's Household" on September 1, and it was printed in the October issue.[47] Even more important, Fields accepted Nathaniel Hawthorne's essay "Near Oxford" on September 18 and still managed to publish it in October.[48] By the time Whitman's submission reached Fields on October 9 he might have been working on a slightly longer backlog. In early November, for example, Fields accepted Wasson's essays "Light Literature" and "Ease in Work," which did not appear until the January and February 1862 issues.[49] However, in Lowell's October 8 letter enclosing Whitman's poems, he also writes, "I set about a poem last night—*à propos* of the times and hope to finish it tomorrow, and if it turn out to be good for anything, I will send it at once and you can print it or no as you like."[50] M. A. DeWolfe Howe argues that the poem "appears to have been 'The Washers of the Shroud,' published in the November, 1861, *Atlantic*," but James C. Austin counters, "If that were the case . . . the presses must have been stopped to insert it, for the November issue was probably being printed by October 8."[51] However, the earlier example of Hawthorne's essay refutes this argument. If Fields decided to accept Hawthorne's essay on September 18 for the October issue, surely he could have accepted Lowell's poem on October 9 (or even later) for the November issue. Further support for this comes from Lowell himself, who later affixed the epigraph "October, 1861" to "Washers of the Shroud," the only poem from his "War Poems" (which were all dated) to come from 1861.[52] Thus if Lowell still had not completed "Washers of the Shroud" on October 8, but it appeared in the November issue, then Fields's rejection of Whitman's "1861" must have been for some reason other than timeliness. Indeed, in December Fields accepted John Greenleaf Whittier's poem "Port Royal, 1861"—and even incorporated a revision sent by Whittier after the New Year—with no apparent concern that the date in the title limited the publication of the poem.[53]

That information, coupled with the fact that Fields returned all three poems because they were "of the present," might suggest that the rejection had less to do with concern about the production schedule than Fields's belief that the war would draw to a close before the poems appeared. That explanation is unlikely, however, as he certainly did not shy away from war poetry. The November issue contained not only Lowell's "Washers of the Shroud," but also Oliver Wendell Holmes's more overtly war-related "The Flower of Liberty." Still clinging to the notion of reconciliation between North and South, Holmes wrote:

> Behold its streaming rays unite
> One mingling flood of braided light,—
> The red that fires the Southern rose,
> With spotless white from Northern snows,
> And, spangled o'er its azure, see

The sister Stars of Liberty!
Then hail the banner of the free,
The starry Flower of Liberty![54]

In December Fields published yet another flag poem by Holmes, "Union and Liberty," a ballad steeped in vagaries and clichés with a refrain designed to be set to music:

Up with our banner bright,
Sprinkled with starry light,
Spread its fair emblems from mountain to shore,
While through the sounding sky
Loud rings the Nation's cry,
UNION AND LIBERTY! ONE EVERMORE![55]

As 1861 drew to a close, Fields accepted three more overtly war-related poems. At the beginning of December he took Whittier's "At Port Royal, 1861," published in February 1862, and "Mountain Pictures," published serially in March and April.[56] At the end of the month Fields also famously accepted Julia Ward Howe's "Battle Hymn of the Republic," which ran on the front page of the February issue. Like "Union and Liberty," Howe's "Battle Hymn" was meant to be sung. She later recalled that she had composed the lyrics after a visit to the front on November 18; from her carriage she had sung "John Brown's Body" to the approval of the soldiers.[57] At the urging of her minister, she decided to compose more encouraging words that would also be appropriate to camp life:

I have seen Him in the watch-fires of a hundred circling camps;
They have builded Him an altar in the evening dews and damps;
I can read His righteous sentence by the dim and flaring lamps:
His day is marching on.[58]

Howe later reported that the poem was paid only "small heed" upon its appearance: "[But] I knew, and was content to know, that the poem soon found its way to the camps, as I heard from time to time of its being sung in chorus by the soldiers."[59]

It would appear that in many ways Fields shared Howe's ambition. All the poems published during this period in the *Atlantic* can be divided into two categories: the inspiriting popular poems (such as Howe's and Holmes's) with regular rhythms and stock imagery that lend themselves easily to group singing, and the more traditionally literary poems, where the themes of war are steeped in history (such as Lowell's) or veiled in nature imagery, such as Whittier's "Mountain Pictures," in which the author begs, "let me hope the battle-storm that beats / the land" will leave "A greener earth and fairer sky behind, / Blown crystal-clear by Freedom's Northern wind!"[60] Fields was clearly willing to dedicate space to poetry about the war, but his stylistic tastes were decidedly different from Whitman's approach in "1861."

Indeed, Whitman denounces the very kind of poetry published in the *Atlantic* at the outset of "1861":

> Arm'd year! year of the struggle!
> No dainty rhymes or sentimental love verses for you, terrible year!
> Not you as some pale poetling, seated at a desk, lisping cadenzas piano;
> But as a strong man, erect, clothed in blue clothes, advancing, carrying a rifle on your shoulder.[61]

If the version read by Fields began this way, it's not hard to understand why he returned the poems. And if he did object to Whitman's poetry, his position had not changed by the war's end, when he rejected John Burroughs's essay "Walt Whitman and His Drum-Taps."[62]

Their different aesthetics, however, never seems to have grown personal between Fields and Whitman, as it later did between Whitman and Lowell. Fields eventually published one poem by Whitman, "Proud Music of the Sea-Storm," in February 1869, and, after Whitman suffered a stroke in 1873, Fields was one of his occasional benefactors. In his later years, after examining his letter submitting "Proud Music" to Fields, Whitman made a comment to Horace Traubel that perhaps best sums up Fields's real reason for rejecting "1861": "I sometimes growl a little about the editors but after all they are a good lot—they do the best they can. Besides, I am an incongruity to most of them—I make the sort of noise they don't like—I upset the things they do like: why should I expect to be received?"[63]

• • •

As other publications rejected his poetry, the *New York Leader*, under Clapp's literary editorship, became Whitman's primary outlet for the remainder of 1861 and 1862. In all, Whitman published three poems and six essays in the *Leader* during those years, providing the primary record by which we know his work and his changing attitudes in the early years of the war. Given the central position the *Leader* occupies in Whitman's Civil War writings, there has been surprisingly little attention given to his publications there and no discussion of the convergence of circumstance that led to his prominent place in the *Leader*'s stable of writers.

When John Clancy became one of the editors of the *Leader*, then an all-Irish weekly, in February 1857, he was already a rising political star among the Tammany Hall Democrats in New York's Sixth Ward. By year's end he had bought a controlling interest in the paper to become its editor in chief, despite having relatively little background in writing or editing.[64] His political fortunes were on the climb, but Clancy's journalistic inexperience showed, and subscriptions plummeted. In 1859, in hopes of increasing the circulation, he sold one-third interest to Charles Graham Halpine, a popular writer for the *Leader*'s chief competitor, the *Irish-American*. The move paid off. By the outbreak of the war Halpine had successfully increased the *Leader*'s weekly circulation from a few hundred to eleven thousand. As William Hanchett has observed, Halpine's strategy was to lure educated readers from the *Irish-American* by offering them "a lively smorgasbord of literary and political features," including serialized novels, feature stories, travel essays, and poetry, featuring many of his own poems and some by Clancy.[65] His part ownership of the *Leader* was the realization of Halpine's greatest ambitions.

Then came the attack on Fort Sumter and Lincoln's call for volunteers to defend the Union. On April 20, 1861, the new issue of the *Leader* carried a poem titled "The Sixty-Ninth." Though the poem is signed "Sigma," it is clearly Halpine's own, addressed to his wife, Margaret, and published on the very day Halpine himself enlisted in the 69th New York:

> Come, Margaret, to the window,
> See the Sixty-ninth go by!
> Brave, honest, gallant fellows
> Ready for right to die.

Three days later, on April 23, the 69th formed their lines on Great Jones Street. After hours of speeches, presentations of battle flags and Union colors, singing "The Starry Flag" (a song composed by Halpine's good friend John Savage especially for the occasion), and other formalities, the troops at last were given the order to march and turned onto Broadway. A horse-drawn wagon bearing the inscriptions "Sixty-ninth, remember Fontenoy" and "No North, no South, no East, no West, but the whole Union" led the procession.[66] The flag of Ireland flew alongside the American Flag. Well-wishers thronged the sidewalks shouting encouragement and throwing bouquets. The 69th and George Whitman's unit, the 13th New York State Militia, met at the docks and, joined by the 8th New York, were transported to Annapolis and on to the defense of Washington.

Halpine's absence created a literary gap at the *Leader*. Within a few weeks of his departure John Clancy hired Henry Clapp to write theater reviews and attract literary contributions. During the three months of Halpine's planned hiatus the poetry catered mostly to the *Leader*'s narrow Irish readership, including poems with the titles "Col. Corcoran's Brigade" (May 4), "Sixty-ninth" (June 1, also signed "Sigma"), "Camp Song of the Sixty-Ninth" (June 22), "Song, dedicated to Col. Corcoran and the Sixty-Ninth Regiment" (July 13), and "Mary O'Connor, The Volunteer's Wife" (July 20). Every issue in June led with Halpine's column, "The Sixty-Ninth in Camp," detailing the regiment's activities protecting Washington at Fort Corcoran. In mid-July Halpine's three-month stint expired, and he returned to his editorial duties in New York. In so doing he missed fighting in the First Battle of Bull Run by a matter of days. The 69th suffered heavy losses, including the wounding of Colonel Hunter, to whom Halpine served as adjutant.

In late July Halpine published George Cooper's "Welcome, Sixty-Ninth," a poem heralding the return of the 69th's late enlistments to New York, and, in August, an anonymous elegy, "Lines on the Death of Captain Haggarty of the Sixty-Ninth New York State Militia, who fell at the Battle of Manassas, 21st July." Guilt-ridden that his comrades had fought bravely and died without him, Halpine sold back his interest in the *Leader* to John Clancy and reenlisted as a general volunteer on September 5 for the standard commitment of three years or the duration of the war.

With Halpine permanently removed from literary control, Clancy apparently turned such tasks over to Clapp. Beginning in September Clapp's presence at the *Leader* became strongly felt as he brought all of his talented young followers to its pages. William Winter, George Arnold, and Ada Clare joined the full-time staff. Clapp also reprinted poetry from the large-circulation magazines, including Holmes's "The Flower of Liberty" from the *Atlantic Monthly*, and more purely literary poems by Bayard Taylor and Whittier. In October he also reprinted Fitz-James O'Brien's "The Tenement House" from *Harper's Monthly*, with a harsh note decrying an unscrupulous Connecticut soldier who had sent it to a newspaper in Hartford as his own. At first glance this appears to be one of the *Leader*'s typical defenses of an Irish writer who was then engaged in recruiting Irish soldiers for the McClellan Rifles, but, in fact, Halpine had taken every opportunity to thwart O'Brien's career. The feud dated back to O'Brien's negative review of Halpine's first book of poetry in 1854 and Halpine's naming a villain "Knightly Fitz-James" in one of his serialized novels published in the *Irish-American* in 1857. O'Brien favored literary excellence over Irish nationalism, and his appearance in the *Leader* is the clearest indication of the publication's shifting emphasis under Clapp.

It was no doubt Clapp's advocacy of Whitman that brought him to the *Leader* as well. Winter remembered that each night at Pfaff's as Clapp "assumed the sceptre as Prince of Bohemia," Whitman always sat to his right, "clad in his eccentric garb of rough blue and gray fabric,—his hair and beard grizzled, his keen, steel-blue eyes gazing, with bland tolerance, on the frolicsome lads around him."[67]

On October 5, 1861, Walt Whitman's second Civil War poem, "Little Bells Last Night," appeared in the *Leader* (cover dated October 12):

War-suggesting trumpets, I heard you;
And you I heard beating, you chorus of small and large drums;
You round-lipp'd cannons!—you I heard, thunder-cracking, saluting
　　the frigate from France;
I heard you solemn-sweet pipes of the organ as last Sunday morn I
　　pass'd the church,
Winds of Autumn!—as I walk'd the woods at dusk, I heard your
　　long-stretch'd sighs up above so mournful,
I heard the perfect Italian tenor, singing at the opera; I heard the
　　soprano, in the midst of the quartet singing;
Lady! you, too, I heard, as with white arms in your parlor, you play'd
　　for me delicious music on the harp;
Heart of my love!—you, too, I heard, murmuring low, through one
　　of the wrists around my head—
Heard the pulse of you when all was still ringing little bells last night
　　under my ear.[68]

By the time he published this poem in *Sequel to Drum-Taps* in late 1865 under the title "I heard you, Solemn-sweet Pipes of the Organ," Whitman had removed the first three lines, as well as the seventh. The contemporary poet James Wright has argued that Whitman removed these four lines because they were apostrophes, leaving behind only the lines that are parallel in structure but also advance the narrative incrementally, so that "we discover the form of the poem as we read it, and we know what it is only after we have finished."[69] Although this is a compelling argument for the form Whitman discovered in revision, it ignores the more obvious fact that removing those lines strips out all references to the war.

In this first version the first two lines are not merely apostrophes; they also serve as a direct continuation of "Beat! Beat! Drums!," which the readers of the *Leader* would have seen only two weeks earlier. Thus the poem assumes a continued readership. The appearance of the poem's third line, however, is puzzling. The phrase "round lipp'd cannon" also appears in "1861," which was under consideration at the *Atlantic Monthly* even as "Little Bells" appeared in the *Leader*. Likewise, "The Errand-Bearers," the poem Whitman had published the previous summer, contained the lines "When the thunder cracking guns arouse me with the proud roar I love, / When the round-mouth'd guns, out of the smoke and smell I love, spit their salutes." Rather than simply extending the reach of "Beat! Beat! Drums!" for the recent readership that poem enjoyed, Whitman refers to two poems, one that he may have assumed would soon be published and another more than a year old, which would have been known only by his most loyal readers and close friends. Moreover, these three poems collectively formed the most nationalistic work to date in Whitman's oeuvre; "Little Bells" opens by harkening to these patriotic hymns, but the lines that follow overturn that grand rhetorical style. Whitman follows with a litany of other sounds, the sounds of nature and of art, that he has also heard and heard recently. He emphasizes that he heard the sound of the pipe organ "as last Sunday morn I pass'd the church," and refers to the sorrowful moans of the wind in the woods as the "Winds of Autumn!" These are not wistful recollections of idyllic prewar days, but the recent sounds of beauty and, at the poem's end, tender love, heard even over "war-suggesting trumpets." Such sentiments would have appealed directly to Clapp and the writers at Pfaff's, but they would have found little favor among the *Leader*'s readership, who by now were interested only in songs of war.

In the wake of the devastation to the 69th New York at Bull Run, blame was consistently placed on inadequate leadership, and calls grew in New York for an all-Irish brigade free from Union incompetence. No one was more adamant than Captain Thomas Francis Meagher, commander of

Company K of the 69th. A hero of Bull Run, Meagher was invited by the
3rd New York Irish Volunteers to command their regiment in early August, and two weeks later his name was being used to encourage Irish enlistment in Boston. He insisted, however, that his sole aim was to reform
the 69th as part of the proposed Irish Brigade.[70] In late August he agreed
to assume the colonelcy of the 69th, then withdrew on September 5,
when it appeared that the reformed regiment would not be joined with
other Irish regiments.[71] Meagher's stubborn withdrawal may have been
driven by his growing power within the Irish community; when he spoke
on August 29 at Jones' Woods, thousands of Irish supporters turned out,
and the *New York Times* carried the full text of his speech the following
day. Meagher spoke to ten thousand in Bridgeport, Connecticut, on September 14, and to four thousand in Boston (with another two thousand
turned away) on September 23.

With Irish nativism and eagerness for a swift conclusion to the war already at a fever pitch, bad news reached New York on September 28. The
New York Times reprinted from the *Chicago Tribune* a detailed account of the
fall of Lexington, Missouri. The article recounted the ten-day siege and
described the suffering of Colonel James A. Mulligan's 23rd Illinois, com-
monly known as the "Western Irish Brigade," in excruciating detail. In the
days after losing their access to the river, Mulligan's troops stood in the rain
with their blankets spread, letting them saturate and then wringing them
into their canteens. When, on September 24, Mulligan finally gave the
tearful order to surrender with his men on the brink of death from dehy-
dration, the *Tribune* reported that many of the men "threw themselves
upon the ground, raved and stormed in well nigh frenzy," demanding to be
led back into battle.[72] The lack of support for Mulligan's men, isolated and
unassisted for nearly two weeks, only deepened resentful feelings toward
Union commanders among the New York Irish.

On October 5, in the very issue where "Little Bells Last Night" appeared, the *Leader* carried an announcement that Meagher would soon
return to speak in New York: "*The Irish Brigade for the American Union.* —
In aid of this patriotic organization *Thomas Francis Meagher* will deliver

an ORATION in the Academy of American Music, corner Fourteenth street and Irving Place, *Sunday Evening*, October 6th on the 'Irish Soldier,' his history and present duty—his obligations to the American Republic! The National Cause, its justice, sanctity and its promised glory. The triumph of the National Arms assured! The New World vindicates itself against the Old!"[73]

That night Meagher addressed "an overflowing house," heralding the bravery of Irish soldiers (including a tribute to "the gallant Mulligan, of Lexington"). He urged Lincoln, however, not to succumb to pressure to abolish slavery, saying that the South had been "exasperated" by Horace Greeley's editorials, by "the sermons of [Henry Ward] Beecher" and "the Phillipics of [Wendell] Phillips," and "the poetry of Whittier." After each name was added to the list, Meagher waited for the chorus of boos and hisses to die down, but when the crowd failed to respond to Whittier's name, Meagher remarked that he guessed the crowd "didn't know much about poetry," and the audience erupted into laughter.

Whitman may or may not have been in attendance at the Academy of American Music—he certainly had a taste for such public spectacles—but he would have read the transcript carried in various New York newspapers. Not only had Whitman's own brother recently reenlisted at the urging of his Scots-Irish friend Fred McCready, but Fitz-James O'Brien, Whitman's close friend from Pfaff's, was then engaged in a frantic effort to find enough recruits to contribute his ragtag bunch, known as the McClellan Rifles, to the Irish Brigade.

Whitman could not resist responding to this urgent need for Irish enlistments together with this public ridicule of poetry's ability to stir Irish interest in the war. On October 27 the new issue of the *Leader* (dated November 2) hit newsstands with Whitman's poem "Old Ireland" prominently displayed on the front page:

> Far hence, amid an isle of wondrous beauty,
> Crouching over a grave, an ancient sorrowful mother,
> Once a queen—now lean and tattered, seated on the ground,
> Her old white hair drooping dishevel'd round her head;

At her feet fallen an unused royal harp,
Long silent—she too long silent—mourning her shrouded hope
    and heir;
Of all the earth her heart most full of sorrow, because most full of
    love.

Yet a word, ancient mother;
You need crouch there no longer on the cold ground;
Oh! you need not sit there, veil'd in your old white hair, so
    dishevel'd,
For know you the one you mourn is not in that grave,
It was an illusion—the heir, the son you love, was not really dead;
The Lord is not dead—he is risen again, young and strong, in
    another country;
Even while you, veiled, wept there by your fallen harp, by the grave,
What you wept for was translated, pass'd from the grave,
The winds favor'd and the sea sail'd it,
And now with rosy and new blood, again among the nations
    of the earth,
Moves to-day, an armed man, in a new country.[74]

Besides speaking to the *Leader*'s urgent cause of Irish recruitment, Whit-man's poem also reimagines a widely distributed scene from popular li-thography. Beginning in 1861, following First Bull Run, Currier & Ives and other lithographers issued hand-tinted prints that featured a mother bent next to her son's grave, her face covered by her handkerchief, while in the background soldiers march away to battle. In these prints blanks were left for the name of the soldier, his regiment, where he was killed, and the date. Without a similar way to particularize and personalize the dead Irish at Bull Run and Lexington, Whitman instead abstracts and in-verts the scene depicted by Currier & Ives so that the specific mother mourning the loss of her soldier son becomes "an ancient sorrowful mother" of all Ireland whose son, lost on Irish soil, "was not really dead." Instead, the soldier is likened to "the Lord" and is "risen again, young and strong, in another country." Yet the son is not resurrected as a for-giving savior but as "an armed man."

The extent to which this poem speaks to the particular moment of its first publication may best be seen in Whitman's postwar revision of the poem. By the time it appeared in *Drum-Taps* in May 1865, the final two lines read, "And now with rosy and new blood, / Moves to-day in a new country,"[75] thus removing all reference to the "armed" Irish and the notion that their fighting would restore their rightful place "among the nations of the earth." By that time the Irish-led killing of freed slaves during the New York draft riots in 1863 had changed public opinion about the armed sons of Ireland and the restorative value of their violence. Perhaps, as with the revision of "Little Bells Last Night," Whitman simply sought to obscure the original impetus for the poem once the war had ended, or perhaps his early idealism was tempered by violence even before the draft riots.

On the night of November 2, 1861, the copies of the *Leader* containing "Old Ireland" were being replaced with the new issue of the *Leader*, and *Vanity Fair* featured a caricature by Ned Mullen, another among the Pfaff's crowd, of Fitz-James O'Brien's strong-arming a street tough into enlisting.[76] Eerily, that very night O'Brien shot a man named Davenport, one of the sergeants of his regiment, when O'Brien caught him out without a pass. By O'Brien's account the shooting was accidental, but subsequent investigation revealed that Davenport had been shot twice. O'Brien explained that the first shot was accidental and the second must have been fired in the ensuing struggle. He was tried and acquitted, but he was stripped of his captaincy and demoted to the lieutenant position of aide-de-camp. The controversy deeply hurt recruiting efforts, and rather than becoming an all-Irish regiment, the McClellan Rifles were later transformed into the 90th New York.[77]

Both "Little Bells Last Night" and "Old Ireland" were significantly revised for their postwar publications and never again included references to the Civil War. But in these first published versions they reveal the dual cultures Whitman was struggling to assimilate: the purely literary audience at Pfaff's and the purely popular audience of the general readership he sought through wide-circulation newspapers and magazines. Perhaps precisely because they are caught in this moment of Whitman's artistic and psychological hesitation neither poem is as wholly successful as "Beat! Beat! Drums!," a poem that succeeds more fully on both levels.

On the morning of October 30, 1861, the 51st New York prepared to leave the Palace Garden "for the seat of war." The *New York Times* reported, "The regiment numbers over nine hundred men, all of whom are fully uniformed, armed and equipped. Long before the time named for their departure, Fourteenth-street in the vicinity of Palace Garden was crowded with people anxious to see the men off. Punctual to the time mentioned in the orders for departure line was formed, and the regiment marched down Broadway to Pier No. 1 North River, where the boat was taken for South Amboy, *en route* to Washington."[78] With his brother George's departure, Whitman's flurry of writing and publishing poetry ended just as abruptly as it had begun. There is no evidence that he sought to publish "Kentucky," "1861," or the other two unidentified poems rejected by the *Atlantic Monthly* after October 1861. Clapp's support of Whitman was, by this time, sufficient that one can reasonably assume that Whitman could have published his poetry in the *Leader* whenever he wished.

For the time being, however, Whitman seems to have returned his focus to earning enough money to support his aging mother, his invalid brother Edward, and his ill-tempered brother Jesse, who some time in November was fired from his job at the Brooklyn Navy Yard.[79] In December he returned to writing the "Brooklyniana" series of articles for the *Brooklyn Standard*, which he continued intermittently for nearly a year. Even though he wrote these articles for much needed money, nothing would have prevented Whitman from publishing his already completed poems in the *Leader* or elsewhere. Surely Clapp would have jumped at the chance to publish "1861" in one of his November or December numbers.

There is certainly no evidence that Clapp's opinion of Whitman's work ever wavered; indeed, at the end of November at Pfaff's, George

Clapp, Henry's brother, handed Whitman a copied extract of a letter sent
to him by Mary Greenwood Couthouy, "a lady in New England" and the
wife of Joseph Pitty Couthouy, a distinguished conchologist and then
lieutenant in the U.S. Navy. In her letter she told George, "The oftener
I read 'Old Ireland' the more I like it"; she added that her father had recently written to her to say "I like Walt Whitman's 'Little bells last
night'—pretty and tender. Of course not as much as his Grand Drum
call."[80] George Clapp may have given this letter to Whitman as encouragement, evidence that his poetry in the *Leader* was being read and considered as a growing body of work, but increasingly Whitman was turning his efforts toward prose and his attention toward the reminders of
death that surrounded him in Brooklyn.

CHAPTER FIVE

Dead and Divine, and Brother of All

Young man, I think I know you—I think this face of yours is
the face of the Christ himself;
Dead and divine, and brother of all, and here again he lies.
"A Sight in Camp in the Daybreak Grey
and Dim," 1865

For a moment, standing in the silence of a wagon path far from home and looking into the deep woods around him, George Whitman was reminded of Long Island, of the dense scrub oak along the railroad cut east of Farmingdale and the pine barrens riddled with burned trunks that stretched into the dark forest near Deer Park. Walt had written off those woods as "monotonous" and "gloomy,"[1] but in this brief reverie, the tall black trees reminded George of home.

Then shots rang out, and everyone rushed for cover.

It was February 8, 1862. The 51st New York, as part of the Burnside Expedition, was pursuing rebel troops under the command of Confederate General Henry A. Wise, the former governor of Virginia, on Roanoke Island, off the coast of North Carolina. Wise's men had caught sight of the advance lines, and now George with shattering suddenness was under fire for the first time. His regiment took to the woods following the 1st Brigade on the double-quick and pressed through thickets into a swamp, their boots filling with water and sinking in mud to their knees, as Minie balls sheared off branches and bark all around them. When they finally emerged on the 1st's right flank, the men were ordered to charge.

The next day George's letter to his mother still rang with the excitement of the moment. "Away we went," he wrote, "the water flying over our heads as we splashed through it."[2] But as soon as the 2nd Brigade advanced, the rebel troops withdrew into the woods, leaving everything behind. Knapsacks, haversacks, guns, and ammunition lay scattered among the dead. George picked up a few things, including the paper on which he wrote his letter and the envelope in which he mailed it. His regiment gathered the Confederate wounded—among them O. Jennings Wise, the general's son, shot mortally through the hip—and took them to a nearby house before pressing into the woods in pursuit. The dead were all along the retreat: an old man with a white beard, a young man still clutching his rifle, another sprawled in the bushes struggling for his last breath with the top of his head blown off. Little wonder the remaining Confederate troops, when they were finally found, raised the white flag "and wilted without a strugle."[3]

If George was at all affected by what he had seen, he gave no indication in his letter. "I was as calm and cool during the whole affair as I am at any time," he told his mother. "So Mammy I think we done a pretty good days work yesterday marching 15 or 16 miles and fighting with boots filed with water for 4 hours." In fact, he had seen several reporters in the field asking questions after the battle, and he hoped Walt would send along a copy of a New York newspaper. "I should like one giveing a discription of the battle I supose you will see a good account of it."[4]

Indeed, the account that ran a week later in the *New York Times* seemed as swept up in the exhilaration of battle as George's letter, and as indifferent to its effects. The writer recounted how the "panic-stricken rebels" had fled in disarray, while Union troops "poured into their battery." The 51st planted its battle flag first and sent up a holler as "never awaked such echoes before in the lonely forests of Roanoke." But the reporter also confessed that, walking among the same Confederate dead that George had looked on, he saw the body of a particularly handsome young officer. "I thought of the parents of this rash misguided man," he wrote, "and though I had no clue to his identity, could not resist the desire to remove a lock of his hair as a memento."[5]

With George now in the heat of battle, Walt walked the streets of Brooklyn, obsessed by visions of anonymous death. In the last edition of *Leaves of Grass* he had bragged that he was "willing to disregard burial-places, and dispense with them."[6] But that seemed to change in the first months of 1862. The trustees of St. Ann's Episcopal on Fulton had voted to sell its churchyard and relocate the bodies of those buried there. The church discreetly erected a board fence during the exhumation in the early winter, but after the first of the year the barrier was removed and passersby could stop to watch the workmen dig out the foundation for the planned new buildings. "The cellar yawns deeper and wider every day," Whitman wrote in the *Brooklyn City News*, "and before another winter is upon us, St. Ann's Church, instead of having that old memento of the graves of its founders and ancestors, with all its clustering associations to point to and gaze upon, and become pensive over, will be the thrifty owner of a row of valuable dry-goods and jewelry stores."[7]

In the pages of the *Eagle* Whitman lamented the passing of many familiar sights of Brooklyn in an irregular series of articles published under the heading "An Old Brooklyn Landmark Gone." He was troubled by the demolition of historic buildings and the felling of old trees, making way for new shops and roads, but nothing seemed to concern him more than the removal of the long-neglected cemeteries: "Fast, fast, fade and vanish the landmarks of old Brooklyn. The men of the earlier years of the century have nearly all departed—and the women. The old trees have been all cut down. The old edifices, one after another, are going. Even the old graveyards have had their bones and coffins dug up from the earth, and already the places that knew them, know them no more."[8]

This notion—that the dead might be forgotten by the living, exiled even from their final resting places—was deeply troubling to Whitman. He recoiled from the idea of anonymity, of namelessness, and most of all from the appearance of willful erasure at the hands of future generations. "By blood, by marriage, by some or another tie, thousands are yet connected there in those old grave-yards," he wrote in the *Brooklyn Standard*, "soon every trace of them, however, to be utterly rubbed out."[9] Within three months, he predicted, "a row of magnificent stores will uprise and be completed on this ground; and then but a few years more and the recollection of the former sacredness of the spot will have passed entirely away. Gorgeous with rich goods, seen through plate glass windows, and splendid with glittering jets of gas at night, and resonant with the hum of voices of crowds, is, or will be, the spot. A fit illustration of the rapid changes of the kaleidoscope of alteration and death we call life."[10]

For the singer of progress to so disdain the arrival of gas jets, the bard of Broadway to disparage "the hum of voices of crowds," indicates the degree of his disquiet. Whitman was consumed by the unalterable and eradicating anonymity of the forward march of time—though, ironically, he chose not to sign his name to any of the articles he published in Brooklyn.

He continued to seek refuge in the bustling hubbub of Pfaff's, but now the dank, subterranean confines of the Broadway rathskeller felt like a tomb. In an incomplete poem drafted at the time, Whitman reimagined the main room and the cave under the sidewalk as "The Two Vaults." The one dark hole that held the long table where the Bohemians convened now became

> The vault at Pfaff's where the drinkers and laughers meet to eat
>   and drink and carouse,
> While on the walk immediatly overhead, pass the myriad feet
>   of Broadway
> As the dead in their graves, are underfoot hidden
> And the living pass over them, recking not of them.[11]

With an uncharacteristic air of mock exhortation, Whitman urges, "Laugh on laughers! Drink on drinkers! / Bandy the jests!" All those around proceed blithely unaware of their place in the underworld, while the poet looks up longingly toward the street:

> The lamps are lit—the shops blaze in—the fabrics and jewelry are
>   seen through the plate glass windows
> The thick crowds, well-dressed—the continual crowds as if they
>   would never end
> The curious appearance of the faces—the glimpses first caught of the
>   eyes and expressions, as they flit along.
> (You phantoms! oft I pause, yearning, to arrest some one of you!
> Oft I doubt your reality—I suspect all is but a pageant.)[12]

In a subtle and effective inversion, it is the voice of the poet, speaking from the vault, who doubts the existence of those walking above ground, even as they pass unaware of those who lie beneath their "myriad feet."

The poem seeks to wrestle with Whitman's established ideas of identity when confronted by the effacing reality of death. The anonymity of the 1855 edition, published without an author's name on the title page, had been a literary device, an intentional mystery maintained until the poet revealed himself to the reader as "Walt Whitman, an American, one of the roughs, a kosmos."[13] This anonymity—the anonymity of strangers, poet and reader, on the cusp of acquaintance ("Whoever you are, now I place my hand upon you, that you be my poem")[14]—is considerably different from the insurmountable anonymity of death. As Whitman wrote in the 1856 edition, pondering the decomposition of bodies into nourishing soil, "Now I am terrified at the earth! it is that calm and patient."[15] If the body was the soul's container and conduit, what did its disintegration mean?

It is precisely that question and its accompanying pangs of terror that seem to have returned in 1862 as Whitman was simultaneously confronted by the possibility of his brother's death and the grim finality of bodily decomposition. Most of all, however, he feared the disappearance from memory, the eradication of identity as embodied in a name. He was reminded of an account of an exhumation in Brooklyn, performed a generation before, during the demolition of an old thatched-roof Dutch church: "In removing the traces of the church, the workmen came upon the dead body buried there, dressed in the complete uniform of a British officer of rank. The body was in remarkable preservation, in the midst of its showy uniform, buttons, epaulettes, gold lace, cocked hat, sword by its side."[16]

He had heard the story directly from an aged Brooklynite named Andrew Demarest, who was present on the morning the crew prepared to remove the body. A large crowd gathered, including, Whitman wrote, "a lady who distinctly remembered the burial of the officer." She told the crowd that the man was a casualty of the Battle of Brooklyn in 1776 and had been buried there after Washington's retreat. As a small child, this old woman had watched the funeral, but she could not remember the officer's name. Now Demarest, telling the story to Whitman, could not remember the name of the old woman, though she "was one of the Duffield family."[17] The cycle of erasure continued.

Whitman confessed, "The subject we have opened has a volume contained within it," the story not just of the British officer but of the Revolutionary soldiers he fought, in particular the so-called Wallabout Martyrs. During the War for Independence, some twelve thousand American rebels died aboard the infamous British prison ships anchored off the shore of Long Island. Whenever another man died, the remains were "brought ashore and dumped in the sand, in careless heaps, uncoffined, uncared for, with just enough dirt thrown over them to prevent the neighboring air from becoming pestilential."[18] As if to show his close identification with them, Whitman described these men as "unnamed Revolutionary patriots, 'roughs.'" But whereas Whitman gladly saw himself and the Wallabout Martyrs as roughs and he the American heir to their Revolutionary patriotism, he recoiled at the realization that they had moldered into namelessness, a fact that cast doubt on his belief in his place among the "men and women of a generation, or ever so many generations hence."

Worst of all, no one else in Brooklyn seemed the least bit troubled by their mistreatment. Whitman told readers of the *Standard* that longtime residents remembered that "nothing was more common in their early days than to see thereabout plenty of the skulls and other bones of these dead—and that thoughtless boys would kick them about in play. Many of the martyrs were so insecurely buried that the sand, being blown off by the wind, exposed their bleached skeletons in great numbers."[19]

In 1808, to properly commemorate the sacrifices of these soldiers, the Tammany Society paid for the erection of a wooden vault, inscribed with the story of those who had died, and the remains were buried with the utmost pomp. The procession was led by a trumpeter dressed in black, astride a black stallion, trailing black banners, followed by thirteen coffins to represent the dead from each of the thirteen colonies, each attended by eight veterans of the war as pallbearers. Once the coffins were safely in the ground, however, the memorial, too, was forgotten and allowed to become dilapidated. Now, more than fifty years later, as the nation spiraled into Civil War, Whitman bemoaned that the vault was in a "ruinous condition" and "probably the most slatternly and dirtiest object to be seen anywhere in Brooklyn."[20]

The image of this grand military procession for the Wallabout Martyrs opened a still deeper vault in Whitman's mind and commingled with memories of a similar military burial he had witnessed firsthand. On June 4, 1829, when Whitman was just ten years old, a sailor, angry at being whipped by a superior, set fire to the powder magazine of the U.S. steamer *Fulton*, blowing apart the frigate and killing all those aboard. The ship was moored in port at the Brooklyn Navy Yard, near Whitman's grammar school, and he remembered "the dull shock that was felt in the building as of something like an earthquake." But he remembered even more clearly the funeral of one of the officers that followed just a few days later. In the pages of the *City News* he wrote:

> We climbed up with other youngsters on the fence, and saw the
> whole procession and funeral service. It was a solemn scene. The
> downcast faces, the tears of many, the wailing notes of the music that
> came like living voices of lamentation—the blue-dressed sailors,
> hand-in-hand—the army and navy officers in their uniforms and

with uncovered heads—the black pall draping that coffin in which lay the mutilated body—the procession, so slow—the ministers, the sublime service, the weeping group around the grave—and, to end all, the volley that was fired in military fashion;—and then the return marching off to a lively air from the band—we saw the whole.[21]

Many years later, recalling the scene yet again, Whitman would confess that he had been brought to tears, particularly by what he described in the *Standard* as "the muffled drums beating, the bugles wailing forth the mournful peals of a dead march."[22]

Such memories are a striking reversal of Whitman's urgent recruitment fervor reflected in "Beat! Beat! Drums!," which he concluded by exhorting, "Make the very trestles shake under the dead, where they lie in their shrouds awaiting the hearses. / So strong you thump, O terrible drums—so loud you bugles blow." Not only does the prospect of George's death seem to have dawned on Whitman in the early months of 1862, but also the realization that even should George be returned to Brooklyn and buried with full military honors, he might shortly be exhumed, a forgotten and nameless corpse, and relocated to a place where no one knew him. Whitman himself could remember the burial of the *Fulton* officer, but now each day he passed the empty hole of the graveyard, in which a work crew was laying the foundation for a block of shops. That officer, like the British officer killed during the Battle of Brooklyn and the Wallabout Martyrs, had received an illustrious burial with attending procession, throngs of mourners, and salutes fired over his grave. Yet, in the span of Whitman's own lifetime, the officer had been forgotten, and his grave, like all the others, had been desecrated.

These fears would only intensify for Whitman as his brother's own sense of mortality deepened. The next letter the family received from George arrived on Confederate letterhead. In the upper left-hand corner was the image of a cannon discharging under a fluttering Confederate battle flag. In the opposite corner were the death-defiant printed lines:

> Bright Banner of Freedom with pride I unfurl thee;
> Fair flag of my country with I behold thee.

Gleaming above us in freshness and youth,
Emblem of Liberty, Symbol of truth;
For the Flag of my country in triumph shall wave,
O'er the Southerner's Home and the Southerner's Grave.

Next to these verses George had written cavalierly, "This is some of the paper we found her[e] it is first rate to write acounts of Union Victories on."

Once again George's carefree tone seemed to belie the horrors he had witnessed, this time at the Battle of Newbern, North Carolina. "The balls fairly rained upon me," he told his mother, but he assured her that he "did not get a scratch."[23] The battle was little more than a series of skirmishes fought for control over a railroad line, which the Union troops were eventually able to secure; nevertheless, the casualties to the 51st New York were quite heavy. By George's own estimate, one hundred of the regiment's 650 men were killed or wounded. George found Major Charles LeGendre, who had been instrumental in recruiting the 51st, motionless in the mud; a ball had struck him in the back of the neck, just below his collar, and passed all the way through, exiting at his cheek. George wrapped him in the blanket he wore draped around his shoulders and carried the major a quarter-mile to the nearest surgeon's tent. Among the dead were George's friend Bob Smith, who had served with him in the 13th New York State Militia, and a litany of others: "The Chaplain of our regt was killed. one Captain wounded (probably mortaly) our Leuit killed. one Leuit had a leg taken off and 2 other Leiuts was shot through the Leg. we had 3 orderly Sergts killed and 16 or 18 privates."[24]

But it was not until he revisited the battlefield the next day that George understood what had nearly happened. The Confederates had erected excellent and extensive breastworks with a deep water-filled trench running between them and the position Union troops had chosen for their advance. Had the rebel troops not abandoned their entrenchments, the Union soldiers would have faced near-certain slaughter. His vision now cleared of cannon smoke and the haze of adrenaline, George stood exactly where his regiment had fought the day before. The trees were riddled with Minie balls or shorn off into stumps. The way ahead of their advance, he told his mother, "was almost impassable." He stood there and watched as the last of his dead comrades were collected for burial. He confessed, "When I saw the almost impregnability of the enemys position I was almost scared."

. . .

When the young writer John Burroughs called at the offices of the *New York Leader* hoping for information about Walt Whitman, he found Henry Clapp minding the office, seeing the articles into type, but everyone else gone for the day, already drinking and eating.[25] "Walt Whitman is at Pfaff's almost every night," Burroughs wrote his friend Myron B. Benton. "He lives in Brooklyn, is unmarried, and 'manages,' Clapp says, to earn 6 or 7 dollars per week writing for the papers. He wrote a number of articles for the 'Leader' some time ago, on the Hospitals. Do you remember them? I do not like to believe that he can write in any other style than that of 'Leaves of Grass.' "[26] Whitman, it would appear, didn't like anyone to believe that either.

Nevertheless he left clues for those who knew him then—and scholars in the future—to follow his trail, away from the desecrated graveyards of Brooklyn in winter, toward a springtime spent memorializing those soldiers who still lived in the warehouses of the wounded in the hospitals of New York. None but the closest of Whitman's friends knew the six articles in the *Leader* were his because they appeared under the name "Velsor Brush," a pseudonym constructed from his mother's maiden name, Van Velsor, and the maiden name of his paternal grandmother, Hannah Brush.

Whitman chose a name that stretched into his family's past to tell this new story of familiar-faced strangers. In his description of his first impression of the hospital it is as though visions of the Brooklyn graveyards still haunt his mind: "Along each side of this apartment are ranged the beds, single iron cots, with their heads to the wall, and an ample space down the middle of the room between the two rows. . . . On the wall at the head of every occupied bed hangs a little card-rack, upon which is inscribed the name of the patient."[27] Whitman read those cards with the same portentous feelings he had ascribed to headstones of the long departed, evoking the same gulf of anonymity that came from knowing little more than a person's name and vital statistics. "What a volume of meaning, what a tragic poem there is in every one of those sick wards!" he wrote. "Yes, in every individual cot, with its little card-rack nailed at the head."[28]

But he returned to the hospital time and again in the following weeks—more than twenty times by the end of March—and slowly he came to know the worst cases, especially among the sick and wounded soldiers sent there from the battlefronts and training camps. He discovered that these soldiers were often young men in their late teens or early twenties, many far from rural homes in the Northeast and away from their families for the first time. They needed medical attention, but what they craved most were smaller comforts: a newspaper or book to pass the hours, a favorite fruit or candy, a few minutes of conversation.

Whitman noticed how responsive the soldiers grew in the presence of the ward's two most matronly nurses: Mrs. Jackson, a Swede who had worked in the hospital for thirty years, and an African American woman nicknamed Aunty Robinson, who had been there for twenty years and was singled out by Whitman as the one he "should want to be nursed by" if he ever found himself in the hospital. He watched, too, an anonymous aristocratic woman, whom he dubbed the "Benevolent Lady among the Soldiers." She came frequently to the hospital to distribute gifts and sweets to the soldiers; the gestures were always small, but, he noted, "Often and often have the soldiers mentioned her, and shown me something she has given them."[29]

In time, Whitman found that he went to the hospital "just to help confinement—and indeed, just as much, too, for the melancholy entertainment and friendly interest and sympathy, I found aroused in myself toward and among the men."[30]

One Sunday night Whitman passed an entire evening, which he described as "one of the most agreeable . . . of [his] life," among seven young soldiers from the 13th Maine. Each was well enough to return to duty and soon to depart for Ship Island, Mississippi. He marveled at their

warmth and innocent eagerness to rejoin their comrades. This last evening to be shared with their frequent visitor was almost as intimate as a
family gathering: "We drew around together, on our chairs, in the dimly-
lighted room, and after interchanging the few magnetic remarks that
show people it is well for them to be together, they told me stories of
country life and adventures, &c., away up there in the Northeast. They
were to leave the next day in a vessel for the Gulf, where their regiment
was; and they felt so happy at the prospect. I shook hands with them all
round at parting, and I know we all felt as if it were the separation of old
friends."[31] Thus, as Whitman came to know these soldiers, he saw them
less and less as silent and anonymous ciphers and more as individual
young men with families and stories of their own.

In some ways, however, this familiarity seemed only to heighten Whitman's sense of the hospital as a kind of living cemetery. In one of his articles
for the *Leader* he wrote, "After I have passed through them of late, especially
in the South Building, which is now filled with soldiers, I have many hours
afterwards, in far different scenes, had the pale faces, the look of death, the
appealing eyes, come curiously of a sudden, plainly before me. The worser
cases lying quite helpless in their cots—others, just able to get up, sitting
weak and dispirited in their chairs—I have seen them thus, even through all
the gayety of the street or the jovial supper party."[32] Not only did these men
literally wear "the look of death," but their visages haunted Whitman's
thoughts far from the hospital wards, coming to him like apparitions.

One night in late March at Pfaff's, Whitman had an anonymous encounter
of another kind. Someone identifying herself by the pseudonym "Ellen
Eyre" inscribed an address at which she could be reached via mail—"Mrs.
Ellen Eyre, station 'D,' New York"—and under it Whitman entered "765
Broadway 3d story front room," the address on Broadway near 9th Street,
just one block from Pfaff's, at which "Mrs. Eyre" was living.[33] The follow-
ing night Whitman received a hand-delivered letter addressed to "Mr.
Walt Whitman /At Pfaffs Restaurant / BroadWay / New York":

Tuesday March 25th 1862

My dear Mr. Whitman

I fear you took me last night for a female privateer—It is true that I
was under *false colors*—but this flag I assure you covered nothing pi-
ratical although I would joyfully have made your heart a captive,
Women have an unequal chance in this world—Men are its monarch
and, "full many a rose is born to blush unseen, And waste its sweet-
ness in the desert air."

Such I was resolved should not be the fate of this of the fancy I
had long nourished for you—A gold mine may be found by a Divin-
ing Rod but there is no such instrument for detecting in the crowded
Streets of a great City the unknown Mine of latent affection a man
may have unconsciously inspired in a woman's breast.

I make these explanations in extenuation not by way of apology—
My social position enjoins precaution & mystery, and perhaps the
enjoyment of any friends society is heightened while in yielding to its
fascination I preserve my incognito, yet mystery lends an ineffable
charm to love and when a woman is bent upon the gratification of
her inclinations—She is pardonable if she still spreads the veil of
decorum over her actions—Hypocrisy is said to be "the homage that
Sin pays to virtue," and yet *I* can see no vice in that generous sympathy with which we share our caprices with those who have inspired
us with tenderness.—

I trust you will think well enough of me soon to renew the pleasure you afforded me last P.M. and I therefore write to remind you
that there is a sensible head as well as a sympathetic heart, both
of which would gladly evolve wit & warmth for your direction &
comfort—You have already my whereabouts & my home [hours?]—
It shall only depend upon you to make them yours and me the happi-
est of women.

> I am always
> Yours Sincerely
> *Ellen Eyre.*[34]

What Whitman did with this letter, what further contact he may have
had with "Ellen Eyre" is unknown, and for more than a century the true

identity of the woman who called herself Ellen Eyre likewise remained a mystery. But the solution, revealed here for the first time, presents as many new questions as it answers.

Some time in early 1862 a con man named William Kinney rented an office on Broadway between Eighth and Ninth, then a prominent medical district, under the false name Dr. B. Coffin.[35] He had presented his landlord with prominent references, including Samuel Ward Jr., son-in-law to William B. Astor, and was granted a lease without further investigation. He appears to have begun seeing patients during the daytime hours; at night, however, he began running another, even more complicated scam.

Posing as a woman and calling himself Mrs. Ellen Eyre, he would send letters to the prominent men of New York—doctors, judges, attorneys. The men would agree to meet this mystery woman at the time and place appointed by her in the letter. What exactly transpired thereafter is veiled in niceties of the period, but the letters from several suitors, published later in the *Sunday Mercury*, are highly suggestive. One invited Eyre for some "twilight entertainment," another thanked her for "your 'loving kindness' at our last meeting." One man, offended at being asked for money, wrote that he never considered "our tender relations in the light of a financial operation."

It appears, however, that at least some of the men were never aware that "Ellen Eyre" was actually a man. When Kinney was arrested in March on charges of extorting money by blackmail, he was "dressed in female apparel" and released by Inspector Dilks "under promise of doing so no more, and leaving the impression that it was indeed a woman."[36]

Only later did police discover the full extent of the con, when in June an unidentified man received the following letter:

> Monday, June 9—P.M.
> My Dear Sir—Having a communication to make to you, which may prove agreeable, I take the liberty of requesting that you meet me this evening, between half-past nine and ten o'clock, on the south

side of West Ninth street, between Nos. 120 and 130. You will doubtless be surprised to receive this communication from me, whose identity you will be at a loss to conceive; but when I see you I will explain all. Should any prior engagement prevent your meeting me as proposed, and you intimate the same in a line addressed to Mrs. Ellen Eyre, station D, New York Post Office, indicating the evening, after eight o'clock, that will be convenient for you to meet me, I shall be too happy to respond. Meanwhile, believe me, very sincerely yours,

Ellen Eyre

Enclosed was a plain white card that read:

Mrs. Ellen Eyre, of No.—Ninth street, at the first door on the left as you enter from the street. The bell marked "office" is on the left of the front door. Can be found any P.M., from eight till ten o'clock, as above.

Rightly suspicious, the man contacted his attorney, who turned the case over to Detective William Wilson, who worked fraud cases for the New York Police Department. Wilson and the attorney composed a "decoy letter":

Wednesday—A.M.

The gentleman whom Mrs. E. did the honor to address a note on Monday last, appointing a meeting for that evening, was unable to attend. He is never at leisure in the evening, but will be happy to meet Mrs. E. at Brady's Gallery, corner of Broadway and Tenth street, on Thursday at three o'clock.

Wilson then waited outside the post office at Station D near Astor Place. Between five and six o'clock a black footman entered the post office and presented a note to the postmaster: "Please deliver to the bearer my letters, and oblige. Ellen Eyre." Detective Wilson followed the man back to the house on Ninth Street and entered to find "Dr. Coffin" inside. In their search of the apartment police found a carpetbag of love letters from duped men and thousands of dollars' worth of women's clothing. At last they understood that the deception was carried forward in person, some sexual favors were performed, and afterward, "under threats of exposure of improper intimacy," the men would pay—anywhere from ten dollars to three hundred dollars—"in order to hush the affair."[37]

With this new knowledge that "Ellen Eyre" was, in fact, a young man dressed as a woman who attempted to lure Whitman to his nearby apartment, the opening of the letter to Whitman must be read in an entirely new light. In particular, "female privateer," a slang term for a prostitute, takes on a different weight. In "I fear you took me last night for a female privateer" the emphasis now seems to be on "female" rather than "privateer." The letter continues, "It is true that I was under *false colors*," which was then both a general term for a deception and slang for cross-dressing, and it seems that Whitman questioned "Eyre" about his "incognito."

Is "Ellen Eyre" attempting to elicit an admission from Whitman that he saw through the disguise, or is the young con man intent on extending his deception? If the latter, how complete could the deception have been? If Whitman clearly recognized his attire as a disguise, did he also recognize that "Ellen Eyre" was attempting to disguise not just his identity but his gender? Was Whitman's interest, in other words, in the young woman "Ellen Eyre" or the young man who arrived at Pfaff's under the shadowy light of the cellar's torches in the garb of a woman?

Our only clue comes in a notebook entry several weeks after Eyre's arrest. In a list of young men he had met recently, Whitman records "Frank Sweezey, (July 8th, '62.) 5th av. brown face, large features, black moustache (is the one I told the whole story to, about Ellen Eyre)—talks very little."[38] As Jonathan Ned Katz observed—before Eyre's real identity was known—"The 'whole story' of Eyre, recounted by the talkative Whitman, created a shared intimacy between himself and Sweezey. . . . Sharing the 'whole' Eyre story *only* with Sweezey, apparently, Whitman made this passing stranger a confidant."[39]

But perhaps Sweezey was more than a passing stranger. The notation "is the one I told the whole story to" suggests that the conversation about Eyre had occurred on an earlier occasion. Sweezey is also one of dozens of men who Whitman met on the omnibus riding down Fourth Avenue and back up on Fifth. Earlier in May, on this same omnibus, he recorded speaking to the "somewhat feminine" Daniel Spencer, then returned to the entry in September to add the annotation "slept with me."[40] In the same notebook he lists brief descriptions of more than a hundred young men—only men—another three of whom he notes "slept with me."

Might the Ellen Eyre incident have served as an unlocking of Whitman's repressed sexuality? Or was the anecdote of the incident a way to test the reactions of potential partners, as he apparently did with Frank Sweezey?

In mid-July, a free verse poem, "Wounded," appeared in the new issue of *Continental Monthly*.[41] The narrative focused on two "comrades in arms" who were injured together in battle and taken to their "hospital-home" in an unnamed northern city. Now, convalescing, the two men have ventured out together:

> Up the quiet street in the early Sunday morning, came with slow
>   steps and silently, two wounded soldiers:
> One with shattered arm and a cruel sabre-cut on his forehead;
> One with amputated leg, hobbled slowly along on crutches.

With its long lines, irregular rhythms, and eccentric punctuation, the poem roughly approximated Whitman's stylistic hallmarks. For those closest to Whitman who knew about the *New York Leader* articles, the lines about the "Lady in Gray" must have seemed to echo Whitman's description of the "Benevolent Lady among the Soldiers":

> At home in a hospital kindly nursed and tended, hearing for the first
>   time the name of God—not taken in vain: seeing the good
>   DEEDS of true woman . . .
> Knowing that should he die, he would ask no gentler sounds to cheer
>   him on his road to the Hereafter, than the prayer he once heard
>   read by the Lady in Gray to a dying soldier in the same
>   hospital: . . . thus pass he again back to life.

Seeing the lines in the pages of the *Continental Monthly,* James Del Vec-chio, Whitman's friend and the editor of the *Brooklyn Standard*, repub-lished the poem on July 16, adding under the title "By Walt Whitman." Two weeks later, on July 31, the Oneida *Circular,* either trusting the *Stan-dard* or drawing the same conclusion (the *Circular* exchanged subscrip-tions with both publications), also published the poem with an attribu-tion to Whitman and added an editorial introduction that read simply: "The following picture is well drawn."[42] Thus "Wounded" became the most circulated work by Walt Whitman to appear in 1862; indeed, it was the only poem published under his name that year. But Whitman wasn't the poem's author.

In fact, the poem was the work of a longtime Whitman admirer, Henry P. Leland. Two years earlier, in June 1860, Leland had sent Whit-man an impassioned defense of *Leaves of Grass* when it was under fire for indecency and a poem in the Whitmanic mode titled "Enfans de Soixante-Seize," both of which had originally appeared in the Philadel-phia *City Item.*

"Enfans de Soixante-Seize" seems designed to show the extent to which Leland had assimilated Whitman's style:

> I hear the sharp crack of a pistol!
> Pitcairn at the head of the red coats shouts fiercely
> Rebels, disperse! Throw down your arms and disperse
> Then comes the rolling of musketry . . . dead in their tracks fall
> Four of my countrymen . . . This was at Lexington
> Martyrs for Liberty . . . pallid in death, with the holes letting souls
>   out, drilled by blue lead
> From your cold, pale, and inanimate corpses rose with fierce wrath
>   to a new life, long slumbering Liberty.[43]

Though it is at best an approximation of Whitman, it flattered the poet's wounded ego to see a young writer emulating his poetic experiments, but he did not maintain correspondence with Leland beyond this brief period.

Leland's brother, Charles, took over as editor of the fledgling humor weekly *Vanity Fair* at the end of July 1860. In less than a year as editor he would publish at least a dozen references to Whitman.[44] Charles Leland's short run at the magazine ended when he was fired for publishing an outspoken antislavery screed titled "Good—for Good" in the April 27, 1861, issue. But his fiery editorial attracted the attention of J. R. Gilmore, the new owner of the *Knickerbocker*, who offered Leland the editorship.

Leland began publishing a series of vehement editorials in the *Knickerbocker* denouncing the South and calling for an end to slavery. After the disaster at Bull Run he took a slightly different tack in the pair of articles that led the October and November issues.[45] The first renewed his call for the emancipation of the slaves but avoided arguing on moral grounds, instead insisting that victory over the South would never be total until the point of contention was eradicated. In the second, he contended that emancipation would produce a massive new population of soldiers at the same time that it drained away the workforce of the Confederacy: "Within two days' foot-travel of Mason and Dixon's Line are nearly one million blacks!"[46] The idea excited enough interest that Gilmore told Leland he wanted to start a new magazine devoted to emancipation in the heart of northern abolitionism: Boston.

Just before Christmas 1861, the first issue appeared. Unlike the *Knickerbocker*, the contributions to the *Continental Monthly* were all anonymous, though Leland was named as editor and his "Editor's Table" column never failed to mention emancipation. His contributors, however, were not yet so willing to attach their names to the cause of ending slavery; for many, their political positions required anonymity. In his *Memoirs* Leland revealed that Secretary of State William Henry Seward "contributed to it two anonymous articles," and another contributor, whose identity he did not disclose, had appeared twice in the magazine "*by official request, to me directed.*"[47]

Henry P. Leland was also a frequent contributor to the *Continental Monthly*, but of poetry and criticism. His passion for emancipation had convinced him to enter officer training for the Union Army in Philadelphia. He graduated as a first lieutenant but was never officially commissioned due to ill health. In 1862 he attempted again to enlist, this time as a sergeant, and was invalided once more. He spent his convalescence in army hospitals where the sick and wounded from the battlefront were beginning to crowd the corridors. Perhaps Henry had surmised Whitman's identity as "Velsor Brush" or had been informed by one of his friends at Pfaff's and had written "Wounded" as a tribute.

. . .

Letters to Mother Whitman from George arrived regularly throughout April and May as the 51st lay in camp near Newburn, North Carolina. The men pitched their tents along the Trent River, so they had fresh water and cooling breezes. Despite a serious bout of heat rash, George insisted, "I am hearty as ever and take things prety easy, and [am] comfortable this hot weather."[48] Most days were passed drilling and reading the papers for news from the front. When one of his mother's letters expressed discouragement "with the way the war is progresing," George replied that he had been reading the same papers and didn't find there "any thing very discouraging."[49]

The relative calm of the Whitman household was disrupted when Lincoln issued a call for additional short-term soldiers to defend Washington. Walt's brother Andrew, nicknamed "Bunkum," enlisted with George's old unit, the 13th New York State Militia, and just three days later on May 31 the regiment left for Fort McHenry in Baltimore.[50] George responded to Andrew's enlistment with brotherly ribbing. "So Bunkum has gone Sogering too has he," George asked. "Well they will have good times in Baltimore."[51] But Andrew was at Fort McHenry for only a few days when the regiment was ordered to Fort Monroe, opposite Norfolk, Virginia, where they were officially mustered into service for a term of three months.

The conditions were miserable. One soldier in the 13th described the camp near Suffolk as "the meanest God-forsaken place you ever saw" and wrote to his father to complain of the stifling heat near the Dismal Swamp and "the lumps caused by the pigeon-sized mosquitos."[52] As the weeks wore on George grew worried that he hadn't heard from his brother. "Has

Andrew written to you since he went Sogering," he asked his mother. "Poor Bunkum I wonder how he is getting along, what Co is he in I wish he would write to me."[53] In July George's unit was relocated to Camp Lincoln near Newport News, Virginia, opposite Norfolk and not more than twenty-five miles from Andrew in Camp Crooke. "I think after we get paid I shall try to go down to see Bunkum," George told his mother and proposed a reunion of brothers. "If Jeff aint too busy he might take a run down here it would not cost much for him or Walt to get on board one of the transports that come to Fortress Monroe from New York and there is a boat that runs from the Fort here."[54]

The gathering of brothers never materialized, and increasingly even written communication via the overtaxed military mail delivery was growing difficult. For many families and soldiers alike, the most reliable way of keeping track of loved ones was through the newspapers. In Newport News George could get any of the New York papers "the next day after they are printed so that we keep pretty well posted."[55] But the news from Camp Crooke, where Andrew remained ominously silent, was often dispiriting, and the *Eagle* continued to give space to whatever bad news came to hand. Illness was reportedly rampant; then, in early August, the hospital steward of the 13th Regiment died from unknown causes. An anonymous member of Andrew's unit wrote, "As the body entered our lines, the coffin draped in the dear old Flag, every head was uncovered, and a death-like stillness prevailed. The solemn funeral service was performed, the body lowered to its resting place, three volleys fired over the open grave, the last sad offices finished, and we all returned silently to our tents. How solemn the burial of our young soldier, so far from home and friends! Who can measure the solemnity of the tens—yes, hundreds of thousands of such burials that have been performed."[56]

Everyone in the Whitman family must have been relieved to learn that the 13th would be back in Brooklyn on September 12 to be mustered out of service. But death followed the regiment home. Their final obligation was escorting the remains of one of their comrades who had died of typhoid on the transport. They marched his coffin to Greenwood

Cemetery amid the solemn rolls of the snare drums, and his "body was consigned to the grave with military honors."[57]

During the long summer of 1862 the relentless stream of such news took its toll on New Yorkers. The wild enthusiasm for daily newspapers had cooled into a fatigued passivity. *Vanity Fair* noted, "Placidity . . . [is] displayed now daily by the Northern Mind when the 'barbaric yawp' of the newsboy announces another episode of the War. Men don't leap from their downy couches at midnight, now, and stoop wildly from their windows, like white specters, grasping ravenously at the half *Herald* upward hurled at them by the vociferous distributor."[58] Readers grew eager for diversions and escapism.

In September and October Whitman returned to the "Brooklyniana" series, publishing four articles in the *Brooklyn Weekly Standard* about a vacation excursion to Greenport, Long Island. The pieces described frolicking in the waves, declaiming Shakespeare, boiling pots of crabs, and generally enjoying carefree days on the beach. At the end Whitman thanks his "lucky star" for this chance "merely to sail—to bend over and look at the ripples as the prow divided the water—to lie on my back and *to breathe and live* in that sweet air and clear sunlight—to hear the musical chatter of the girls, as they pursued their own glee—was happiness enough for one day." These articles have led many critics to disparage Whitman for remaining "strangely abstracted" during the fall of 1862.[59] In fact, as Jerome Loving has shown, the last four parts of "Brooklyniana" were constructed almost entirely from his series "Letters from a Travelling Bachelor," originally published in the *Sunday Dispatch* in 1849 and 1850.[60]

As summer gave way to fall in Brooklyn, Whitman's feelings about the war were anything but abstracted. The papers were reporting that a great fight had occurred near the old Bull Run battleground and that the 51st New York had saved "a battery from falling into the hands of the enemy, thus maintaining the reputation whose groundwork was laid at Roanoke, and worked out in permanent colors at Newbern," but the *New York Times* also cautioned that in "both fights in which it was engaged," on August 29 and 30, "the Fifty-first suffered severely."[61] Those ominous words, combined with George's uncharacteristic silence, spread deep worry throughout the Whitman family. On September 11 Walt's sister Hannah wrote from her home in Burlington, Vermont, to their mother, "Have you heard from George I have felt very anxious I have expected a letter every day from home I wish dear Mother you or Walt would write a line just as soon as you get this. I know George is safe but not hearing makes me feel anxious. he has always written immediately after any battle. I think perhaps he has written to you. he wrote me a very *kind good affectionate* letter about four weeks since, I thought very much of it."[62]

All evening and into the night of September 18 Whitman circled Manhattan on the omnibuses. Earlier that day word had begun to appear in the newspapers of an epic battle in Maryland, not far from Harpers Ferry, somewhere between Sharpsburg and Antietam Creek. On the heels of his victory at Second Bull Run, General Robert E. Lee had pressed north in hopes of winning a major battle on the Union side of the Mason-Dixon line. The report in the *New York Times*, though still sketchy, assured its readers that the Union lines had held—but at a heavy cost. The dead were said to number many thousands, and thousands more were wounded or captured. But the Confederate Army had been turned back in what the *Times* described as "the greatest battle of the war."[63]

That same day Whitman heard news of the death of William Giggie, a friend of his from Pfaff's. Bill had enlisted in the 1st New York Infantry within days of the firing on Fort Sumter. A month later his younger brother, Arthur, enlisted in the same regiment, and they mustered into Company E together. Bill was twenty-eight years old at the time, Arthur twenty-two. As Whitman learned, the brothers not only had been together at Second Bull Run, but Bill had died before Arthur's eyes. In a brief entry in his notebook Whitman wrote, "I heard of poor Bill's death—he was shot on Pope's retreat—Arthur took him in his arms, and he died in about an hour and a half—Arthur buried him himself."[64] How could Walt keep his mind from his own brother, who, after all, had also been at Bull Run and, even if he had survived, may well have fallen prey to the carnage of the day before at Antietam?

To make matters bleaker still, Walt heard that Elanson Fargo had been killed on Pope's retreat as well. Fargo, nicknamed "Erie" after his hometown in Pennsylvania, had enlisted in the 9th New York State Militia (subsequently redesignated the 83rd New York Infantry) in October 1861 and, along with the rest of the 83rd, had been with George's 51st Infantry since the Battle of Cedar Mountain in early August. To learn in a span of two days that two friends had been killed would have been hard enough, but these young men—these dear sons to Walt—were also in battle with George, from whom the family had had no word since Second Bull Run at the end of August. As he sat with his thoughts on the number 15 omnibus, Whitman ran into Erie's old friend Joseph Cornell. Perhaps he was on this car in hopes of seeing Cornell, or perhaps it was pure coincidence. Whitman records only that the two rode up and down Seventh Avenue reminiscing about their dead comrade. Lost in conversation, they crossed Brooklyn Ferry together and walked all the way from the landing to Amity Street, where they parted.[65]

Later, on a scrap of paper, Whitman penciled just two lines: "Battles, the horrors of fratricidal war, / The news of my friends mortally wounded." Then he struck the words "The news of" and wrote "the deaths of."[66] It was not the news that mattered—how the word of their death affected Whitman—but the deaths themselves, the result of this horrific fratricide.

Soon after, Walt's mother received a letter from George. Written shortly after Second Bull Run and the Battle of Chantilly, it attested to his well-being, but only as of September 5. There was still no way of knowing whether he had survived Antietam. In this period of doubt and piecemeal reports in the pages of the daily newspapers, Whitman received two shocking eyewitness accounts of the battle and the carnage that lay in its wake.

The first came to him from his old friend Fred Gray. Just before his departure for war, Gray had met Whitman at the Pisan Raffaele on Church Street for a farewell dinner and rounds of red wine. Gray was a favorite of Walt's and the namesake of what he dubbed the "Fred Gray

Association," a motley union of young men who gathered at Pfaff's with no loftier goal than pursuing a nightly bacchanal and the easy camaraderie it inspired. But now Gray at twenty-eight was finally growing up. As a well-educated son of a Manhattan doctor, he had been assigned as an aide-de-camp on the staff of Major General William Farrar Smith, copying orders, answering correspondence, serving with a pen rather than a rifle. Nevertheless, as he was headed for the seat of war there was cause for nostalgia. As a keepsake, Gray gave Whitman a beloved copy of Frederick H. Hedge's *Prose Writers of Germany*, which Gray had received from his father in 1856. He asked Whitman to keep the book and make an entry in it each time they were again together. When Whitman returned to the quiet of his room at the end of their night, he noted in the book: "F. S. Gray . . . requested me to keep this book. He goes in a few days on Gen. Smith's staff, down in the Army in Va."[67]

Just a few short months later, Gray was back in New York on a two-day furlough after having served at Antietam and received special mention by General Smith as one of the members of his staff who served "faithfully and gallantly through the battle."[68] He spent the evening with Whitman at Pfaff's, recounting the carnage he had seen. When he returned home that night Whitman took out *Prose Writers of Germany* and added a brief note about their evening together, concluding, "He gave me a fearful account of the battlefield at ½ past 9 the night following the engagement— He crossed it on duty."[69] The scene witnessed by Gray—and recounted to Whitman—must have been difficult to comprehend. Upwards of twenty thousand men had been left sprawled, dead or wounded, on the field that night, more than the ambulance trains could carry away. Some time after, Whitman drafted the short poem "Look down, fair moon":

> Look down, fair moon, and bathe this scene;
> Pour softly down night's nimbus floods, on faces ghastly, swollen,
>   purple;
> On the dead, on their backs, with their arms toss'd wide,
> Pour down your unstinted nimbus, sacred moon.[70]

The poem may also have been influenced by the grisly images of the battlefield photographed by one of Whitman's friends and displayed in the gallery of another.

The morning after the battle Alexander Gardner and his assistant, James F. Gibson, arrived on the field at Antietam. Gardner was a member of General George B. McClellan's staff, serving as something like the Civil War's official photographer, an idea hatched by Gardner's longtime friend and former employer, Mathew Brady. Because of his official capacity, Gardner had unfettered access to the battlefield and he went quickly to work, setting up his tripod, making his exposures, and developing his glass-plate negatives on the spot in his traveling darkroom. The images Gardner captured were not the first photographs of war; there were no charges, no cannon fire, no muskets or drawn sabers. What Gardner captured was the grim aftermath of battle, the undeniable reality of young men torn apart, pierced through, sprawled in open fields, huddled in wagon traces, their limp bodies dragged and stacked for mass burial.

When the photographs were unveiled a month later at Brady's walk-up gallery on Broadway in New York, announced only by a small placard inscribed "The Dead of Antietam," they touched off a controversy. What were the ethics of portraying scenes of such carnage? The *New York Times* reporter recoiled at what he saw: "[If Brady] has not brought bodies and laid them in our door-yards and along the streets, he has done something very like it." The camera lens—that cold, unblinking Cyclops—did not embellish the scene or soften the loss of a loved one with visions of false heroics. These portraits of the dead were "taken as they fell, their poor hands clutching the grass around in spasm of pain, or reaching out for a help which none gave." The reporter conceded, "[Such brutal imagery] has done something to bring home to us the terrible reality and earnestness of war," but the full lists of the dead from Antietam had not yet been released, and many next of kin were still awaiting letters, so he confessed he "would scarce choose to be in the gallery, when one of the women bending over [the photographs] should recognize a husband, a son, or a brother in the still, lifeless lines of bodies, that lie ready for the gaping trenches." He imagined especially how a mother, seeing "the boy whose slumbers she has cradled," would react to these scenes: "How can this mother bear to know that in a shallow trench, hastily dug, rude hands have thrown him. She would have handled the poor corpse so tenderly, have prized the boon of caring for it so dearly."[71]

Despite this unspeakable human toll and the new vividness Gardner brought home, President Lincoln recognized the significance of the Union victory at Antietam. In the most pitched battle of the war, the first southern effort at attack, federal troops had carried the day—and at all costs. The president seized on the opportunity to deliver the Emancipation Proclamation, declaring an end to slavery in all states still in open revolt on January 1, 1863. George Whitman puzzled over Lincoln's announcement. "I don't know what effect it is going to have on the war," he wrote Walt, "but one thing is certain, he has got to lick the south before he can free the niggers, and unless he drives ahead and convinces the south, before the first of January, that we are bound to lick them, and it would be better for them to behave themselves and keep their slaves, than to get licked and lose them. I don't think the proclamation will do much good."[72]

Though Walt's response is apparently lost, we may suppose his sentiment to be roughly equivalent to one expressed by a *New York Times* correspondent on the day after the Proclamation was issued. Gauging the reaction in Washington, the reporter was surprised to see "less excitement here than was anticipated," which he believed "may be regarded as an evidence that all other questions have become trifling beside the great cause of saving the Government."[73] Indeed, this seemed to be the reaction across the North, even in copperhead strongholds like New York. If the institution of slavery meant constant instability or, worse yet, a permanent fracture of the nation, then pro-slavery advocates had "gradually brought themselves to acquiesce in the growing necessity of its extinction." So although Lincoln's announcement was met with condemnation in the rebel states, in the North it provoked few demonstrations and no riots, merely a widespread, wary silence.

In early October Lincoln traveled to the Antietam battlefield to meet the officers who had led the victory there and to see the toll for himself. Formal events and affairs took up most of the day, but as the sun set Lincoln insisted on seeing the battle site. By the time McClellan led him onto the field the moon was high in the sky, as it had been that terrible night weeks earlier. A reporter from the *New York Herald* wrote:

> Hundreds of dead horses, many of which had been burned, were lying on the field. Hundreds of human graves, where the dead of both armies lay buried, were seen at different points on the ground. The field was still strewn with clothing of the wounded and the dead. In one place there was a monster grave, over which there was this inscription—"Here lies the body of General Anderson and eighty other rebels," and on another mound we could read by the early moonlight—"Here lie the bodies of sixty rebels. The wages of sin is death."[74]

On Tuesday, December 16, the *New York Herald* printed a list of soldiers from the 51st New York Infantry killed or wounded at Fredericksburg, including an entry for "First Lieutenant G. W. Whitmore, Company D." It was midmorning when Whitman saw the misspelled name and in a fevered hour informed his family and made arrangements to leave New York for Washington, DC, where the wounded were being transported. His mother hurried to the bank to withdraw fifty dollars from the savings she had been setting aside for George. Jeff secured from Moses Lane, his boss and the chief engineer at the Brooklyn Water Works, a letter of introduction to Captain Joseph J. Dana, assistant quartermaster of the Union Army, identifying Walt as "a particular friend" and requesting "any assistance you can render."[75] Walt went to City Hall, where he obtained a similar letter from Brooklyn mayor Martin Kalbfleisch to Moses Fowler Odell, the Democratic congressman from Brooklyn. In a hasty note Kalbfleisch explained, "[Whitman] visits Washington to see his brother Lieut Whitman of the 51st N.Y. who is wounded."[76]

Whitman took the ferry across the East River, crossed Manhattan Island, then boarded another ferry to Jersey City, where he could take the train to Philadelphia and transfer to the rail line to the capital. But in the "jam and hurry, changing cars, at Philadelphia," his pocket was picked; he arrived in Washington "without a dime."[77]

Whitman sought help from his former publisher Charles Eldridge, by then working in the office of the paymaster general. Eldridge later joked, "Any pickpocket who failed to avail himself of such an opportunity as Walt offered, with his loose baggy trousers, and no suspenders, would have been a disgrace to his profession."[78]

With Eldridge's help, Whitman spent the next day "hunting through the hospitals, walking all day and night, unable to ride, trying to get information, trying to get access to big people." He may have seen in the *New York Times*, as Jeff did back in Brooklyn, that George was now listed under his correct name with a wound to his "face." Jeff wrote immediately with this news to Walt, telling him, "We are trying to comfort ourselves with hope that it may not be a serious hurt."[79] Meanwhile Walt had concluded that George must still be in camp near Fredericksburg and began working bureaucratic channels to obtain a pass. Congressman Odell refused even to see him, but Colonel Dana referred him to Lieutenant Colonel W. E. Doster, provost marshal, with his endorsement for "a pass to Falmouth."[80] Doster, in turn, referred Whitman to General Samuel P. Heintzelman, who offered him passage on a government boat that ran Aquia Creek to a rail line that would connect him to Falmouth, across the Rappahannock from Fredericksburg.

It was Friday afternoon when he arrived and made his way to Ferrero's brigade. "When I found dear brother George, and found that he was alive and well," Walt wrote his mother, "O you may imagine how trifling all my little cares and difficulties seemed—they vanished into nothing."[81] George had sustained a deep gash from a shell fragment—"You could stick a splint through into the mouth," Walt wrote—but the wound had not been deemed serious enough for him to be confined to the hospital.

Walt sent the good news to Washington via messenger to be telegraphed home to Brooklyn.

Whitman spent the following days visiting the two makeshift hospitals set up in commandeered houses along the Rappahannock. The first was Conway House, the family home of Whitman's old acquaintance and supporter Moncure Conway. After the battle, Union troops "battered down the doors, and, finding no one, began vengeance on the furniture." But in the midst of the destruction one of the young soldiers from Washington recognized the portrait on the wall as his former minister. The black servants were ordered into the room to identify the person in the portrait. Conway himself recounted, "Old Eliza cried, 'It's mars' Monc the preacher, as good abolitionist as any of you!'" Thus, instead of destroying the house, the soldiers converted it into quarters for the wounded; its grand parlors and bedrooms, even the wide halls and grand foyer, were filled with beds.[82]

In the dooryard outside the Lacy House, the second hospital, where more severe cases were taken, Whitman witnessed a grisly scene: "Out doors, at the foot of a tree, within ten yards of the front of the house, I notice a heap of amputated feet, legs, arms, hands, &c., a full load for a one-horse cart. Several dead bodies lie near, each cover'd with its brown woolen blanket."[83] Whitman approached the three bodies lying on untended stretchers. In his notebook he wrote, "Three dead men lying, each with a blanket spread over him—I lift one up and look at the young man's face, calm and yellow. 'Tis strange." Then, almost as an afterthought, he added a parenthetical line directly addressing the young man: "I think this face of yours the face of my dead Christ." Nearly the entirety of the poem "A Sight in Camp in the Daybreak Grey and Dim" resided in that short entry:

> A sight in camp in the day-break grey and dim,
> As from my tent I emerge so early, sleepless,
> As slow I walk in the cool fresh air, the path near by the
> hospital-tent,

Three forms I see on stretchers lying, brought out there, untended
   lying,
Over each the blanket spread, ample brownish woolen blanket,
Grey and heavy blanket, folding, covering all.

Curious, I halt, and silent stand;
Then with light fingers I from the face of the nearest, the first, just
   lift the blanket:
Who are you, elderly man so gaunt and grim, with well-grey'd hair,
   and flesh all sunken about the eyes?
Who are you, my dear comrade?
Then to the second I step—And who are you, my child and darling?
Who are you, sweet boy, with cheeks yet blooming?

Then to the third—a face nor child, nor old, very calm, as of
   beautiful yellow-white ivory:
Young man, I think I know you—I think this face of yours is the face
   of the Christ himself;
Dead and divine, and brother of all, and here again he lies.[84]

Whitman later added poetic touches and tropes—the persistent grays of
the daybreak, the blanket, and the old man's hair, for example—but most
of the poem is only a more elaborate version of that notebook jotting.
The poet tells the young man, "I think I know you," a moment of insight
and unexpected kinship. When Whitman lifted the woolen blankets to
look into the faces of the dead, the fear of recognition was potent. But
what he sees is not the face of his own brother, but "the face of the Christ
himself; / Dead and divine, and brother of all."

Whitman was not only composing poetry on the spot, he was also
hastily composing a retrospective of the 51st New York, which he hoped
to publish in the *Eagle* as a counterbalance to the dire letters that ordi-
narily filled its columns. He had seen how vital the newspapers were to the
soldiers, both as a source of information and as a means of diversion. "At
dark a horseman will come galloping through the camp, with something
white thrown across the pommel of the saddle in front of him," he wrote
in his notebook, "and you will hear the cry, papers! papers! Then quite a

rush out of the tents, and the shinplasters fly around lively."[85] But he also knew that word of the health of young soldiers and accounts of their bravery could console their anxious families back home in Brooklyn.

On Sunday, December 28, 1862, Whitman broke camp at Falmouth and began his journey back north via the Aquia Creek Railroad. At the end of the rail line, as passengers transferred to a government steamer continuing north up the Potomac, he found a large number of wounded waiting at the landing. "I went around them," he wrote later. "Several wanted word sent home to parents, brothers, wives, &c., which I did for them, (by mail the next day from Washington.); On the boat I had my hands full." And for the first time, he saw for himself, as a soldier—beyond his ability to aid or comfort—died en route. By the time Whitman arrived in the capital in the evening, he felt he had found his own small place within the greater war. He was determined to stay in Washington to report, and he was equally committed to ministering to the soldiers in the hospitals.

Conclusion

> Breaking up a few weeks since, and for good, my New York
> stagnation—wandering since through camp and battle
> scenes—I fetch up here in harsh and superb light—wretchedly
> poor, excellent well, (my only torment, family matters)—
> realizing at last that it is necessary for me to fall for the time in
> the wise old way, to push my fortune, to be brazen, and get
> employment, and have an income—determined to do it, (at any
> rate until I get out of horrible sloughs).
>
> Whitman to Emerson, December 29, 1862

With his arrival in Washington, Whitman reemerges into the light of existing scholarship. The next three years of his life are well-documented in his own prose and poetry and in numerous biographies and critical analyses. The war-time Whitman, as we have known him, commences from this point and proceeds uninterrupted to the end of the war. However, if this retrospective of his years from 1860 to 1862 has been successful, we now will see Whitman in a new light and gain a new understanding of the networks he built and relied on in Washington.

He stayed in a spare bedroom afforded him by fellow Thayer & Eldridge author William D. O'Connor. He found employment with the help of Eldridge himself. Back in New York John Swinton published the

majority of Whitman's prose about Washington's military hospitals in
the *New York Times*. Moncure Conway and Franklin B. Sanborn would
raise money for Whitman's hospital efforts in the pages of their Boston
weekly, *The Commonwealth*. After having sought and missed Whitman at
Pfaff's in late 1862, John Burroughs finally found him on the streets of
Washington and eventually became his first biographer. In 1863 James
Redpath would form a publishing concern in the mold of Thayer & Eldridge and, before folding, would discuss publishing Whitman's hospital diary. After the close of the war Henry Clapp managed to restart the
Saturday Press and published Whitman's elegy for Lincoln, "O Captain!
My Captain!" In that same week, William Dean Howells, now home
from Vienna, would write the first negative review of Whitman's war
poems.

Even the very shape of *Drum-Taps* was determined by the early Civil
War. Had Thayer & Eldridge not collapsed, Whitman would have published many of the *Drum-Taps* poems in *The Banner At Day-Break*. Had
he owned the plates of the 1860 edition, he would likely have typeset the
poems of *Drum-Taps* to match those in *Leaves of Grass*, instead of the
other way around, as he did in preparing the 1867 edition.

In short, the years 1860–1862, no longer lost to us, can now be seen
as the foundation for all that followed and in themselves prove as critical
to Whitman's transformation as they were to the transformation of the
country. Moreover, we must judge Whitman's productions of this period,
even his silences, not as refusals to engage the war but as profound productions of the volcanic upheaval of the nation and a vital record of those
quicksand years.

ABBREVIATIONS

Corr.   *Walt Whitman: The Correspondence*, vols. 1–6, edited by Edwin Havi-land Miller (New York: New York University Press, 1961–1977).

Corr.   *Walt Whitman: The Correspondence*, vol. 7, edited by Ted Genoways (Iowa City: University of Iowa Press, 2004).

CRE   Walt Whitman, *Leaves of Grass: Comprehensive Reader's Edition*, edited by Sculley Bradley and Harold W. Blodgett (New York: New York University Press, 1965).

CWL   Jerome M. Loving, ed., *Civil War Letters of George Washington Whitman* (Durham, NC: Duke University Press, 1975).

DT   Walt Whitman, *Drum-Taps* (New York: Self-published, 1865).

LG 1856   Walt Whitman, *Leaves of Grass* (Brooklyn, NY: Self-published, 1856).

LG 1860   Walt Whitman, *Leaves of Grass* (Boston: Thayer & Eldridge, 1860).

NUPM   Walt Whitman, *Notebooks and Unpublished Prose Manuscripts*, edited by Edward F. Grier (New York: New York University Press, 1984).

PW   Walt Whitman, *Prose Works 1892*, vols. 1 and 2, edited by Floyd Stovall (New York: New York University Press, 1984).

UPP   *The Uncollected Poetry and Prose of Walt Whitman: Much of Which Has Been but Recently Discovered with Various Early Manuscripts Now First Published*, vol. 2, edited by Emory Holloway (1921; reprinted Gloucester, MA: Peter Smith, 1972).

WWWC   Horace Traubel, *With Walt Whitman in Camden*, 9 vols. (1906; New York: Rowman and Littlefield, 1961).

NOTES

INTRODUCTION

1. Whitman, *Prose Works 1892*, 115. Hereafter *PW.*

2. *PW,* 116.

3. *PW,* 116.

4. *PW,* 116–17.

5. Traubel, *With Walt Whitman in Camden*, 1:157. Hereafter *WWWC.*

6. *PW,* 30–31; 30n–31n.

7. *PW,* 54.

8. Whitman, *Notebooks and Unpublished Prose Manuscripts*, 764. Hereafter *NUPM.*

9. Wilson, *Patriotic Gore*, ix.

10. Wilson, *Patriotic Gore*, ix.

11. Wilson, *Patriotic Gore*, x.

12. Aaron, *Unwritten War*, xix.

13. Aaron, *Unwritten War*, xvii–xviii.

14. O'Brien, *The Things They Carried*, 78.

15. Aaron, *Unwritten War*, xvii.

16. See, for example, James M. Perry's study of battlefield reporting and the politics of newspapers' editorial stances, *A Bohemian Brigade: The Civil War Correspondents, Mostly Rough, Sometimes Read* (New York: Wiley, 2000); Joshua Brown's *Beyond the Lines: Pictorial Reporting, Everyday Life, and the Crisis of Gilded-Age America* (Berkeley: University of California Press, 2002), an examination of

pictorial reporting as represented by *Frank Leslie's Illustrated*; and Brayton Harris's overview of technological advances and competition in reporting, *Blue & Gray in Black & White*.

17. Alice Fahs, *The Imagined Civil War: Popular Literature of the North and South, 1861–1865* (Chapel Hill: University of North Carolina Press, 2000), 3–4.

18. *WWWC*, 4:452.

19. Greenspan, *Walt Whitman and the American Reader*, 184–85.

20. See Loving, *Walt Whitman*, 227–32.

21. Loving, *Walt Whitman*, 3.

22. Folsom and Price, *Re-Scripting Walt Whitman*, 77.

23. Morris, *Better Angel*, 45, 46.

24. Killingsworth, *Cambridge Introduction*, 8.

25. Garner, *Civil War World*, 2.

1. THE RED-HOT FELLOWS OF THOSE TIMES

1. "The Remains of John Brown," *Chicago Press and Tribune*, December 8, 1859, 3; "News of the Day," *New York Times*, December 5, 1859, 4; "Abolition on and off the Stage," *New York Herald*, December 5, 1859, 1.

2. See "John Brown," *New York Times*, December 5, 1859, 8. For an eyewitness description of the mob and viewing of Brown's body by Louisa Williamson, see Reynolds, *John Brown*, 399.

3. These and other details of Hinton's life, unless otherwise noted, derive from Hollis, "R.J. Hinton."

4. Redpath, *Roving Editor*, iv.

5. Redpath, *Public Life*, 8.

6. This same description, written by Hinton, appears in "John Brown," *New York Times*, December 5, 1859, 8, and "The Remains of John Brown," *Chicago Press and Tribune*, December 8, 1859, 3.

7. On September 26, 1894, Hinton wrote William Sloane Kennedy detailing his role in recommending the book: "The Thayer and Eldridge edition was made through me." Kennedy, *Fight of a Book*, 242.

8. "Review of Mr. Yancy's Speech," *The Liberator*, October 26, 1860, 172.

9. McPherson, *Battle Cry*, 200–201; "By Telegraph," *Chicago Press and Tribune*, December 6, 1859, 1.

10. "Redpath's Life of John Brown," *The Liberator*, December 23, 1859, 202; advertisement in *National Era*, January 5, 1860, 3.

11. Advertisement in *The Liberator,* January 20, 1860, 11.

12. "Life of Capt. John Brown," *The Liberator,* January 20, 1860, 11.

13. "Mr. Giddings and Howe before the Inquisitorial Committee," *The Liberator,* February 10, 1860, 23; "The Quickest Path out of the Country," *Vanity Fair,* February 18, 1860, 119.

14. Quoted in Loving, "Broadway."

15. Winter, *Old Friends,* 65.

16. This advertisement ran constantly in the early issues of *Vanity Fair.* See, for example, *Vanity Fair,* January 14, 1860, 47.

17. "Death of Charles I. Pfaff," *New York Times,* April 26, 1890, 2.

18. Winter, *Old Friends,* 63.

19. This statement ran regularly in Clapp's own advertisements for the *Saturday Press.* See, for example, *Vanity Fair,* January 14, 1860, 47.

20. Winter, *Old Friends,* 58.

21. "Editor's Drawer," *Harper's New Monthly Magazine,* July 1868, 283.

22. This line was later quoted by (and often mistakenly attributed to) Mark Twain. See Mark Twain, "Harry Hill's," *San Francisco Alta California,* August 18, 1867. Twain describes one of his fellow passengers on a train as "a solemn, unsmiling, sanctimonious old iceberg that looked like he was waiting for a vacancy in the Trinity, as Henry Clapp said of Rev. Dr. Osgood."

23. Jay Charlton [pseudonym for Jay C. Goldsmith], "Bohemians in America," 162; Parry, *Garrets,* 44.

24. Winter, *Old Friends,* 140.

25. "At the Café," *Vanity Fair,* December 31, 1859, 12.

26. *Vanity Fair,* January 14, 1860, 47.

27. Whitman placed ads in the *New York Times, New York Evening Post, New York Tribune, Brooklyn Eagle, Brooklyn City News,* and *Brooklyn Daily Times.* See manuscripts in the Oscar Lion Collection.

28. Walt Whitman, "A Ballad of Long Island," *Brooklyn City News,* December 24, 1860, reprinted in *Leaves of Grass Imprints,* 60–61.

29. "Walt Whitman's Poem," *Saturday Press,* December 24, 1860, 2. The manuscript, in Whitman's hand, is held at the New York Pubic Library.

30. "Walt Whitman's New Poem," *Cincinnati Daily Commercial,* December 28, 1859, 2.

31. "Walt Whitman's New Poem," *Cincinnati Daily Commercial,* December 28, 1859, 2.

32. "All about a Mocking-Bird," *Saturday Press,* January 7, 1860, 3.

33. "Waifs from Washington.—VI," *Saturday Press*, January 14, 1860, 2. The original reads "*musical* skates," but in the next week's issue the author complained that his spelling had been altered by the copy editor.

34. "Waifs from Washington.—VI," *Saturday Press*, January 14, 1860, 2.

35. In the version of "You and Me and To-Day" in the *Saturday Press*, the seventh section begins differently from the version published in the 1860 *Leaves of Grass:*

> I know that the past was great, and the future will be great,
> And I know that both curiously conjoint in the present time, in myself and
>   yourself

whereas the version published in the 1860 edition reads:

> I know that the past was great, and the future will be great,
> And I know that both curiously conjoint in the present time,
> (For the sake of him I typify—for the common average man's sake—your
>   sake, if you are he;).

The poems titled "Poemet" later appeared as "Calamus No. 17" and "Calamus No. 40," and the three sections of "Leaves" later appeared as "Calamus No. 21," "Calamus No. 37," and "Enfans d'Adam No. 15," all in the 1860 edition of *Leaves of Grass*.

36. Clark, " 'Saerasmid' "; see Winter, *Old Friends*, 88.

37. Freedman, *William Douglas O'Connor*, 96–97.

38. Feinberg Collection. Complete text in Allen, *Solitary Singer*, 236–37.

39. Higginson, *Cheerful Yesterdays*, 232.

40. William Wilde Thayer, "Autobiography of William Wilde Thayer," p. 21, unpublished manuscript, dated November 1, 1892, Feinberg Collection.

41. See Hinton, *John Brown*, 520; Thayer, "Autobiography," 19.

42. Thayer, "Autobiography," 20.

43. "Execution of Stevens and Hazlett," *The Liberator*, March 23, 1860, 46.

44. Quoted in Cady, *Young Howells*, 52.

45. Quoted in "Stephens [*sic*] and Hazlett Sympathy Meeting," *Portsmouth* (OH) *Times*, April 7, 1860, 1.

46. "Another Brown Raid—The South Forewarned," *Pittsburgh Dispatch*, quoted in *Portsmouth* (OH) *Times*, April 7, 1860, 1.

47. Exact release dates are always difficult to pinpoint, but Fred Vaughan records having seen the April issue of the *Atlantic* in New York by March 19, and the *Chicago Press and Tribune* reviewed the new issue on March 22 ("The Professor on Parties," 3).

48. "New Publications," *New York Times*, April 24, 1860, 3.

49. "The April Magazines," *Saturday Press*, April 24, 1860, 2.

50. "Bardic Symbols," *Daily Ohio State Journal*, March 28, 1860, 2. Whitman's stint as an omnibus driver was reported with great delight and exaggeration by his detractors, but it does appear to be rooted in fact. Several of Whitman's confidants during this period remembered that he filled in for sick drivers.

51. "Bardic Symbols," *Daily Ohio State Journal*, March 28, 1860, 2.

52. Eldridge, " 'A Woman Waits for Me,' " 39.

53. Tilton, *Letters*, 8:458.

54. *NUPM*, 422.

55. For a description of the proofing office, see Trowbridge, "Reminiscences," 170.

56. *Walt Whitman: The Correspondence*, vol. 1, 1961, 1:49. Hereafter *Corr.*

57. Thayer, "Autobiography," 16.

58. *PW*, 281.

59. *PW*, 279n44.

60. Eldridge, " 'A Woman Waits for Me,' " 39.

61. *Corr.*, 1:49. Whitman's letter is now lost, but Vaughan wrote on March 27, 1860, "You tell me Mr. Emmerson (one m to many I gues?) came to see you and was very kind." Feinberg Collection.

62. *WWWC*, 3:439.

63. Henry Clapp Jr. letter, May 14, 1860, Feinberg Collection, reprinted in *WWWC* 2:375.

64. Henry Clapp Jr. letter, March 27, 1860, Feinberg Collection, reprinted in *WWWC* 1:236–37.

65. *WWWC*, 4:196.

66. Winter, *Old Friends*, 293–94.

67. Henry Clapp Jr. letter, May 12, 1860, location unknown, reprinted in *WWWC*, 4:195–96.

68. Henry Clapp Jr. letter, May 14, 1860, Feinberg Collection, reprinted in *WWWC*, 2:375–76.

69. *Corr.*, 1:55.

70. Malin, "Plotting," 85–86.

71. Thayer, "Autobiography," 24.

72. Myerson, *Whitman*, 7.

73. Thayer, "Autobiography," 24.

74. "More of the Harpers' Ferry Affair," *New York Illustrated News*, April 21, 1860, 368.

75. "A Distinction without a Difference," *Vanity Fair*, April 21, 1860, 261.

76. Malin, "Plotting," 86.

77. James Redpath, letter to Thomas Wentworth Higginson, April 20, 1860, quoted in Malin, "Plotting," 84.

78. W[hipple], "Echoes of Harper's Ferry," 79.

79. From the *Boston Saturday Evening Gazette*, April 21, 1860, reprinted on the inside back over of *Leaves of Grass Imprints*.

80. *Saturday Press*, May 5, 1860, 2; *Saturday Press*, May 12, 1860, 2.

81. *Corr.*, 1:52.

82. *Corr.*, 1:52.

83. Thayer, "Autobiography," 17.

84. *Corr.*, 1:52.

85. Henry Clapp Jr. letter, March 12, 1860, Feinberg Collection.

86. "The Chicago Convention," *New York Times*, May 15, 1860, 1.

87. "The Wigwam," *Chicago Press and Tribune*, May 16, 1860, 1; "News of the Week," *Prairie Farmer*, May 17, 1860, 320; "Pickpockets About," *Chicago Press and Tribune*, May 17, 1860, 4.

88. "The Convention Week in Chicago," *Chicago Press and Tribune*, May 17, 1860, 1.

89. "The Chicago Convention," *New York Times*, May 15, 1860, 1.

90. "The Scene in the Wigwam," *Chicago Press and Tribune*, May 22, 1860, 1.

91. McPherson, *Battle Cry*, 220.

92. "The Scene in the Wigwam," *Chicago Press and Tribune*, May 22, 1860, 1.

93. "The Scene in the Wigwam," *Chicago Press and Tribune*, May 22, 1860, 1.

94. "The Republican Ticket for 1860," *New York Times*, May 19, 1860, 1.

95. "New Publications," *New York Times*, May 19, 1860, 9.

96. "Walt Whitman: Leaves of Grass," *Saturday Press*, May 19, 1860, 2.

2. THE REPRESENTATIVE MAN OF THE NORTH

1. January Searle, untitled article, *New York Illustrated News*, May 26, 1860, 43.

2. Reprinted in "Gossip with Readers and Correspondents," *The Knickerbocker*, July 1860, 102.

3. Allen, *Solitary Singer*, 260.

4. Juliette H. Beach, "Harriet Prescott," *Saturday Press*, April 7, 1860, 2.

5. "Political Anti-Slavery Convention," *The Liberator*, June 15, 1860, 1.

6. "Honest Abe," *Saturday Press*, May 26, 1860, 3.

7. "Sanguinary," *Saturday Press*, May 26, 1860, 3.

8. "Notes of the Week," *Saturday Press*, June 2, 1860, 2.

9. Juliette H. Beach [Calvin Beach], "Leaves of Grass," review, *Saturday Press*, June 2, 1860, 2.

10. William Thayer letter, June 5, 1860, Feinberg Collection.

11. Hinton, *The Life*, 106.

12. Juliette H. Beach letter, June 7, 1860, Feinberg Collection.

13. Ceniza, "'Being a Woman,'" 123–24.

14. *Saturday Press*, June 9, 1860, 3.

15. Ceniza, "'Being a Woman,'" 191.

16. Mary A. Chilton, "Leaves of Grass," review, *Saturday Press*, June 9, 1860, 3.

17. Ceniza, "'Being a Woman,'" 193, 194.

18. "'Leaves of Grass'—Smut in Them," *Springfield Daily Republican*, June 16, 1860, 4.

19. Heenan, "Swimming," 1.

20. *Corr.*, 1:55.

21. For a detailed description of this period, see Sentilles, *Performing Menken*, 50–90.

22. Quoted in Hyman, "'Where the Drinkers,'" 59.

23. William Thayer letter, June 14, 1860, Feinberg Collection.

24. "A Woman," "Walt Whitman," *Saturday Press*, June 23, 3.

25. Susan Garnet Smith letter, July 11, 1860. Original is lost but is described by Horace Traubel (*WWWC*, 4:313).

26. Wilhelmina Walton letter, August 16, 1860, Feinberg Collection.

27. K. B. Yale letter, September 23, 1860, Feinberg Collection.

28. Walt Whitman, "A Broadway Pageant," *New York Times*, June 27, 1860, 2.

29. Allen, *Solitary Singer*, 242.

30. *Milwaukee Daily Sentinel*, June 30, 1860, 1. "Peter Funks" was a made-up name used by auctioneers to inflate prices when no one counterbid against an eager bidder. Soon, though, it became the nineteenth-century equivalent of "Joe Schmoe."

31. "Rough Poetry," reprinted in *Saturday Press*, July 21, 1860, 3.

32. "Editor's Easy Chair," *Harper's New Monthly Magazine*, September 1860, 555.

33. "Watches Given Away," *The Liberator*, April 4, 1860, 223.

34. Thayer & Eldridge letter, June 14, 1860, Feinberg Collection.

35. *Frank Leslie's Illustrated Newspaper*, June 23, 1860, 80, Feinberg Collection. The advertisement was certainly placed by Thayer & Eldridge. On June 14

they sent a letter about the scheme to Whitman, instructing him, "If you will look in the next number of Frank Leslie, an advertisement headed 'a Good Book given away' will explain what we mean." Thayer & Eldridge letter, June 14, 1860, Feinberg Collection.

36. Thayer & Eldridge letter, July 27, 1860, Feinberg Collection.

37. Thayer & Eldridge letter, June 14, 1860, Feinberg Collection.

38. *New York Illustrated News*, June 16, 1860, 91.

39. Thayer & Eldridge letter, June 14, 1860, Feinberg Collection.

40. Thayer & Eldridge letter, June 14, 1860, Feinberg Collection.

41. *Saturday Press*, June 30, 1860, 3.

42. See back cover of Hinton, *The Life*.

43. *Saturday Press*, June 30, 1860, 3.

44. "A Nine Years Resident Driven Away," *The Liberator*, January 20, 1860, 10.

45. "Abolition Bibles," *Illinois State Democrat*, July 4, 1860, 3

46. "Persecution of a Northern Bookseller in Arkansas," *The Liberator*, October 12, 1860, 163.

47. Sumner, *The Works*, 128. The original of this letter along with Sumner's thankful declination are now in the Sumner papers at the Houghton Library, Harvard University.

48. "Walt Whitman," *New Orleans Sunday Delta*, June 17, 1860, 1.

49. "A New American Poem," *Southern Field and Fireside*, June 9, 1860, 20.

50. *Golden Era*, July 22, 1860, 1.

51. "A Specimen from Walt Whitman," *New Orleans Sunday Delta*, June 24, 1860, 1.

52. "Editor's Table," *Southern Literary Messenger*, July 1860, 74.

53. "Editor's Table," *Southern Literary Messenger*, August 1860, 155.

54. "Why, Juliette!" *Virginia Free Press*, July 12, 1860, 1.

55. The reviewer in 1860 compares Whitman to many of the same antecedents as the 1856 reviewer cited, and the erudite, allusive style is quite similar in both pieces.

56. "Notes on New Books," *Washington Daily National Intelligencer*, February 18, 1856, 4.

57. "Short Notes on New Books," *Daily National Intelligencer* (Washington, DC), July 14, 1860, 2.

58. *Daily National Intelligencer*, August 7, 1860. Many of the books advertised by Philp & Solomons in 1860 have a familiar pro-slavery bent. However, it should be noted that when the firm began publishing books, their titles included Alexander Gardner's pro-Union *Photographic Sketch Book of the War*.

59. Whitman, *Leaves of Grass*, 1860, 289, 297–98. Hereafter *LG* 1860.

60. "The Hairy Poet of Brooklyn," *Houston Telegraph*, June 26, 1860, 2.

61. *Louisville Daily Journal*, June 28, 1860, 2.

62. *Corr.*, 1:55.

63. Henry P. Leland, review, *Philadelphia City Item*, early June 1860, reprinted in *Saturday Press*, June 16, 1860, 1.

64. Conway, *Autobiography*, 317–18.

65. *Dial*, March 1860, 200.

66. "Echoes of Harper's Ferry," *Dial*, June 1860, 389.

67. Conway, *Autobiography*, 309.

68. Conway, "Critical Notices," 517.

69. William Dean Howells, "Letters from the Country," *Ohio State Journal*, July 4, 1860, reprinted in Price, "The Road to Boston," 95–98.

70. [William Dean Howells], "A Hoosier's Opinion of Walt Whitman," *Saturday Press*, August 11, 1860, 2, reprinted from the *Ashtabula Sentinel*, July 18, 1860, 4.

71. Howells, *Literary Friends*, 72.

72. Howells, *Literary Friends*, 71–72.

73. Howells, *Literary Friends*, 75.

74. Howells, *Literary Friends*, 75.

75. *Brooklyn Daily Eagle*, July 9, 1860, 1.

76. "Leaves of Grass," *Saturday Review*, July 7, 1860, 19–21.

77. *Corr.*, 7:57. In volume 7 of the *Correspondence*, I incorrectly guessed that this letter dated from 1879. Thanks to Kenneth M. Price for correcting this date and calling it to my attention.

78. *Corr.*, 1:52.

79. Charles Eldridge letter, July 27, 1860, Feinberg Collection.

80. Von Frank, "Secret World," 59.

81. William Thayer letter, August 17, 1860, Feinberg Collection.

82. Whitman, "A Brooklynite Criticised," n.p. A facsimile of the article from Whitman's scrapbooks is published in Stephen Railton's *Walt Whitman's Autograph Revision of the Analysis of* Leaves of Grass (New York: New York University Press, 1974), 144.

83. Whitman, "A Brooklynite Criticised," n.p.

84. Whitman, "A Brooklynite Criticised," n.p.

85. William Thayer letter, October 11, 1860, Feinberg Collection.

86. "Our New York Correspondence," *Charleston Mercury*, October 30, 1860, 4.

3. THE VOLCANIC UPHEAVAL OF THE NATION

1. "The Storm of Saturday," *New York Times*, November 5, 1860, 8.
2. "A Paper Factory Consumed," *Brooklyn Eagle*, November 5, 1860, 3.
3. "Brooklyn News," *New York Times*, November 5, 1860, 1.
4. "False Alarm," *Brooklyn Eagle*, November 5, 1860, 3.
5. "The Storm of Saturday," *New York Times*, November 5, 1860, 8.
6. "After the Storm a Calm," *New York Evangelist*, November 8, 1860, 1.
7. "Another Secession Blast," *New York Times*, July 24, 1860, 4.
8. Greeley, "The Menaces," 1860, 1.
9. "Mr. Kendall's Reply," *New York Times*, September 20, 1860, 1.
10. "Mr. Kendall's Reply," *New York Times*, September 20, 1860, 1.
11. "At the Newspaper Offices," *New York Times*, November 7, 1860, 8.
12. "The Metropolis," *New York Herald*, November 7, 1860, 2. As improbable as it may seem, a thorough search of the New York and Brooklyn newspapers from 1840 to 1860 turned up only one reference to "glorious jam"—Walt Whitman's description of the streets of New York as "one continued, ceaseless, devilish, provoking, delicious, glorious jam!"—in the *New York Aurora* in 1842. Followed, as it is, on the heels of "roughs" (also in quotation marks), one must assume that the unidentified writer knew Whitman's work, and most likely the man, very well.
13. Goodwin, *Team of Rivals*, 277.
14. "The Metropolis," *New York Herald*, November 7, 1860, 2.
15. "At the Newspaper Offices," *New York Times*, November 7, 1860, 8.
16. "At the Newspaper Offices," *New York Times*, November 7, 1860, 8.
17. "Agents Wanted," *The Liberator*, November 2, 1860, 175.
18. Most of the book's advertisements described it as two hundred pages long at 16mo size. Only the advertisements in *The Liberator* described it as a "handsome brochure of 150 pages."
19. Whitman, *Drum-Taps*, 10. Hereafter *DT.*
20. *DT,* 11.
21. *DT,* 11.
22. *DT,* 22.
23. This previously unpublished manuscript is among the "Brooklyniana" documents in the Feinberg Collection.
24. *NUPM*, 436.
25. *NUPM*, 437.
26. "Book Notices," *New York Illustrated News*, November 24, 1860, 42.

27. Thayer & Eldridge, letter to William D. O'Connor, n.d., 1860, Feinberg Collection, quoted in Freedman, *William Douglas O'Connor*, 120.

28. William Thayer letter, December 1, 1860, Feinberg Collection.

29. William Thayer letter, October 11, 1860, Feinberg Collection.

30. William Thayer, letter to Whitman, December 5, 1860, Feinberg Collection.

31. Thayer, "Autobiography," 22.

32. William Thayer, letter to Whitman, December 5, 1860, Feinberg Collection.

33. "Senator Seward on the Crisis," *New York Times*, December 24, 1860, 4.

34. *PW*, 26.

35. "Kansas Admitted!," *New York Times*, January 29, 1861, 4.

36. Yale Collection of American Literature, Beinecke Rare Book and Manuscript Library.

37. Thayer & Eldridge letter, February 6, 1861, Feinberg Collection.

38. For advertisements of the books by Clare and Higginson, see, for example, "Notices of New Publications," *Boston Daily Advertiser*, October 24, 1860, 2. Higginson's essays on slave revolts eventually appeared in *Travellers and Outlaws* (1889).

39. *PW*, 499–500.

40. *PW*, 100.

41. Lincoln, *Collected Works*, 229–30.

42. *PW*, 500.

43. "The Inauguration Ceremonies," *New York Times*, March 5, 1861, 1.

44. *PW*, 499–501.

45. "The Inauguration Ceremonies," *New York Times*, March 5, 1861, 1.

46. McPherson, *Battle Cry*, 264.

47. "The March of Events," *New York Evangelist*, March 14, 1861, 5.

48. "The Evacuation of Fort Sumter," *The Independent*, March 14, 1861, 4.

49. "The Great Literary Question of the Day," *Vanity Fair*, March 9, 1861, 118.

50. "The Cab-Age," *Vanity Fair*, April 13, 1861, 179.

51. "Answers to Correspondents," *Frank Leslie's Budget of Fun*, February 1, 1861, 2.

52. Lincoln, *Collected Works*, 323.

53. *PW*, 26.

54. *New York Times*, April 14, 1861, 1.

55. "War at Last," *New York Times*, April 13, 1861, 4.

56. This previously unpublished fragment is in the Feinberg Collection, Item 132, Box 28. Two additional lines have been cut off at the bottom of the manuscript,

apparently by Whitman himself, as the text on the verso wraps around the excision.

57. *Brooklyn Daily Eagle*, April 19, 1861, 2.

58. *Brooklyn Daily Eagle*, April 18, 1861, 2.

59. *PW*, 1:25–26.

60. "The Enthusiasm in New York," *The Independent*, April 25, 1861, 1.

61. See Loving, *Civil War Letters*, 39. Hereafter *CWL*.

62. William Thayer, letter to Walt Whitman, April 19, 1861, Feinberg Collection.

63. "The War Excitement," *Brooklyn Eagle*, April 20, 1861, 2.

64. *Brooklyn Daily Eagle*, April 23, 1861, 2.

65. Whitman, *Leaves of Grass: Comprehensive Reader's Edition*, 678–79. Hereafter *CRE*.

66. *DT*, 6–7.

67. *PW*, 2:430.

68. *Corr.*, 1:56.

69. *Walt Whitman: The Correspondence*, vol. 7, 2004, 13. Hereafter *Corr.*

70. *NUPM*, 438.

71. William Thayer letter, April 19, 1861, Feinberg Collection.

72. *NUPM*, 1456–57.

73. *NUPM*, 1457.

74. This list of titles includes Elizabeth R. Torrey, *The Ideal of Womanhood;* Harriet Farley, *Happy Hours at Hazel Nook;* Lewis Holmes, *The Arctic Whaleman;* and C. W. Dana and Thomas Hart Benton, *The Great West.*

75. See the lists of "New Publications Received" in *North American Review* and "Recent American Publications" in the *Atlantic Monthly.* Unfortunately, most other major magazines, such as *Harper's, The Living Age,* and *Putnam's Monthly,* did not publish such lists. The *New Englander* briefly published a list in fall 1860 but halted the practice in April 1861, which itself may indicate that fewer books were received.

76. Tryon, "The Publications," 309–10.

77. Tryon, "The Publications," 329.

78. Child, *Selected Letters*, 356.

79. The following northern publishers were in business in 1861 (those that failed that year are marked with asterisks): A. S. Barnes & Burr*; A. Williams & Co.; Baker and Godwin; C. S. Francis & Co.*; Carlton and Porter; Charles Scribner; Crocker and Brewster; Crosby, Nichols, Lee & Co.; D. Appleton & Co.; E. C. & J. Biddle; G. G. Evans*; G. P. Putnam; Gould and Lincoln; H. H. Lloyd

& Co.*; Harper and Brothers; J. B. Lippincott & Co.; J. E. Tilton & Co.; James Challen and Son; James Munroe & Co.*; John P. Jewett & Co.*; Mayhew and Baker*; Sheldon & Co.; T. O. H. P. Burham; Thayer & Eldridge*; Ticknor and Fields; W. A. Townsend & Co.; Walker, Wise, & Co.; William Gowans*.

80. "Notice," *American Publishers' Circular and Literary Gazette*, June 22, 1861, 213.

81. Whitman, *Drum-Taps (1865) and Sequel to Drum-Taps (1865–6)*, xxiii.

82. "Recent American Publications," *Atlantic Monthly*, July 1861, 123.

83. "Editor's Easy Chair," *Harper's New Monthly Magazine*, September 1861, 556.

84. Holmes, "Bread and the Newspaper," 348.

85. See, for example, column 1 of the *Brooklyn Standard*, June 8, 1861, 1.

86. Mancuso, "Civil War," 293.

87. *Corr.*, 1:56–57.

88. "The War Excitement," *Brooklyn Eagle*, May 11, 1861, 2.

89. "Serious Charges against the Colonel of the 13th Regiment," *Brooklyn Eagle*, June 25, 1861, 2.

90. *CWL*, 40.

91. *Corr.*, 1:56.

92. *CWL*, 40.

93. *Corr.*, 1:56–57.

4. WAR-SUGGESTING TRUMPETS, I HEARD YOU

1. Quoted in Harris, *Blue & Gray*, 71.

2. *New York Herald*, July 22, 1861, 4.

3. Quoted in Harris, *Blue & Gray*, 71.

4. *PW*, 27.

5. Stedman, *Battle of Bull Run*, 34.

6. *PW*, 27.

7. The original of this poem is in the Feinberg Collection. The complete text appears in *CRE*, 612.

8. Version from the *New York Weekly Graphic*, February 7, 1874, quoted in *PW*, 30–31, 30n–31n.

9. "Newspapers and the War," *New York Times*, August 16, 1861, 4.

10. "Newspapers and the War," *New York Times*, August 16, 1861, 4.

11. "Newspapers and the War," *New York Times*, August 16, 1861, 4.

12. "Newspapers and the War," *New York Times*, August 16, 1861, 4.

13. "Local Military Movements," *New York Times*, September 20, 1861, 8.

14. "Beat! Beat! Drums!," *Harper's Weekly*, September 28, 1861, 623.

15. Kaplan, *Walt Whitman*, 263.

16. Jay Charlton [pseudonym for Jay C. Goldsmith], "Bohemians," 166–67.

17. Kennedy, *Fight of a Book*, 69–70.

18. Goldsmith, "Bohemians," 166–167.

19. *Corr.*, 4:40.

20. Kennedy, *Fight of a Book*, 70.

21. In his bibliography "Walt Whitman's Poetry in Periodicals," William White cited the original appearance of "Beat! Beat! Drums!" as *Harper's Weekly* and the *New York Leader* on September 28, 1861. *The Serif* 11 (Summer 1974): 31–38. Shortly thereafter, however, a librarian, William T. O'Malley, notified White that the special collections at the University of Rhode Island Library contained a clipping of Whitman's "Beat! Beat! Drums!" from the *Boston Daily Evening Transcript* on September 24, 1861. Not realizing that both *Harper's Weekly* and the *Leader* published one week in advance of their cover dates, White revised his original listing to reflect that the poem had first appeared in the *Boston Daily Evening Transcript* on September 24, 1861, and subsequently in *Harper's Weekly* and the *New York Leader* on September 28. White, " 'Beat! Beat! Drums!': The First Version," 43, 44. In fact, the sequence of publication was *Harper's Weekly* on the morning of September 21, the *New York Leader* on the evening of the 21st, a previously unrecorded appearance in the *Brooklyn Daily Eagle* on the 23rd, and the *Transcript* appearance on the 24th.

22. *Harper's Weekly* always appeared on newsstands one week prior to its official publication date. The clearest evidence of this appears in the issues published just after the bombardment of Fort Sumter. The April 20 issue leads with an advertisement mentioning "the possible outbreak of civil war." The issue was evidently already on press when word of war reached New York late on April 12 and was rushed into extras just after midnight on April 13. The same advertisement appears on the second page of the April 27 issue, but "the possible outbreak of civil war" has been revised to "the actual outbreak of civil war" (258). That same issue carries the poem "The Seventh," written after the recruitment meeting of the 7th New York on "Friday Evening, *April* 19" (259). Thus it appears that each issue was assembled and printed each Friday, eight days before its cover date, and distributed to newsstands the following morning.

23. For examples, see *Harper's Weekly*, September 14 and October 5, 1861. The September 21 issue did not contain poetry.

24. All descriptions from *Harper's Weekly*, September 28, 1861, 623.

25. "The Editor's Easy Chair," *Harper's Monthly*, September 1861, 556.

26. See "The Seventh" (April 27), "Fort Sumter" (May 11), "Volunteered" (May 18), "Not Dead" (May 25), "The Midnight March" (June 1), "Ellsworth, A Battle Hymn for Ellsworth's Zouaves" (June 8), "The War" (July 6), "Up with the Flag" (August 10), "To Talkers" (August 24), "On Guard" (September 7), "Our Brother" and "Peace" (September 14).

27. *Harper's Weekly*, May 11, 1861, 295.

28. *Harper's Weekly*, June 8, 1861, 357.

29. *Boston Daily Evening Transcript*, February 13, 1861, 2.

30. Chamberlin, *Boston Transcript*, 121.

31. *Boston Daily Evening Transcript*, June 12, 1861, 2.

32. "The Advertizer," *Brooklyn Daily Eagle*, July 19, 1849, 2.

33. "To the Wars," *Brooklyn Eagle*, September 28, 1861, 1.

34. See "On Drafting," *Brooklyn Eagle*, September 17, 1861, 2.

35. *Circular*, October 3, 1861, 137.

36. *Circular*, October 3, 1861, 139.

37. Goodman and Dawson, *William Dean Howells*, 67.

38. Walt Whitman, "Beat! Beat! Drums!," *Daily Evening Bulletin* (San Francisco), November 9, 1861, 4.

39. See Carter, "Before the Telegraph."

40. Details derived from Long, *Civil War*, 114–17.

41. James E. Miller Jr. attempted an "arranged text" version of "Kentucky" (published with a literal transcription and annotation by William White in *Prairie Schooner*, Fall 1958, 172–78); however, he significantly misreads the manuscript marks. Most important, he seems not to have recognized that the "obvious" repetitions—as described by Bradley and Blodgett (*CRE*, 663)—were earlier iterations of a single draft. In fact, it appears that Whitman worked on a single section, making changes and interlineations until the manuscript became too confusing to read; he copied out the lines at that stage and began to rework them further. Therefore, the "repetition, set down three times, of the title," again as noted by Bradley and Blodgett, was representative of three progressive drafts of the opening stanza.

42. *CRE*, 294.

43. Walt Whitman, letter to James Russell Lowell, October 1, 1861, in *Corr.*, 1:57; Walt Whitman, letter to James Russell Lowell, October 2, 1861, in *Corr.*, 7:53.

44. See Austin, *Fields*, 50–51.

45. Lowell, *New Letters*, 102.

46. *WWWC*, 2:213.

47. Austin, *Fields*, 250.

48. Austin, *Fields*, 215.

49. Austin, *Fields*, 251–52.

50. Howe, *Reminiscences*, 102.

51. Howe, *Reminiscences*, 101; Austin, *Fields*, 53.

52. See Lowell, *Complete Poetical Works*, 4:1.

53. Austin, *Fields*, 188.

54. Holmes, "The Flower of Liberty," 550.

55. Holmes, "Union and Liberty," 756.

56. See Austin, *Fields*, 187–188.

57. Howe, *Reminiscences*, 274.

58. Howe, "Battle Hymn," 145.

59. Howe, *Reminiscences*, 276.

60. John Greenleaf Whittier, "Mountain Pictures," *Atlantic Monthly*, March 1862, 299.

61. *DT*, 17.

62. Austin, *Fields*, 364.

63. *WWWC*, 1:217.

64. See Anbinder, " 'We Will Dirk.' "

65. Hanchett, *Irish*, 28.

66. "Sixty-ninth, remember Fontenoy" is a reference to the Irish Brigade's bravery at the Battle of Fontenoy in 1745.

67. Winter, *Old Friends*, 64.

68. Walt Whitman, "Little Bells Last Night," *New York Leader*, October 12, 1861, 2.

69. Wright, "Delicacy," 180.

70. "Capt. T. F. Meagher Declines to Leave the Sixty-Ninth," *New York Times*, August 7, 1861, 2; "The 'Meagher Brigade,' " *New York Times*, August 18, 1861, 1, reprinted from *Boston Herald*.

71. "Local Military Movements," *New York Times*, August 28, 1861, 8; "Capt. T. F. Meagher Declines the Colonelcy of the Sixty-Ninth," *New York Times*, September 6, 1861, 1.

72. *New York Times*, September 28, 1861, 2.

73. *New York Leader*, October 12, 1861, 8.

74. Walt Whitman, "Old Ireland," *New York Leader*, November 2, 1861, 1.

75. *DT*, 66.

76. *Vanity Fair*, November 9, 1861, 211. William Winter later captioned this image in *Mullen's caricature of Fitz-James O'Brien recruiting for the Union Army* and included it in *O'Brien's Poems and Stories*.

77. "A Sergeant of the McClellan Rifles Shot," *New York Times*, November 8, 1861, 8.

78. "Local Military Movements," *New York Times*, November 1, 1861, 2.

79. See Genoways, "Jesse Whitman."

80. Mary Greenwood Couthouy, letter to George Clapp, n.d., Feinberg Collection.

5. DEAD AND DIVINE, AND BROTHER OF ALL

1. Rubin, *Historic Whitman*, 329.

2. *CWL*, 43.

3. *CWL*, 43.

4. *CWL*, 44, 45.

5. "The Burnside Expedition," *New York Times*, February 15, 1862, 1.

6. *LG* 1860, 362–63.

7. "Farewell to the Old Episcopal Graveyard in Fulton Street!" *Brooklyn City News*, January 28, 1862.

8. "An Old Brooklyn Landmark Going," *Brooklyn Daily Eagle*, October 5, 1861, 2.

9. Whitman, *Uncollected Poetry and Prose*, 262. Hereafter *UPP*.

10. *UPP*, 262.

11. *NUPM*, 454.

12. *NUPM*, 455.

13. Whitman, *Leaves of Grass*, 1855, 29.

14. Whitman, "Poem of You, Whoever You Are," in *Leaves of Grass*, 1856, 206. Hereafter *LG* 1856.

15. Whitman, "Poem in Wonder at the Resurrection of the Wheat" (later "This Compost"), in *LG* 1856, 202.

16. *UPP*, 263.

17. *UPP*, 263.

18. *UPP*, 266.

19. *UPP*, 239.

20. *UPP*, 242, 266–67.

21. "Farewell to the Old Episcopal Graveyard in Fulton Street!" *Brooklyn City News*, January 28, 1862.

22. Whitman, *Daybooks*, 615; *UPP*, 265–66.

23. *CWL*, 46.

24. *CWL*, 47.

25. Barrus, *Whitman and Burroughs*, xx, 2.

26. Barrus, *Whitman and Burroughs*, 2.

27. "City Photographs, I," *New York Leader*, March 15, 1862, reprinted in *Walt Whitman and the Civil War*, 27–28.

28. "City Photographs, I," *New York Leader*, March 15, 1862, reprinted in *Walt Whitman and the Civil War*, 29.

29. *Walt Whitman and the Civil War*, 42–43.

30. "City Photographs, IV," *New York Leader*, April 12, 1862, reprinted in *Walt Whitman and the Civil War*, 42.

31. "City Photographs, IV," *New York Leader*, April 12, 1862, reprinted in *Walt Whitman and the Civil War*, 42.

32. "City Photographs, I," *New York Leader*, March 15, 1862, reprinted in *Walt Whitman and the Civil War*, 29.

33. *NUPM*, 446.

34. "Ellen Eyre," letter to Walt Whitman, March 25, 1862, Feinberg Collection.

35. "A Wolf in Sheep's Clothing," *New York Sunday Mercury*, June 23, 1862, 7.

36. "Strange Mode of Black Mailing," *New York Herald*, June 20, 1862, 2.

37. "Strange Mode of Black Mailing," *New York Herald*, June 20, 1862, 2.

38. *NUPM*, 488.

39. Katz, *Love Stories*, 148.

40. *NUPM*, 487.

41. "Wounded" was published in the August 1862 issue of the *Continental Monthly*; however, it appeared on newsstands and was mailed to subscribers in the first half of July.

42. *Circular*, July 31, 1862, 99. On September 19, 1861, a correspondent to the *Circular*, identified only as "T. R. H.," mentioned that he was "connected with the Brooklyn *Standard* with which you exchange" (131). On January 2, 1862, the *Circular* published a laudatory review of the newly established *Continental Monthly* (191).

43. Henry P. Leland, "Enfans de Soixante-Seize," *Philadelphia City Item*, early June 1860, reprinted in *Saturday Press*, June 16, 1860, 1.

44. For an excellent examination of Whitman's appearances in *Vanity Fair*, see Scholnick, " 'An Unusually Active Market.' "

45. Charles Godfrey Leland, "Words to the West," *Knickerbocker*, October 1861, 1–5; "Servile Insurrection," *Knickerbocker*, November 1861, 1–7.

46. "Servile Insurrection," *Knickerbocker*, November 1861, 1.

47. C. G. Leland, *Memoirs*, 243, 244.

48. *CWL*, 53.

49. *CWL*, 59.

50. Details of Andrew Whitman's military service are derived from Murray, "Bunkum."

51. *CWL*, 55.

52. Quoted in Murray, "Bunkum," 143.

53. *CWL*, 56–57.

54. *CWL*, 59.

55. *CWL*, 58.

56. "Burial of a Soldier at Suffolk, Va.," *Brooklyn Eagle*, August 7, 1862, 2.

57. "Military Matters," *Brooklyn Eagle*, September 13, 1862, 2.

58. "The Northern Mind," *Vanity Fair*, June 21, 1862, 303.

59. Morris, *Better Angel*, 45.

60. See Loving, *Walt Whitman*, 8.

61. "Movements of the Fifty-first Regiment New York Volunteers," *New York Times*, September 14, 1862, 3.

62. Hannah Whitman, letter to Louisa Van Velsor Whitman, September 11, 1862, Feinberg Collection.

63. "The Rebellion," *New York Times*, September 18, 1862, 4.

64. *NUPM*, 493.

65. *NUPM*, 493.

66. This manuscript scrap is glued into Whitman's Blue Book of the 1860 edition of *Leaves of Grass*, Oscar Lion Collection, on the verso of a correction affixed to page 269. The date can be approximated by another note: "Article on / Death of Brooklyn's most ancient citizen / *Andrew Demarest—Reminiscences of our* city years ago." Demarest died in early October 1861, and Whitman's proposed article about him appeared as "An Old Landmark Gone," *Brooklyn Eagle*, October 9, 1862, 2.

67. *Walt Whitman: Complete Poetry*, 1099.

68. United States et al., *Antietam—Serial 27*. Vol. 19: *The War of the Rebellion: A Compilation of the Official Records of the Union and Confederate Armies*, 401–3.

69. *Walt Whitman: Complete Poetry*, 1099.

70. *DT*, 66.

71. "Brady's Photographs," *New York Times*, October 20, 1862, 5.

72. *CWL*, 71.

73. "Our Washington Correspondence," *New York Times*, September 25, 1862, 1.

74. "McClellan's Army," *New York Herald*, October 7, 1862, 4.

75. Moses Lane, letter to James J. Dana, December 16, 1862, Whitman miscellaneous correspondence file, Feinberg Collection.

76. Martin Kalbfleisch, letter to Moses Fowler Odell, December 16, 1862, Whitman miscellaneous correspondence file, Feinberg Collection.

77. *Corr.*, 1:58.

78. Calder, "Personal Recollections," 196.

79. T. J. Whitman and Whitman, *Dear Brother Walt*, 18.

80. James J. Dana, letter to W. E. Doster, December 17, 1862, Whitman miscellaneous correspondence file, Feinberg Collection.

81. *Corr.*, 1:59.

82. Conway, *Autobiography*, 356.

83. *PW*, 32.

84. *DT*, 46.

85. *NUPM*, 506.

BIBLIOGRAPHY

ARCHIVES

Charles E. Feinberg Collection of the Papers of Walt Whitman, Library of Congress, Washington, DC.
Oscar Lion Collection, New York Public Library.

PUBLISHED MATERIAL

Aaron, Daniel. *The Unwritten War: American Writers and the Civil War.* New York: Knopf, 1973.

Allen, Gay Wilson. *The Solitary Singer: A Critical Biography of Walt Whitman.* New York: New York University Press, 1955.

Anbinder, Tyler. "'We Will Dirk Every Mother's Son of You': Five Points and the Irish Conquest of New York Politics." *Eire-Ireland: Journal of Irish Studies* 36 (Spring–Summer 2001): 29–46.

Austin, James C. *Fields of the Atlantic Monthly: Letters to an Editor, 1861–1870.* San Marino, CA: Huntington Library.

Barrus, Clara. *Whitman and Burroughs Comrades.* Boston: Houghton Mifflin, 1931.

Cady, Edwin Harrison. *Young Howells and John Brown: Episodes in a Radical Education.* Columbus: Ohio State University Press, 1985.

Calder, Ellen M. "Personal Recollections of Walt Whitman." In *Whitman in His Own Time*, edited by Joel Myerson. Iowa City: University of Iowa Press, 2000.

Carter, John Denton. "Before the Telegraph: The News Service of the San Francisco Bulletin, 1855–1861." *Pacific Historical Review* (1942): 301–17.

Ceniza, Sherry. " 'Being a Woman . . . I Wish to Give My Own View': Some Nineteenth Century Women's Responses to the 1860 *Leaves of Grass*." In *Cambridge Companion to Walt Whitman*, edited by Ezra Greenspan. Cambridge, UK: Cambridge University Press, 1995.

Chamberlin, Joseph Edgar. *The Boston Transcript: A History of Its First Hundred Years*. Freeport, NY: Books for Libraries Press, 1969. (Originally published 1930.)

Charlton, Jay. "Bohemians in America." In *Pen Pictures of Modern Authors*, edited by William Shepard. New York: G.P. Putnam's, 1882.

Child, Lydia Maria Francis. *Lydia Maria Child: Selected Letters, 1817–1880*. Edited by Milton Meltzer, Patricia G. Holland, and Francine Krasno. Amherst: University of Massachusetts Press, 1982.

Clark, George Pierce. " 'Saerasmid,' An Early Promoter of Walt Whitman." *American Literature* (1955): 259–62.

Conway, Moncure Daniel. *Autobiography: Memories and Experiences of Moncure Daniel Conway*. Boston: Houghton Mifflin, 1904.

———. "Critical Notices." *Dial*, August 1860, 517–19.

Diffley, Kathleen. *Where My Heart Is Turning Ever: Civil War Stories and Constitutional Reform, 1861–1876*. Athens: University of Georgia Press, 1992.

Eldridge, Charles W. " 'A Woman Waits for Me': The Personal Relations of Whitman and Emerson." *Conservator*, May 1896, 38–39.

Folsom, Ed, and Kenneth M. Price, *Re-Scripting Walt Whitman*. Malden, MA: Blackwell, 2005.

Freedman, Florence Bernstein. *William Douglas O'Connor: Walt Whitman's Chosen Knight*. Athens: Ohio University Press, 1985.

Garner, Stanton. *The Civil War World of Herman Melville*. Lawrence: University of Kansas Press, 1993.

Genoways, Ted. "Jesse Whitman in 1861: A New Letter." *Walt Whitman Quarterly Review* 21 (Fall 2003): 96–97.

Goldsmith, Jay C. "Bohemians in America." In *Pen Pictures of Modern Authors*, edited by William Shepard. New York: G. P. Putnam's, 1882.

Goodman, Susan, and Carl Dawson. *William Dean Howells: A Writer's Life*. Berkeley: University of California Press, 2005.

Goodwin, Doris Kearns. *Team of Rivals: The Political Genius of Abraham Lincoln*. New York: Simon & Schuster, 2005.

Greeley, Horace. "The Menaces of Disunion." *The Independent*, August 16, 1860.

Greenspan, Ezra. *Walt Whitman and the American Reader*. Cambridge, UK: Cambridge University Press, 1990.

Hanchett, William. *Irish: Charles G. Halpine in Civil War America*. Syracuse, NY: Syracuse University Press, 1970.

Harris, Brayton. *Blue & Gray in Black & White: Newspapers in the Civil War*. Washington, DC: Brassey's, 1999.

Heenan, Adah Isaacs Menken. "Swimming Against the Current." *New York Sunday Mercury*, June 10, 1860.

Higginson, Thomas Wentworth. *Cheerful Yesterdays*. Boston: Houghton Mifflin, 1898.

Hinton, Richard J. *John Brown and His Men*. London: Funk and Wagnalls, 1894.

———. *The Life and Public Services of Hon. Abraham Lincoln, of Illinois, and Hon. Hannibal Hamlin, of Maine*. Boston: Thayer & Eldridge, 1860.

Hollis, C. Carroll. "R. J. Hinton: Lincoln's Reluctant Biographer." *Centennial Review* 5 (Winter 1961): 65–84.

Holmes, Oliver Wendell. "Bread and the Newspaper." *Atlantic Monthly*, September 1861, 348.

———. "The Flower of Liberty." *Atlantic Monthly*, November 1861, 550–51.

———. "Union and Liberty." *Atlantic Monthly*, December 1861, 756.

Howe, Julia Ward. "Battle Hymn of the Republic." *Atlantic Monthly*, February 1862, 145.

———. *Reminiscences, 1819–1899*. Boston: Houghton Mifflin, 1899.

Howells, William Dean. *Literary Friends and Acquaintances*. New York: Harper & Brothers, 1911.

Hyman, Martin D. " 'Where the Drinkers & Laughers Meet': Pfaff's: Whitman's Literary Lair." *Seaport* 26 (1991).

Johnson, Arnold Burgess. "Recollections of Charles Sumner." *Scribner's*, August 1874, 486.

Kaplan, Justin. *Walt Whitman: A Life*. New York: Simon & Schuster, 1981.

Katz, Jonathan Ned. *Love Stories: Sex between Men before Homosexuality*. Chicago: University of Chicago Press, 2001.

Kennedy, William Sloane. *The Fight of a Book for the World: A Companion Volume to Leaves of Grass*. West Yarmouth, MA: Stonecroft Press, 1926.

Killingsworth, M. Jimmie. *The Cambridge Introduction to Walt Whitman*. Cambridge, UK: Cambridge University Press, 2007.

Leland, Charles Godfrey. *Memoirs*. New York: D. Appleton, 1893.

———. "Words to the West." *Knickerbocker*, October 1861, 1–5.

Lincoln, Abraham. *The Collected Works of Abraham Lincoln.* Vol. 4. Edited by Roy P. Basler. 9 vols. New Brunswick, NJ: Rutgers University Press, 1953.

Long, E. B., and Barbara Long. *The Civil War Day by Day: An Almanac 1861–1865.* Garden City, NY: Doubleday, 1971.

Loving, Jerome M. "Broadway, the Magnificent! A Newly Discovered Whitman Essay." *Walt Whitman Quarterly Review* 12, no. 4 (1995): 209–16.

———, ed. *Civil War Letters of George Washington Whitman.* Durham, NC: Duke University Press, 1975.

———. *Walt Whitman: The Song of Himself.* Berkeley: University of California Press, 1999.

Lowell, James Russell. *The Complete Poetical Works of James Russell Lowell.* Edited by Horace Elisha Scudder. Cambridge Edition of the Poets. Boston: Houghton Mifflin, 1897.

———. *New Letters of James Russell Lowell.* Edited by M. A. DeWolfe Howe. New York: Harper & Brothers, 1932.

Malin, James C. "Plotting after Harpers Ferry: The 'William Handy' Letters." *Journal of Southern History* 8, no. 1 (1942): 81–87.

Mancuso, Luke. "Civil War." In *A Companion to Walt Whitman,* edited by Donald D. Kummings, 290–310. Malden, MA: Blackwell, 2006.

McPherson, James M. *Battle Cry of Freedom: The Civil War Era.* New York: Oxford University Press, 1988.

Morris, Roy, Jr. *The Better Angel: Walt Whitman in the Civil War.* Oxford: Oxford University Press, 2000.

Murray, Martin G. "Bunkum *Did* Go Sogering." *Walt Whitman Quarterly Review* 10 (Winter 1993): 142–48.

Myerson, Joel, ed. *Whitman in His Own Time: A Biographical Chronicle of His Life, Drawn from Recollections, Memoirs, and Interviews by Friends and Associates.* Iowa City: University of Iowa Press, 2000.

O'Brien, Tim. *The Things They Carried,* Boston: Seymour Lawrence, 1990.

Parry, Albert. *Garrets and Pretenders: A History of Bohemia in America.* New York: Covici, Friede, 1933.

Price, Robert. "The Road to Boston: 1860 Travel Correspondence of William Dean Howells." *Ohio History* 80 (1971): 85–154.

Redpath, James. *The Public Life of Capt. John Brown.* Boston: Thayer & Eldridge, 1860.

———. *The Roving Editor; or, Talks with Slaves in the Southern States.* New York: A. B. Burdick, 1859.

Reynolds, David S. *John Brown, Abolitionist.* New York: Knopf, 2005.

Rubin, Joseph Jay. *The Historic Whitman*. University Park: Pennsylvania State University Press, 1973.

Scholnick, Robert. "'An Unusually Active Market for Calamus': Whitman, *Vanity Fair*, and the Fate of Humor in a Time of War, 1860–1863." *Walt Whitman Quarterly Review* 19 (Winter/Spring 2002): 148–81.

Sentilles, Renée M. *Performing Menken: Adah Isaacs Menken and the Birth of American Celebrity*. Cambridge, UK: Cambridge University Press, 2003.

Shively, Charley. *Drum Beats: Walt Whitman's Civil War Boy Lovers*. San Francisco: Gay Sunshine Press, 1989.

Stedman, Edmund C. *The Battle of Bull Run*. New York: Rudd & Carleton, 1861.

Sumner, Charles. *The Works of Charles Sumner*. Vol. 5. Boston: Lee and Shepard, 1874.

Tilton, Eleanor M., ed. *The Letters of Ralph Waldo Emerson*. Vol. 8. New York: Columbia University Press, 1991.

Traubel, Horace. *With Walt Whitman in Camden*. 9 vols. New York: Rowman and Littlefield, 1906–1996.

Trowbridge, John Townsend. "Reminiscences of Walt Whitman." In *Whitman in His Own Time: A Biographical Chronicle of His Life, Drawn from Recollections, Memoirs, and Interviews by Friends and Associates*, edited by Joel Myerson. Iowa City: University of Iowa Press, 2000.

Tryon, Warren S. "The Publications of Ticknor and Fields in the South, 1840–1865." *Journal of Southern History* 14 (1948): 309–29.

United States, Robert N. Scott, H. M. Lazelle, George B. Davis, Leslie J. Perry, Joseph W. Kirkley, Fred C. Ainsworth, John S. Moodey, and Calvin D. Cowles. *Antietam—Serial 27*. Vol. 19: *The War of the Rebellion: A Compilation of the Official Records of the Union and Confederate Armies*. Washington, DC: Government Printing Office, 1880.

Von Frank, Albert. "The Secret World of Radical Publishers: Thayer and Eldridge of Boston." In *Boston's Histories: Essays in Honor of Thomas H. O'Connor*, edited by James O'Toole and David Quigley. Boston: Northeastern University Press, 2004.

W[hipple], C[harles] K[ing]. "Echoes of Harper's Ferry." *Liberator*, May 18, 1860.

White, William. "'Kentucky': Unpublished Poetic Fragments by Walt Whitman, Edited, with a Commentary." *Prairie Schooner* 32 (Fall 1958): 172–78.

Whitman, Thomas Jefferson, and Walt Whitman. *Dear Brother Walt: The Letters of Thomas Jefferson Whitman*. Edited by Dennis Berthold and Kenneth M. Price. Kent, OH: Kent State University Press, 1984.

Whitman, Walt. "A Ballad of Long Island," *Brooklyn City News*, December 24, 1860. Reprinted in *Leaves of Grass Imprints: American and European Criticisms on "Leaves of Grass."* Boston: Thayer & Eldridge, 1860.

———. "Beat! Beat! Drums!" *Daily Evening Bulletin*, November 9, 1861.

———. "A Brooklynite Criticised." *Brooklyn City News*, October 10, 1860.

———. *Daybooks and Notebooks*. New York: New York University Press, 1978.

———. *Drum-Taps*. New York: Self-published, 1865.

———. *Drum-Taps (1865) and Sequel to Drum-Taps (1865–6)*. Edited by Frederick DeWolfe Miller. Gainesville, FL: Scholars' Facsimiles & Reprints, 1959.

———. *Leaves of Grass*. Brooklyn, NY: Self-published, 1855.

———. *Leaves of Grass*. Brooklyn, NY: Self-published, 1856.

———. *Leaves of Grass*. Boston: Thayer & Eldridge, 1860.

———. *Leaves of Grass: Comprehensive Reader's Edition*. Edited by Sculley Bradley and Harold W. Blodgett. New York: New York University Press, 1965.

———, ed. *Leaves of Grass Imprints. American and European Criticisms on "Leaves of Grass."* Boston: Thayer & Eldridge, 1860.

———. *Notebooks and Unpublished Prose Manuscripts*. Edited by Edward F. Grier. New York: New York University Press, 1984.

———. *Prose Works 1892*. Vols. 1 and 2. Edited by Floyd Stovall. New York: New York University Press, 1984.

———. *The Uncollected Poetry and Prose of Walt Whitman: Much of Which Has Been but Recently Discovered with Various Early Manuscripts Now First Published*. Vol. 2. Edited by Emory Holloway. Gloucester, MA: Peter Smith, 1972. (Originally published 1921.)

———. *Walt Whitman and the Civil War: A Collection of Original Articles and Manuscripts*. Edited by Charles I. Glicksberg. New York: A. S. Barnes, 1963.

———. *Walt Whitman: Complete Poetry and Selected Prose and Letters*. Edited by Emory Holloway. London: Nonesuch Press, 1938.

———. *Walt Whitman: The Correspondence*. Vol. 1. Edited by Edwin Haviland Miller. New York: New York University Press, 1961.

———. *Walt Whitman: The Correspondence*. Vol. 7. Edited by Ted Genoways. Iowa City: University of Iowa Press, 2004.

———. *Walt Whitman's Autograph Revision of the Analysis of Leaves of Grass (for Dr. R. M. Bucke's Walt Whitman)*. Facsimile edition. Text notes by Stephen Railton. New York: New York University Press, 1974.

Wilson, Edmund. *Patriotic Gore: Studies in the Literature of the American Civil War*. New York: Oxford University Press, 1961.

Winter, William. *O'Brien's Poems and Stories.* Boston: James R. Osgood, 1881.
————. *Old Friends: Being Literary Recollections of Other Days.* New York: Moffat, Yard, 1909.
Wright, James A. "The Delicacy of Walt Whitman." In *The Presence of Walt Whitman,* edited by R. W. B. Lewis. New York: Columbia University Press, 1962.

INDEX

Text: 10/15 Janson
Display: Janson
Compositor: Binghamton Valley Composition, LLC
Printer and binder: Thomson-Shore, Inc.